SNIPER

A History of the
US Marksman

OSPREY
PUBLISHING

SNIPER

A History of the US Marksman

MARTIN PEGLER

First published in Great Britain in 2007 by Osprey Publishing,
Midland House, West Way, Botley, Oxford OX2 0PH, United Kingdom.
443 Park Avenue South, New York, NY 10016, USA.

Email: info@ospreypublishing.com

A CIP catalog record for this book is available from the British Library

ISBN: 978-1-84176-979-0

Martin Pegler has asserted his right under the Copyright, Designs and Patents Act, 1988, to be identified as the author of this book.

Index by Alison Worthington
Typeset in Adobe Garamond
Originated by United Graphic Pte Ltd, Singapore
Printed in China through Bookbuilders

07 08 09 10   10 9 8 7 6 5 4 3 2 1

For a catalog of all books published by Osprey please contact:

NORTH AMERICA

Osprey Direct c/o Random House Distribution Center
400 Hahn Road, Westminster, MD 21157, USA
E-mail: info@ospreydirect.com

ALL OTHER REGIONS

Osprey Direct UK, P.O. Box 140, Wellingborough, Northants, NN8 2FA, UK
E-mail: info@ospreydirect.co.uk

www.ospreypublishing.com

CONVERSION TABLE

Mass	Velocity
27.34 grains = 1 dram	1 mph = 88 feet/min
16 drams = 1 ounce	1 mph = 1.467 feet/sec
7,000 grains = 1 pound	1 mph = 0.447 meter/sec
	1 foot/min = 0.5080 cm/sec
1 milligram = 0.01543 grains	
1 gram = 15.43 grains	1 foot/min = 0.01136 mph
1 gram = 0.03527 ounces	1 foot/sec = 0.6817 mph
	1 meter/sec = 2.237 mph
1 grain = 0.0648 grams	1 cm/sec = 1.067 feet/min
1 ounce = 28.35 grams	
1 dram = 1.772 grams	

CONTENTS

DEDICATION

Dedication: To the memory of Lt William D. Hawkins USMC, the first scout/sniper to be awarded the Medal of Honor for his actions on Betio Island, Tarawa, on November 21, 1943. His leadership materially assisted the Marines in capturing the island.

ACKNOWLEDGEMENTS

With thanks …

To the many people who helped me with this book. It nearly remained unwritten as our house move from England to France was blighted by a fire and among the many items lost were ten years of research along with my entire reference library. However, a lot of people have been instrumental in helping me recover information, among whom I would like to thank:

Philip Abbott and Stuart Ivinson at the Royal Armouries Museum, Terry Abrahams, Bob Burbage, Simon Deakin, Harry Furness, Barry Lees, Chris Scott, Paul Tamony, George Yannaghas, and Russ Young for books and information.

Thanks also to the following people for supplying photographs: Danny Pizzini for his superb Whitworth rifle, Roy Jinks, Rocky and Norman Chandler at the Iron Brigade Armory, the US Marines and the US Army Photographic Libraries, and a special mention to the Director and staff of the Springfield Armory Museum, Massachusetts, for allowing me to photograph their reserve collection.

To the many snipers and ex-snipers who were prepared to talk to me, in particular Chuck Mawhinney, Joe, Eric, "Bull", John D., John H., Peter, and all those others who wished to remain nameless. I couldn't (I dare not!) use all of your anecdotes but thank you regardless. I would also like to express my thanks to my publishers, Osprey, and my editor, Anita Baker, in particular for delaying publication and helping me replace many lost reference books.

Finally to my long-suffering wife Kate, who proofread the text while managing to cope with a move to a foreign country, run a new business venture and deal with a stream of visitors while I buried myself for hours each day in my study, pounding a keyboard. Thank you, my love.

FOREWORD

by Chuck Mawhinney

In common with most snipers, I enjoy my privacy and have never wanted publicity for my actions, but over time I have become increasingly annoyed with the negative publicity that surrounds snipers and their work. The media's portrayal of them as paid assassins couldn't be further from the truth, and totally ignores the bravery, dedication, and sheer hard work that goes into training to be a sniper.

My father bought me my first BB gun when I was six years old, and I have been a shooter ever since. Everyone seemed a little worried when we had to qualify on the rifle range, but for me it didn't seem too difficult. Becoming a sniper seemed a natural progression when I went to Vietnam on my first tour just after the Tet Offensive in 1968. The training was thorough and we learned to shoot accurately from ranges of 300 to 1,000 yards. There are so many variables when sniping – distance, weather, target movement – but I seemed to have an inherent knowledge of what was required. I could tell instantly if I'd made a good shot or not. Of all the skills a sniper needs, aside from accuracy, patience is the most important. Approximately 40 percent of my confirmed kills were taken at night while working company perimeters. I'd often shoot and then wait, sometimes for hours, for someone to come to retrieve the body, and then I'd hit them too. This was using an M14 with a starlight scope. After the enemy's first attempt to retrieve the dead soldier, no one else wanted to try. Thus Charlie would still be lying there in the morning. I was often scared, but the work was like the ultimate hunting trip, with a quarry that was dangerous and shot back. It was often very exhilarating and stalking heightened all of my senses. I could see and smell things that I couldn't at any other time.

I was always unemotional about it: I did exactly what I was trained to do and I followed the rules of engagement. If he carried a weapon, he was a target, and I didn't think about the guy as someone with a wife and kids. He was the enemy and my job was to kill the enemy. The way I saw it, every Charlie I shot could potentially kill my fellow Marines, so one more down meant more Marine lives saved. After three tours of duty, I asked to be a gunner on a helicopter, but my request was denied. I was returned to Camp Pendleton first as a drill instructor and then as an instructor on the rifle range. I survived because I worked 100 percent at being a sniper, and I try to do everything that way. I wanted to live. It was the only way, and I've never looked back.

The instructors taught what was needed to help us stay alive, but there is a lot more to sniping. There were questions no one asked, such as where did the shooting skills we were taught come from, and how did we develop such accurate rifles? This book explains all of that, as well as why a lot of guys like me throughout history have chosen to be snipers. None of us did it to be heroes or to get medals – a sniper with that attitude isn't going to live long – we did it because we wanted to make a difference. I hope everyone reading this book will understand that, because it is a story that deserves to be told.

INTRODUCTION

There are few countries in the world that have advanced as quickly industrially, materially, and socially as the United States of America. In a little over two centuries it has progressed from a barely explored wilderness, peopled by predominantly native tribes who had existed primarily as hunter-gatherers for millennia, to the most powerful economic and military power in the world. Ask any American how this was achieved and it is likely you will get a wry grin and a reply along the lines of "God, guns, and guts." Such an answer is given fairly tongue in cheek, but as with so many such ripostes it bears the unmistakable ring of truth. The America we know and accept today was indeed born out of a time where a spirit of adventure was combined with an intense curiosity, a desire for exploration, and a fundamental belief that while God might be master in heaven, on earth it was man who controlled his own destiny. Of course it helped if, on a level playing field, one's destiny could be materially assisted by some form of advantage. To this end the American love affair with technology, and firearms in particular, began at a very early stage.

The first settlers' tools were simple: axes, ploughs, hammers and nails, saws, and a few primitive firearms, all of which existed for one simple function: to provide the ability to stay alive in what was generally an extremely hostile environment. The America of the 17th century was not a place of Disneyesque enchantment, but a vast continent of incredibly diverse geographical and climatic regions, with weather conditions that included blistering deserts in the southwest, dense forest on the east coast, a southeast that was tropical, and, in the Midwest, complete extremes of climate, with summer temperatures reaching 100°F and winters where -50°F was not uncommon. The continent was thinly peopled by Native Americans, for whom internecine warfare was a matter of both tradition and pride. Their attitude to the slow influx of settlers varied widely from region to region. Some tribes became implacable enemies of the whites at a very early stage, while others were happy to coexist in relative harmony. The differences in social attitudes between the Old and the New World did not always assist the settlers, and the widely held belief among the pioneers that land, once settled on, was the property of the new occupier was one that the natives found fundamentally impossible to understand or accept. In time this tension would lead to sad and bloody conflict. As if the climate and resident natives were not enough, there was of course a bewildering selection of hostile animals, ranging from snakes to mountain lions, which regarded anything on two legs as either a potential threat or dinner.

The first settlers were likely to encounter most, if not all, of these problems, and at the outset it was the use of one advanced form of technology, the gun, that enabled them to improve the odds appreciably in favor of their survival. As neither animals nor Native Americans had firearms, the settlers indeed held an overwhelming advantage. For, crude as these early weapons were, they were still capable of delivering a mortal wound at distances that teeth, horns, a bow, or a spear could not. Distance was, in fact, the key to the success of the gun and it was the desire – one may almost say obsession – within the ranks of firearms owners to improve continually both the range and the accuracy of their weapons that led to the eventual development of the rifle.

The legendary prowess of the American rifleman, which has endured from the 18th century to the present day, has its antecedents in the story of exactly how these firearms came to America. The story begins with the diverse and disparate groups of Europeans who brought them over in the 15th and 16th centuries, developing and improving them in times of peace and war.

It is a curious anomaly that the apogee of the 18th - century rifleman, the modern military sniper, has in very recent times suddenly emerged into the limelight from the outer fringes of warfare. The recent conflicts in the Gulf and Iraq have been called, with good reason, snipers' wars and the snipers themselves have changed from being nobody's children to the most sought after military specialists on the battlefield. Their weapons too have evolved from little more than iron tubes containing firework powder, to precision tools capable of placing a bullet with surgical accuracy out to 1,500 yards or more. How this came about is both a complex and fascinating tale involving greed, politics, science, and man's unquenchable desire for technological improvement.

PART I
THE EVOLUTION OF THE RIFLE

Chapter 1

NEW WORLD, NEW WEAPONS

While the founding fathers of America are generally celebrated as having been a small group of Pilgrims landing on a windswept beach in what is now Cape Cod in November 1620, this is not the entire truth. The beginning of the colonization of the Americas stretches back at least a century prior to the Pilgrims' arrival to when three ships commanded by a Genoese sailor, Christopher Columbus, left Palos harbor in August 1492. Among their assorted cargo they carried with them a technology that had changed the face of the Old World and would soon do likewise in the New World. In the inventory of the vessels were included items listed as "ships cannon and one handgonne."[1] The term *handgonne* is frequently encountered at this period and is an important defining term that differentiates between a weapon too large to be man-portable and a lighter form of longarm that can be hand carried and fired from the shoulder or, more commonly, the waist. These simple hand cannon are the first positive evidence of the use of a portable firearm in the Americas. That these weapons proved of practical use is evidenced by the fact that the following year, when Columbus' new ship, *La Navidad*, returned to the recently founded settlement of La Navidad on Hispaniola (now Haiti), it carried with it no fewer than 100 assorted firearms, referred to rather ambiguously as *espignardas*. There is a basic problem in understanding exactly what sort of firearms are being referred to here. It is difficult to be specific about the weapons carried by the Spaniards in the 15th and 16th centuries, as not only did chroniclers have the unfortunate habit of using generic terms to cover every type of firearm, but Spanish contemporary references to firearms types appear utterly different from those in use in the rest of Western Europe. So while the term "musket" is now the accepted modern description for any muzzle-loading, smoothbore shoulder-fired longarm, it had a far more specific meaning during the 15th and 16th centuries. In Europe it applied to a long-barreled shoulder arm that was normally too heavy to be fired without the use of a supporting forked rest. Calibers were large, usually about .75in, and the guns themselves could weigh in excess of 18lb with barrel lengths of up to 65in. Where the term musket actually originated will probably never be known. Historians of early firearms attribute it to the Italian *moschetto*, literally a young male sparrow-hawk, which relates to the tradition of naming cannon after types of birds, such as Falconet or Basiliski. It may even have been a corruption of the name "Muscovites" given to the Russian fur trappers and hunters who traveled the upper reaches of North America, the word for their guns being *muscovetes*. A simpler answer may be that it was simply a corruption of the Spanish term *escopeta* introduced around the first decade of the 17th century. In England, with its variable phonetic spelling of the period, the firearms were variously referred to as "mousquits," "muskets," or "muskitts" and to the French they were *mousquets*. However, there were at this time two basic forms of hand musket in use in Europe, the *harquebus* (or *arquebus*) and matchlock musket, the former being generally understood to be a lighter type than the much larger primitive matchlock guns. The name harquebus was actually derived from the German word *hack-buss*, literally "hook-gun."

For the Spanish in the New World, however, these varied terms mainly seem to apply to the *hacabuche*. In an order dated 1532 by one Pedro de Avila, he asked that "there be supplied 200 espignardas for use by the infantry, and 35 hacabuches each of thirty pounds weight for defence."[2] Clearly for the Spanish, hacabuches (arquebuses) were longarms regarded as being too heavy to be man-portable and were for use mounted on a fixed wall or ship's rail. From known European examples of handguns of the mid-15th century, it is likely that these weapons were nothing more sophisticated than large simple cast-iron tubes, with an ignition hole at the breech end, in a caliber of anywhere between .50in and 1in. Significantly, their weight determined that they required a mount under the barrel to enable them to be fixed on a parapet or ship's rail, and they may even have been what we would now refer to as "swivel guns." Therefore the use of the term *espignardas* for use by the infantry would seem to imply a different type of lighter construction than the arquebus, each gun weighing perhaps 10–12lb and therefore far more practical for carrying.[3]

The difference within the Spanish written definitions of firearms is important, for it is from such documents that can be drawn the first conclusive evidence of the introduction of a form of light, long-barreled shoulder arm into the Americas. These primitive longarms were the ancestors of all that were to follow and they were neither accurate nor particularly powerful, for gunpowder at that period (then known as "serpentine") was of poor quality, generating little in the way of propellant gas. There is, however, little doubt that they were vitally needed, for when Columbus returned with his 100 new firearms the scene was set for a series of confrontations between the Europeans and native tribes that would last for nearly 500 years.

Yet in the time it took Columbus to sail to and fro between Europe and America, there were already major improvements being made in firearms design, and the first matchlock types were already well established. These advances were to do as much with function as form, the introduction of a mechanism for holding the slow-match being of particular relevance. Firing a charge in an early handgonne was a complicated matter of applying a flame to the touch-hole while holding it firmly at waist level and pointing the gun in the general direction of the enemy. While the noise and smoke would certainly frighten the horses and doubtless terrify the enemy, the gun's practical effect as a killing weapon was limited as it was almost impossible to aim accurately. The introduction of the matchlock mechanism simplified the whole process and added a very faint element of sophistication to the weapons. While the barrel was still a simple iron tube, held by bands onto a wooden stock, a simple hinged arm, or "serpentine" (not to be confused with the gunpowder bearing the same name), was introduced. This screwed onto the side of the stock and could pivot on a spindle. Into its jaws was clamped a piece of slow-burning matchcord. The serpentine was actuated by a lever that projected underneath the stock, and this simple trigger system provided the shooter with two main advantages. First, he was able to raise the gun more or less to eye level and take aim. Second, the match enabled ignition to take place at the moment chosen by the firer. The Spanish had introduced it in the form of the *escopeta* at some period in the first decade of the 16th century, although European examples were known well before this date.

THE COLONISTS' FIREARMS

The behavior of the Spanish adventurers and soldiers towards the largely peaceable Indians did not always promote harmony. Their poor treatment of the Tainos tribe, for example, had led to the first of a series of retaliatory attacks, beginning with the massacre of the entire settlement in the stockade of La Navidad in early 1493; but the early Spanish adventurers were mostly neutral in their attitude toward the Native American peoples. However, those who were to follow in Columbus' footsteps and travel to the New World after his death in 1506 were an entirely different breed, whose emergence was to herald the age of the *Conquistadores*, literally "the Conquerors." These Spaniards, not known for their gentle treatment of native peoples, were voracious in both their lust for precious metals and their subjugation of local tribes, usually with extreme brutality.

Yet it was not the West Indies that initially drew the attention of this new type of government-sponsored mercenary, but mainland America. Adventurer and soldier Juan Ponce de Léon had landed in the lush tropical region now known as Florida in early April 1513, where he established the infrastructure that within two decades would become the forts of St Augustine and Santa Elena. Meanwhile, while the Spanish were busying themselves in the

Americas, other European explorers, such as the Cabot brothers sailing under the protection of English king Henry VII, had also been busy, visiting Nova Scotia and Newfoundland and also probably the coast of Florida, at least a decade or more prior to de Léon. Dutch, Flemish, English, French, and Spanish mariners were regular callers on the eastern seaboard of America, looking for fresh food and clean water. That they traded with the Indians is accepted fact, although exactly what was traded is not known. Certainly by 1500 the Indians who inhabited that coastline must have been familiar with firearms even if they did not at the time own any.

While there was little doubt in the minds of these early adventurers of the superiority of their firepower and the value of carrying firearms, some already had misgivings about one of the most fundamental shortcomings of the firearm, and that was its vulnerability due to its poor rate of fire. A good musketeer could load and fire a matchlock three times in a minute, though the accuracy unless at very short range would have been questionable. However, the native tribes resident in Florida, such as the Ais, were both skilled fighters and extremely efficient bowmen and therein lay the problem. Both de Léon and Manuel de Soto, the leader of several expeditions across the Mississippi in the late 1520s, took with them not only muskets but also crossbows because, as de Soto later said:

> The Indians never stand stille but are always running and traversing from one place to another: by reason whereof neither crossebow nor arquebuse can aime at them; and before one crossbowman can make one shotte, an Indian will discharge three or foure arrows; and he seldome missethe what he shootethe atte.[4]

This problem over the relative firepower of the simple but effective technology of the bow and that of the firearm was one that was to rage for decades. Indeed, it was still of considerable military importance during the American Indian Wars of the mid-19th century.

It is an interesting question as to how effective these early muskets really were against the relatively primitive technology of the natives. Certainly their initial use must have been terrifying to say the least, and the invisible missiles that caused such horrible wounds or death must have greatly puzzled the native tribes. But humans are nothing if not quick to learn, and while no written accounts remain by the conquered peoples who suffered under the invasion from the Old World, there are some enlightening comments by the Conquistadores themselves. Smug contemporary accounts of sailors driving off the local Indians in terror by the use of ship's cannon are doubtless true, but then no one with an ounce of sense will stand still in front of a cannon if there is any alternative, and any group under fire would naturally disperse quickly. There is some evidence that the early shoulder arms did not actually have such a devastating effect as had been assumed. General Hernando de Cortés, commanding the Mexican expedition against the Tlaxclans in 1513, wrote that "Far from panicking at the explosion of gunpowder, [the Tlaxclans] drowned its noise with their shrill whistles and threw dust in the air while they rushed the dead and wounded away so no one could see the damage … the cannons had done."[5] Was this an early form of psychological warfare, a damage limitation exercise on the part of the Indians who did not want to give the invaders the satisfaction of seeing the effect of their technology? Whatever the answer, there is no doubt that the early expeditions did not place their faith entirely in the new muskets, for the use of better established weapons was predominant. When Cortés took 508 soldiers to Mexico there were only 12 arquebusiers, the rest being crossbowmen, pikemen, and sword-equipped infantrymen. Similarly, in Pizarro's 1533 expedition into Peru there were a mere three musketeers out of 177 soldiers. Far from the musket becoming the principal weapon carried by the Spanish to the New World, by the 17th century the situation if anything was temporarily reversed. With the abdication and subsequent death of Spain's King Charles I in 1558 the Spanish firearms industry began to decline rapidly to the extent that by 1590 the Venetian ambassador commented that he did not think that "There is another country less provided with skilled workers than Spain."[6] As a result many expeditions were more traditionally armed with swords, pike, bows, and perhaps a very few firearms.

By the mid-16th century the impracticable size and excessive weight of the old arquebus meant that it was slowly being superseded by a smaller, lighter type of musket. It did not take long for these weapons to become popular – being more compact enabled them to be fired offhand without the need for a rest to take their weight. Within two decades the word "musket" had eclipsed most others as a generic term for any and every smoothbore muzzle-loading firearm and it was their introduction in the hands of European settlers who landed on the east coast of America that was to lead eventually to the establishment of a home-grown gunmaking industry that would become unique. The settlers were still cautious about placing too much reliance upon firearms, a sentiment echoed in an instruction issued to Sir Walter Raleigh in 1622 that advised him to arm as many of his men as possible with longbows, by then an almost obsolete form of weaponry. The British government duly dispatched some 400 bows to the new settlement in Virginia. What comments their arrival generated would today make interesting reading.

There was some logic to this decision, though, for aside from the purely practical problems that beset the early musketeers, which included simply keeping their powder and match dry, carrying sufficient ball, and attempting to use their cumbersome weapons in a relatively efficient manner in the confusing mêlée of contemporary battles, there was the important matter of what to do with your musket once it had been discharged. This issue was to become a perennial problem for musketeers and also for riflemen, for whom reloading was an even slower business. A sword or knife does not require a pause in use to be re-sharpened, and a properly used bow can discharge an arrow as fast as it can be strung and loosed off. Medieval English longbowmen said with some truth that they could have ten arrows in the air in the time it took a simple handgonne to be loaded and fired. Even the slower firing rate of the crossbow was faster than that of the musket. Once fired, the gun was of little use except as a club, and arquebusiers were forced either to rely on the protection of other infantry or, more often than not, to throw down their weapons, draw swords, and fight as best they could.

There was also a question mark over the material damage caused by these primitive firearms, for bullets varied considerably in size and weight and few were perfectly spherical, leading to ballistic instability. The wounds inflicted by them were very dependent on the range and part of the body struck, and it should also be remembered that they were propelled by very low-grade gunpowder and their velocity was pitifully slow, with a consequentially rapid drop in efficiency as distance increased. Tests undertaken with a reproduction English handgonne of the late 15th century showed it to have an extremely poor velocity of 547fps (using modern black powder) and an effective range (i.e. actually capable of hitting what it is aimed at) of 25 yards.[7] This dismal performance is reinforced by comments made in 1590, when British adventurer and sailor Sir John Smythe declared that "a properly loaded musket had a range of twenty four to thirty yards," far less than an arrow, and many explorers and settlers complained that the main disadvantage of their guns over the bow was the lack of penetration of the ball. De Soto, too, commented that an Indian arrow:

> where it findeth no armour, pierces as deep as a crossbow. Their [Indian] bowes are very long, and their arrows are made of certain cane like reedes, very heavy and so strong that a sharpe cane passethe therough a targette. Those of cane do split and pierce a coate of maile, and are more hurtful.[8]

The Old World soldiers were often surprised at how little damage their bullets did when faced with Indians carrying shields of wood, leather, or a combination of the two. Cortés had wall guns of a mere .32 caliber and frequently balls fired from them would not penetrate shields even from close range. The Indian warriors learned quickly that in the time it took for musketeers to reload their guns, they were helpless and could be easily struck down. There was a partial remedy for this, though, for the larger-caliber smooth barrels were ideal for using in the manner of a shotgun, with several balls loaded at once. French adventurer Samuel de Champlain was certainly a convert to buckshot and habitually loaded his weapons with multiple balls.

In 1609 his party was attacked by Iroquois Indians and his account makes interesting reading:

> I marched on until I was within thirty yards of the enemy ... when I saw them make a move to draw their bows upon us, I took aim with my arquebus and shot straight at one of their chiefs, and with this shot two fell to the ground and one of their companions was wounded, who died thereof a little later. I had put four bullets into my arquebus. The Iroquois were much astonished that two men should have been killed so quickly, although they were provided with shields made of cotton thread woven together, and wood, that were proof against arrows.[9]

The fighting range of early firearms was also very dependent on the care with which they were loaded as well as the quality of their bores. Some guns proved much better than others in this respect, but an effective range of 50–80 yards was about average. Accuracy was not helped by the requirement for an undersized ball to be loaded into the barrel. After a few shots, fouling in the bore from the gunpowder would prevent a tight-fitting ball from being rammed home, so the use of the undersized bullet solved one problem but created another in the form of the loss of propellant gas that escaped past it on firing. This was referred to as "windage" or "blow-by" and it did nothing to assist either the musket's accuracy or the ball's poor velocity. It was to be a continual problem for muzzle-loaders until the advent of the breech-loading rifles of the 19th century. A reasonably effective cure was made by the use of a patch, a circle of thin greased leather or cloth, which was put on the muzzle of the musket. The ball was placed on top and both components were rammed down into the breech, the patch forming an effective gas seal as well as helping remove fouling. Some idea of how effective this procedure was can be glimpsed from tests undertaken in 1998 using a reproduction snap-lock arquebus from the collection of the Royal Armouries Museum, UK. With a modern, perfectly bored barrel, patched bullets, and good-quality powder, a musket was capable of producing creditable muzzle velocities of 1,337fps; moreover, the projectiles would penetrate 0.24in of steel plate at 30 yards. This was, admittedly, a test under perfect conditions using modern technology – experience in the past was somewhat different.[10]

THE NEW MATCHLOCKS

Early matchlocks were by any standards relatively unsophisticated, with their heavy curved stocks and "fishtail" butts. They were uncomfortable to hold into the shoulder and it was in fact the alternative straighter and slimmer Spanish style of butt that proved the most efficient. This was soon to be the design that was eventually adopted into most contemporary muskets. Innovation was never very far away and by around 1600 the serpentine arm had acquired a lock side-plate with an internal spring and sear against which the trigger pressed, allowing relatively fine control of the serpentine and thus the speed of ignition. Within a couple of decades this mechanism too had been further refined and a sear trigger was being used, doing away completely with the long under-lever and replacing it with a recognizably modern short trigger housed inside a protective trigger guard. The open pan-cover also gained a hinged top cover, which provided some protection from the elements, an important innovation much appreciated by anyone who has tried to shoot a matchlock in a high wind or driving rain.

The keeping of a lighted match ready to discharge a gun was always fraught with difficulties and it was one of the major drawbacks of the matchlock system, as was the constantly glowing match end, the glow and smoke from which advertised the presence of a soldier as effectively as a lighted cigarette. Indian warriors soon became wise to the shortcomings of the matchlocks, and would often attack in poor weather conditions, for without fire at hand to light their matches the Europeans were reduced to swords and crossbows in the event of attack, a fact that the Indians were quick to exploit. Henry Hudson's expedition of 1609 suffered badly when Indians attacked them in a heavy rainstorm, as Captain Raleigh Gilbert had found in 1607:

The Salvadges [savages] perceiving so much, subtilely devised how they might put out the fire ... by which means they sawe they should be free from the danger of our mens pieces [firearms] ... one of the salvadges came ... and taking the fier-brand which one of our company held in his hand ... he presently threw it into the water. Captain Gilbert seeing that, suddenly commanded his men to ... present their peeces, the which, the salvadges seeing presently let go the boats rope.[11]

By the mid-17th century the matchlock had reached the zenith of its mechanical development and it had also been materially helped by an innovative process developed in the gunpowder industry. While gunpowder may appear to be somewhat peripheral to the history of the development of the rifle, in reality its history is quite inseparable from the story of longarm development and is fundamental to understanding how the science of accurate shooting evolved from the primitive to the sophisticated. Any shooter knows that the accuracy of his weapon is based upon the quality of ammunition used, and this is as true today as it was then. Since its introduction into Europe in the 14th century, gunpowder had been both a curse and a blessing. It fulfilled its primary function, that of propelling a ball from a smooth tube, quite admirably, because gunpowder is not a high-explosive but a low-explosive. In practice this means that it will always take the line of least resistance when ignited, thus preferring to push a projectile out of the barrel than to blow up the barrel, as a high-explosive would do. This made it comparatively safe to use, as overcharging a barrel was unlikely to result in component parts of the gun and the shooter being scattered over the landscape.

Around the mid-16th century improvements in the manufacturing processes of gunpowder occurred that had a major impact on firearms performance. Traditionally black powder was mixed dry and ground into serpentine, akin to talcum powder in form, so the dense, slow-burning result was never terribly effective in generating any serious velocity on the part of the projectile; hence the common use of equal weights of powder to ball. However, a new process known as "corning" was found, probably in Germany, which transformed gunpowder. The ingredients were mixed wet and formed into large cakes or corns, then ground to size, creating varying-sized grains depending on preferred use. "Corned" powder no longer resembled serpentine talcum powder, but had the more gritty, granular form that modern shooters are familiar with. This had the benefit of ensuring that, when packed into a breech, there was sufficient air trapped around the grains to ensure a faster and more powerful ignition. The result meant that determining a charge weight was simply a matter of placing a ball in the palm of the hand and covering it with a pyramid of powder. For generations, this would be the accepted method of measuring. This new technique of powder manufacture ensured that by the 1570s it was generally believed that a charge weight one fifth of that of the weight of the ball was sufficient.

While corning improved almost beyond measure the performance of early firearms, it did not change the fundamental problems associated with the propellant itself and, unfortunately, the shortcomings of black powder were many and varied. When ignited it produced 300 times its own volume in thick gray-white smoke, a very limiting factor if firing from a concealed position. Once ignited, gunpowder left behind a thick, corrosive, sooty residue in the bore that could render a musket unusable if left uncleaned for more than a day or so. Most crucially, the powder had to be kept dry as it was hydroscopic, soaking up moisture like a sponge and thus rendering it useless for shooting. Many modern terms of speech come from the gun trade and one of the oldest was the serious admonishment "keep your powder dry, friend."[12] Its generally accepted meaning now is to be prepared for any eventuality, but its contemporary meaning was clearly understood by any man with a musket who had damp powder – he was effectively holding nothing more dangerous than a 5ft, 12lb club. So seriously was the problem taken that it is mentioned in correspondence dated 1560 between Luis de Velasco and Tristan de Luna y Arrellano, who was leading a punitive expedition of 1,500 hardy souls into Pensacola, then a vast swampy wilderness in an area known as La Florida. The damp tropical climate was unhealthy for humans and a poor environment for firearms, with preservation of powder posing a particular problem. Gunpowder was usually kept in wooden flasks or small wooden bottles, each holding one measure charge, with a dozen hanging on a bandolier slung around the musketeer's shoulder. The problem was that the wood became very damp, allowing moisture to penetrate and wet the powder, and the swelling often made it nearly impossible to pull the wooden stoppers out of the bottles. Wood was also vulnerable to fire and containers were notorious for exploding. The leader of the first colony in Virginia, Captain John Smith, was very badly burned by his flask igniting as he placed it in his pocket.

Better methods of carrying powder were always sought and before long practical experience showed that bone or horn flasks were the best containers. Hollowed-out animal horns were waterproof, durable, and fortuitously the ideal shape to be carried comfortably slung over the shoulder. De Velasco wrote of his expedition that its commander "is also taking one hundred and ten or one hundred and twenty horn flasks which will preserve the powder better in a damp cold country than wooden ones, they will last longer and be useful for loading and priming. If they work well let me know and I will send more."[13] This comment on powder horns is particularly instructive as it is the first example of the introduction of the horn in the Americas; for while it is well known that it was the Spanish who introduced the horse as a means of transport into the Americas, it is not so widely appreciated that aside from the widespread use of firearms they also introduced the powder horn. The horn was soon to have almost iconic status as an indispensable accoutrement of the American rifleman and one which was eventually to become its own art form.

Despite their shortcomings, the use of early arquebuses in America is well documented and their numbers were growing. By 1562 the expedition to look for a safe refuge for Huguenot dissidents led by Jean Ribault had with it no fewer than 75 arquebusiers, some 50 percent of his total military force. Carrying firearms was one thing, of course, but using and maintaining them was another. There was little doubt that their effectiveness was limited by terrain, Indian tactics, and the poor quality of their manufacture. The matchlocks coming from Eibar in Spain in the mid-16th century were reckoned to be as good as any produced elsewhere at the time, yet their effectiveness from new was limited by a catalog of problems – barrels that were bored crookedly (a common problem in pre-industrial days), serpentines that did not line up with their pans, and stocks that broke. Care and repair of the firearms was a secondary issue that manifested itself once the expeditions had left the safety of the ship and ventured inland. While onboard there was access to any number of specialists: the blacksmiths could mend metalwork, carpenters repaired stocks, and matchcord could be made (soaked in saltpeter from stocks of sail-maker's rope). In the inhospitable lands of the interior, the men carried with them only the necessities, and frequently not even enough of those. Food was supplemented by what could be hunted, but weapons that broke were frequently irreparable. However, despite the sometimes fraught relationships with the natives, the Spanish and other Europeans often worked closely with friendly tribes, bartering for what they needed and employing natives as load carriers, cooks, and guides. But the Indians' skills did not end there, for if gunsmiths were not available there were many Indians who were skilled at wood- and metal-working and who learned quickly what the Europeans needed. Broken musket stocks were common and there is some proof that Indians were employed to repair or replace them:

> You ask me to send you two Indians who know how to make arquebus stocks. Until now I have not been able to finish with [the] two or three who are making them here ... if there is no one who knows how to make stocks or who can repair the broken ones then ... you will order them sent there and they will be repaired.[14]

It seems entirely logical that if natives were employed to make stocks, then their use for the manufacture and repair of gun parts is highly probable. While it is unlikely they were required to make anything as complex as barrels, even given the resources, their abilities must soon have been every bit as good as those of the Europeans who taught them. It does not take much of a leap of imagination to see that many of these skills once mastered would have been passed on to other allied tribes who were less accommodating to the New World settlers. As early as 1607 Indians of the Powhatan tribes used matchlock muskets against the men of explorer Raleigh Gilbert's expedition, killing several. Captured guns were surely in the hands of natives and their unnerving habit of turning Old World technology against its masters was one that must have begun at a very early stage and was to continue almost unabated into the 20th century. The soldiers themselves were often very ignorant of the most basic maintenance required to ensure their weapons functioned and, in response to a complaint by de Luna on the condition of the muskets carried by his men, de Velasco gave a hint of these problems in one of his letters:

> It pained me to learn what you write me about the little care which the men take to conserve their offensive and defensive arms, for, aside from the fact that they are necessary, they cost a great deal … you will give strict orders how to care for and preserve the arquebuses which came from Spain.[15]

Cost then, as now, was as always a major consideration and an arquebus of the period was valued at 3 ducats, which approximates in today's currency to about £300 or $600.

FROM WHEEL TO FLINT

New technology is seldom truly "new" by the time it reaches the masses, and this is particularly true of firearms. Historians often talk glibly of one form of technology quickly supplanting another. The Iron Age and Bronze Age are talked of in terms of two utterly separate periods, as though in the space of a few years the former metal died out of use while the latter achieved universal acceptance. This of course is an overly simplified view and nowhere near true; most forms of old and new technology were contiguous for decades, if not far longer. Certainly the matchlock was the predominant form of longarm in America for some 150 years and it underwent a number of useful modifications, from simple bar trigger to a sprung or snapping trigger working in much the same manner as a modern one. Priming pans were protected, lock plates became more sophisticated, but in essence the weapon was still ignited by a crude, unreliable system using a piece of burning string.

Around 1520, a new form of lock called the wheellock had appeared in Germany. Relying on a mechanism using a serrated revolving wheel, it worked in exactly the same manner as a cigarette lighter, with a jaw holding a brittle material known as iron pyrites (also called "fools gold") against the wheel, which spun as the trigger was pulled, producing a shower of sparks to drop into the pan. While the wheellock flourished in Europe, particularly in the Low Countries and Germany, it was both comparatively sophisticated and relatively expensive and this placed it out of the mainstream of gun ownership. Some certainly found their way into the Americas, though, for governor Ralph Lane's intriguing narrative history of the colony of Roanoke Island in North Carolina mentions the accidental wounding of an Indian in 1586 by a gun he describes as a *petronel*, which was of wheellock type.[16] Aside from their cost, more important from the viewpoint of the settlers was that wheellocks were difficult to repair, making them unpopular with men whose lives depended on being able to keep their weapons in perfect working order with the minimum of available materials. The Dutch settlers on the eastern seaboard even wrote specifically that when being shipped firearms "we request that the carbines may be snaphaunce, as the people here are but little conversant with the use of the wheel lock."[17] The other shortcoming was that the lock required a key to turn or "span" the lock (hence the origin of the British word "spanner," meaning wrench) to set the spring tension before firing. Loss of this tool, so easily done, immediately rendered the weapon useless as the spring was far too strong to be cocked by hand. Despite these facts, there is certainly evidence of some wheellocks being carried into the interior, de Valasco noting that three were carried by his expedition of 1597 and that another 15 had certainly been supplied from Spain.[18] More crucial from the viewpoint of American firearms development was a new form of lock that was appearing by the final decades of the 16th century. It used flint to strike a spark and quickly became popular in Europe, but it did not reach the American colonies for some time afterwards. It had several names and a number of slightly differing forms and was known variously as the *snaphaunce* or Spanish *miquelet*.

The snaphaunce originated in the Low Countries where its simple mechanism proved to be far more efficient than the old matchlocks. It was a simple form of flintlock, using flint held in a jaw and a striking plate, known as the "battery," against which the flint struck sparks. The use of flint and steel to make fire was an ancient art and had been well known to travelers for centuries, but the name of exactly who thought of combining the two into a firearm lock is lost in the mists of time. Certainly by 1542 German gunsmiths were supplying self-igniting flintlock longarms to Sweden.[19] A few early settlers brought some of these muskets over with them to the east coast of America, and fragmentary remains have been found at Jamestown and in New York State, but relatively few examples exist.

However, a slightly later and more developed form of lock soon appeared, which was known as the "English lock" or "doglock," and remains of these have proven to be quite common. The reason for this is straightforward, for the snaphaunce was never to become a popular mechanism in England, and it had a short life before the introduction of the doglock, which was developed directly from the snaphaunce by English gunsmiths in the late 16th century. This lock was slightly more sophisticated than the snaphaunce, having a recognizably modern flintlock appearance with a cock holding a flint in its jaws and hinged battery plate (soon renamed the "steel" or "frizzen"). The salient feature of the musket was the large hook or "dog" that was visible on the lock plate behind it; when the cock was pulled back, this was dropped into position on a slot cut into the rear face of the cock, effectively providing a "cocked and locked" position. Although crude, it provided a necessary safety feature at a time when a musket often had to be carried loaded, primed, and ready for instant use. Archeological finds from early settlements on the eastern seaboard of the Americas show that these muskets were in widespread use for some 50 years from around 1625 and many complete examples of such weapons are in private collections. They are of second-generation flintlock type, following on from snaphaunces, and with their use came a change in terminology, for around this period the term "firelock" began to appear in common usage, remaining a generic term for any flintlock musket until well into the 19th century.

THE FRENCH LOCK

In contrast to the relatively simple mechanics of the English lock, the introduction of the French or true flintlock was to create a firearm that would find its way into every nook and cranny of American social history, remaining almost unchanged until the late 19th century, long after it had been replaced by cartridge firearms. Its development is one of the few areas of early firearms history where the time, people, and places can be fairly accurately narrowed down and it is to a French gunmaking family, the brothers Jean and Marin le Bourgeoys, that a debt of gratitude is owed. Based in Lisieux, Normandy, between 1570 and 1630, they were inventive, clever, and very skilled, Marin eventually being appointed *L'arquebuzier* (gunsmith) to the French king Henry IV in 1605. At some date between 1605 and 1615 Marin and Jean had perfected an improved flintlock mechanism that relied on elements of other mechanisms, notably Italian and Spanish, but which was in itself a huge improvement in both function and reliability. It incorporated a vital half-cock notch on the sear, with the movement of the tumbler limited by a short steel finger, or pawl, which prevented the cock dropping forward from the half-cock position even if the trigger was pulled hard. This provided a mechanical safety position known as "half-cock" and is where the common expression "going off at half-cock" originates, denoting something that does not work properly, or happens before it was meant to. With the lock perfectly timed – when its internal springs are properly balanced, enabling the cock to drop squarely onto the frizzen the instant the trigger is pulled – a good flintlock musket should be capable of being fired when held upside down, the priming powder igniting before it can fall from the pan. This was to become a simple test for the efficiency of these muskets and one often adopted by

Native Americans, who quickly learned the difference between good quality muskets and poor "trade" muskets. It is inevitable, of course, that few of the military powers in Europe actually took much notice of this new technology; the British were still fighting each other during their Civil War (1642–51) predominantly armed with matchlocks and doglocks, while the other armies of Europe also kept to more tried and trusted (and cheaper) forms of longarm, although snaphaunces did become far more common on the battlefields of Europe than they did in England.

ARMING THE COLONISTS

Notwithstanding the Roanoke settlement, which was mysteriously abandoned sometime between 1587 and 1601, the earliest surviving European settlers on the North American mainland were the 144 hardy souls who had landed in 1607 at Virginia in three ships of The London Company. Rather uninspiringly, they called their settlement James Towne in deference to their king, and the men and women immediately began erecting a stockade, mindful of the depredations the natives could inflict on them. Under John Smith's leadership the settlers were well catered for in terms of firepower, his report of 1609 listing "24 peeces of ordinances [cannon], 300 muskets, snaphaunces and fire-lockes, shot powder and match."[20] This short description is interesting in that it gives definite information about the weapons used, and also proof of the fact that firearms technology was overlapping – the list contains one of the first mentions of the use of the new flintlocks [firelocks] by the settlers, albeit in conjunction with the existing generation of matchlocks. While most longarms in use up to this time were of military pattern (in part because the bulk were supplied by government agencies financing expeditions) there began to occur a gradual change in the type and quality of firearms found in the colonies.

One type of musket much in use was the Russian *samopal*, a form that was quite different from those commonly found at the time and that has been largely overlooked by firearms historians. This is in part due to the relatively few specimens that have survived in North America and because the men who used them left behind little in the way of written history. These muskets were carried by the hardy Russian hunters and trappers who had moved east through Alaska and gradually worked their way south down the northwest coast, eventually reaching the Pacific coast. Some stayed, setting up trading posts in California. The trading post of Fort Ross was established and run by Russian émigrés in the late 18th century. The samopal was to remain almost the same for nearly two centuries, altering only in that it was modified from matchlock to snaphaunce then flintlock, but with no change in the basic design. It was a fully stocked musket, with a long slim barrel of comparatively small caliber, around .40in or less, and the fore-end had a pivot to enable a bipod to be used. A patch-box was often fitted to the side or underside of the butt and, as far as can be ascertained, the barrels were smoothbore, giving the hunter the option of using ball or shot, depending on his quarry. It is not impossible that some of these guns and their owners also headed east towards the Appalachians and even into New England, where the practical design of their weapons would have caused considerable interest among the inhabitants. To what extent the samopal was responsible for the ultimate design of the Kentucky and Tennessee rifles is a moot point, but Russia's early use of small calibers and the fitting of a patch-box was to be much copied by American gunsmiths in a relatively short period of time.

While the Spanish in central America tended to continue using military weapons during their conquests, from the early 17th century among Dutch, Russian, Swedish, British, and a dozen other nationalities there was an increasing tendency towards carrying their own, commercially manufactured muskets, and many of these were of good-quality sporting patterns. It was the adoption by civilians of the new weapons that was to spread their influence across the North American continent, for it was in the hands of the early settlers from Europe that much of the innovative new weapons technology was to appear. Indeed it was not uncommon for soldiers who accompanied the expeditions to be armed with old-fashioned and outdated matchlocks, while the civilians with them had the latest flintlocks. The reason behind this was simply one of self-preservation; few settlers would risk their lives by using anything less than the best firearms they could afford, while soldiers used what they were given. In addition, the new flintlocks made hunting game, especially birds, a far more practical proposition, with no glowing, smoking match or unreliable priming. The speed of ignition and reliability of the new flintlock meant that even taking birds on the wing was now possible and it led to a great upsurge in hunting. At the time it was even given its own unpronounceable term "pteryplegia" and shooting for sport had, by the mid-17th century, become the new sport of the gentry:

I have today been hunting with my compatriots and we have indulged in some splendid shooting, I took four brace of turkey my friend likewise and also many lesser birds. It is indeed a great joy yette I am mindful of the benefits to our cooking potts thatte such sporte brings.[21]

There were other technical innovations as well; many are now overlooked and forgotten, but at the time they provided great impetus for the future development of the longarm and its eventual supremacy as a weapon for both military and hunting use. By about 1600 at least two methods of testing the efficiency of gunpowder had been invented. In 1587 a British writer named William Bourne had commented on the use of a machine "for the testte of divers powders, the use of which in canon and musketts is much improved."[22] Bourne certainly did not invent the machine, for it most probably first appeared in the Low Countries or France, but his is the first mention of such a device. Its introduction in the early 17th century gave powder manufacturers and shooters their first scientific indication of how good or bad any particular powder was, and as a result the quality of gunpowders began to improve. When the settlers landed in Virginia they were armed with a mixture of matchlocks and flintlocks and it is unlikely any of these weapons were other than smoothbored. These guns, long fowling pieces or simply "fowlers," were forms of musket commonly used for hunting and seldom encountered in warfare, but they are an interesting and important development in the story of the American rifle. Such guns were usually of long barrel length and quite solid construction, though nowhere near as cumbersome as the early military matchlocks. They were designed to take multiple small balls for the hunting of waterfowl as well as larger balls for self-defense, which they could fire out to considerable distances, possibly up to 300 yards. Their practicality was such that prospective emigrants in England were strongly advised by Edward Winslow to "Bring ... a musket or fowling peece. Let your peece be long in the barreled; and fear not the weight of it, for most of our shooting is from standes [blinds or cover]."[23]

In November 1620, 109 exhausted pilgrims (or "Saints" as they had originally been called) on the vessel *Mayflower* landed thankfully at Cape Cod and, after some false starts, established the colony of New Plimoth. They had some foretaste of the problems they faced when their captain, Myles Standish, was attacked by Native Americans, but despite a rain of arrows he and a companion used flintlock muskets to keep the natives at bay until more men arrived with firearms. Many of the guns in use were long fowlers and their use was a demonstrable success, so much so that when the Massachusetts Colony was established particular reference was made to their weapons in a surviving inventory. There were:

> 80 bastard muskettes with snaphaunces foure foote in the barrill, without rests.
>
> 6 longe fowlinge peeces with musket boare, 6 foote long and $^1/_2$
>
> 4 longe fowlinge peeces with bastard musket boare $5^1/_2$ foote longe.
>
> 10 ffull muskets, 4 foote barrill with matchlocks and rests.
>
> 90 bandeleers for the muskets each with a bullet bag[24]

Also supplied were 1lb of shot per bandolier, ten horn flasks for the fowling guns with a 1lb powder capacity, and four barrels of gunpowder. The colonists were clearly not going to be caught napping. The difference in bore sizes quoted was due to the fact that musket bore was generally accepted as 12 bore (12 balls to the pound) or .78in, while bastard muskets used a smaller ball of between .65 and .70in and were the early form of a weapon that was to soon become known as the *fusil*. At around the same time, Dutch and Swedish immigrants also began establishing colonies along the Hudson and Delaware rivers and they brought with them both matchlock and snaphaunce muskets. From the late 1630s the increasing levels of trade between settlements along these rivers meant that they were all soon very well aware of the new flintlock arms and they lost little time in replacing their old weapons with the new ones. Unlike some other settlers, the Dutch had little compunction in trading their old guns with the native Mohawks and other tribes of the Iroquoian nations, and this trade began to encourage the early use of firearms among the Indian tribes. It was a trade that was to have unpleasant consequences for the settlers, as the natives quickly began to understand the significance of firearms and the advantages that their ownership conferred.

The Spanish failure to keep their hard-won territories in New Florida is testament to how possession of modern technology did not necessarily provide the user with any long-term material advantages. Indian bows worked regardless of climate and did not explode, unlike the powder store in St Augustine when struck by lightning in 1592, leaving the fort almost defenseless. Even those weapons that were kept in store succumbed to the two evils of poor climate and lack of maintenance, a report of 1653 showing that none of the 184 matchlocks stored there were in working condition, some having rotted beyond repair, while the powder had decayed through dampness to a point where it too was of no practical use.[25]

Aside from the problems of climate and Native Americans faced by the Spanish, by the 1660s British colonists were firmly establishing themselves in the Carolinas and taking on an increasingly aggressive stance against the Spanish. Neither was the situation helped by the Madrid government, which had continually ignored pleas for military help from Florida and the east coast. Indeed, many soldiers had not been paid for so long that they had sold or traded their weapons with the Indians to buy food, a situation that did not materially help the balance of power. The new governor of Florida, Juan Cabrera, even resorted to purchasing commercial muskets from English and American traders.[26] There was also a subtle change in attitude towards the Indians, as they were increasingly being employed as paid mercenaries by the warring colonists, in part because of their ability to wage stealthy warfare in the woods and forests. It was not a skill that the Europeans possessed. Like the Dutch, the Spanish frequently armed their Indian allies in order that they could assist them in fighting off the encroaching English and French. There exists a letter dated June 1686 in which Spanish policy is clearly outlined, for Governor Cabrera wrote to request that an armed scout party be sent into lower Alabama and should comprise "Twelve soldiers ... armed with muskets ... and also twenty Indians with firearms and twenty with bows and arrows."[27] The sight of white colonists fighting each other must have amused the Indians, but they were nothing if not opportunists and the chance to arm themselves at the white man's expense would not have been lightly passed over.

The late 17th century was to herald the start of a new era of brutal warfare between not only the colonists but also the crowned heads of Europe, leading to revolution. By the middle of the 17th century, there was increasing organization and order being applied to the settlements of colonists who had been, and still were, establishing themselves along the eastern coast and, more frequently, moving westwards to settle and explore the interior of central America. The weapons carried, aside from the traditional swords and pole arms, were predominantly firearms and comprised wheellocks in relatively small numbers and matchlocks and flintlocks in equal numbers. By the latter quarter of the century, flint weapons were to become predominant. There was as yet no form of firearms standardization for any type of firearm, a problem that was by no means unique to the colonies, and a particular problem for the emerging militia units. But order would soon be brought to the chaos by the arrival of professional armies, which would shortly engage in a long drawn-out series of wars that would change, and help to define, America.

Chapter 2
WINDS OF CHANGE

By the latter part of the 17th century, a change was occurring in the balance of power in America. While the Spanish were by no means a spent force, their depredations into southern America had ceased as their home government was forced to deal with a series of complex foreign policy problems closer to home. These included both the Second Dutch War and the Thirty Years' War, and the political situation had been further confused by the death of King Philip IV in 1665. His successor, Mariana of Austria, was a woman with very different views on foreign policy, and this shift materially derailed Spanish plans for expansion. Nevertheless, at the time of Philip's death Spain had no fewer than 40 missions in La Florida as well as colonies in Mexico and Texas. All were under continual threat, though. The Mexican Spanish were actually being driven out of the province for 12 years after the Pueblo revolt of 1680 and the Texan community were under repeated attack from the Comanche Indians, who were materially assisted by French-supplied firearms, in addition to suffering more frequent raids by British colonists from the southern states.

This was the period when the flintlock musket really became the predominant firearm in North America, its supremacy due mainly to the French for the trading influence of La Compagnie de la Nouvelle France (The New France Company, equivalent to the Hudson Bay or East India companies), which had grown hugely in power, wealth, and influence. If the Spanish introduction of their arquebus firearms had been something less than an technological *tour de force* in America, the same cannot be said of the French flintlock. In common with most other colonists, French traders had initially been equipped with matchlocks, but the introduction of the Bourgeoys' perfected flintlock mechanism in the second decade of the 17th century meant that French colonists and explorers were to become armed with the new musket far sooner than most of their contemporaries. By the 1640s the political influence of La Compagnie had become enormous, bolstered by support from the new king, Louis XIV (1638–1715), whose interest in seeing his dominions flourish was a determining factor.

Things were not easy for the French in North America, though, for the powerful Iroquois had sided with the British to fight their ancient enemy the Huron, who were strongly allied to the French. This internecine warfare of course predated white influence in America, but was won, initially at least, by the Iroquois, who had been well supplied with firearms by British and Dutch traders. It was a well-known fact that illegal gun running to the Indians was a large and very profitable business, particularly as so many matchlocks and snaphaunces were now being replaced with flintlock muskets. It only reflects human nature that many settlers, sensing quick and handsome profits, had turned to supplying forbidden articles to the Indians, the highest on the list being weapons and alcohol, despite their trade being expressly forbidden by their respective governments. The Dutch had even introduced the death penalty for gun running in 1620; the Spanish likewise never officially condoned it, and their government was outraged to discover that adventurers such as de Soto were prepared to trade with Indians. The British Crown also responded to the increasingly frequent level of attacks from firearm-equipped Indians with an edict of 1641, stating "In trucking or trading with the Indians no man shall give them for any commodity of theirs, silver or gold, or any weapons of war, either guns or gunpowder, nor sword ... which might come to be used against ourselves."[1] Of course, such declarations were cheerfully ignored by almost everyone, not least the governments who themselves supplied weapons to Indian allies; the increasingly belligerent attitude of some of the tribes towards the white men did nothing to assist harmonious relationships. Indeed, relationships between the settlers and the natives had soured to the point that Dutch authorities offered a bounty for the scalp of any Indian; thus it was Europeans, not the indigenous peoples, who introduced the practice of scalping into the New World.

THE FRENCH INFLUENCE

In 1666 the French decided that the Iroquois were becoming too powerful and were threatening to loosen the grip France held on its territory in New France. Crucially, the French were one of the first major military powers to have adopted wholesale the flintlock system for their armies, due in the main to the influence of the forward-thinking Minister of War, François Le Tellier (1641–91). The real significance of the French use of the musket lay not so much in its novelty as a flintlock weapon, but in its early adoption as a standard military pattern and the fact that it was developed to be specifically issued to line infantry.

Up to the mid-1600s, military muskets used in Europe were of varying makes, differing calibers, and varying barrel lengths, and almost all were heavy and of large caliber. There were some few exceptions, the *caliver* being an early form of light musket with a shorter barrel and of lighter weight, but it was the French who were to pioneer the introduction of the *fusil*, which appeared around 1645. It was a radical departure from those cumbersome longarms that had previously been in service, being of much slimmer and lighter construction. It had been developed almost directly from the line of sporting fowling guns that had found such favor in Europe after 1620. Thus, by 1665 French line regiments were being issued with the new musket as well as some light infantry regiments, who were being supplied with them for use by scouts, skirmishing parties, and guards. This distribution is not to infer that the French totally abandoned the old, heavy martial matchlock overnight, for they did not. The two forms of technology were to overlap for many years – it was not until 1699 that the matchlock was finally declared obsolete for French military service. For the infantry occupying the scattered stockades and forts across North America, the matchlock continued to remain in service long after that date, for it was a good enough weapon when fired from a solid platform that could support its weight. But the new fusil was far better suited to the type of warfare encountered in North America; an average fusil musket, as supplied by a French commercial contractor, weighed 8–9lb, was 60in long, and was fully stocked to the muzzle. It had little in the way of adorning metalwork, save a simple steel lockplate held by two screws and two brass thimbles to retain the wooden ramrod. Its caliber was still about .76in, similar to that of most other military firearms. As a foot soldier's weapon it was less cumbersome to wield, faster to load and fire and far lighter to carry than its predecessors, and it was to provide the cornerstone for an entire gunsmithing industry in the New World.

In 1666, for the first time the French sent a regular army unit, Le Régiment de Carignan-Saliers, to North America entirely equipped with the new muskets. The use of these hardened professional soldiers effectively sealed the fate of the Iroquois, who suffered a bitter series of defeats, and for two decades they posed no further military threat to the French dominion. This outcome fortuitously left the French free to pursue their expanding territorial ambitions along the Mississippi River where a number of trading forts were established, ultimately bringing the French into increasing conflict with already established British, Dutch, and German traders. It should be understood, however, that at this time, despite the number of Spanish and French colonies that had been established or were in the process of being established in the New World, by far the largest majority of colonists were still the English, some 4,646 having settled on the east coast by 1630. This figure rose dramatically after the English Civil War (1642–51) as disenchanted Royalist supporters left Britain, bringing the numbers close to 50,000 by 1660.[2] In the wake of France's desire to expand its lucrative trading interests and the arrival of increasing numbers of English speaking settlers, it was to be only a matter of time before the two nations embarked on a collision course.

MUSKETS AND MILITIA

Of course, it was not only the French who were troubled by Indian depredations: attacks on settlements were commonplace across North America. The British colony at Jamestown had been attacked by the Powhatan tribe in 1622, the colonists losing almost a quarter of their inhabitants. Even the New Englanders, who were relatively well disposed towards their native neighbors, had been on the receiving end of an attack by the Pequot Indians, who had been well supplied with firearms by traders. This clash escalated into a full-scale uprising within five years, a state of affairs that so affected the settlement of Rhode Island that it was decreed in 1638 that "Every inhabitant of the Island shall be always supplied with one musket, one pound of powder, twenty bulletts, and two fadem [approximately 12ft] of match."[3] Such requirements obviously indicate the use of matchlocks at this date, but interestingly within five years this requirement had changed, when the Virginia Assembly stated that men taking part in the reprisal attack on the Pamunkey Indians should carry "1 good fixed gunne."[4] This referred specifically to a flintlock pattern of musket, with a cock, pan-cover, and battery, or frizzen, which may have been of either snaphaunce or early doglock pattern.

Beset by enemies on all sides, the colonists responded by forming their own armed Watch Bands or militias. These were not professional soldiers, but men aged between 18 and 45, equipped at the expense of their colonies, prepared to fight for the defense of life and property. The Massachusetts Bay Colony had gained permission from King James I to form their militia in March 1628, the purpose being:

> To encounter, expulse, repel and resist by force of arms ... and by all fitting ways and means whatsoever, all such person and persons who shall, at anytime hereafter attempt ... the destruction, invasion, detriment or annoyance to the said plantations or inhabitants ... or the hurt of the said company or inhabitants.[5]

In retrospect, this action by the British government condoning the raising of an American military force seems rather ironic in view of future events, but at the time it was to set the scene for the raising of militia units right across the British-inhabited colonies. The movement became a patriotic duty, with men taking it as a matter of personal pride rather than a civic duty to serve and protect their new homeland. These units were initially unskilled at drill, but increasingly took part in musters during which basic military training was instilled in them, as well as skill-at-arms training. Although often denigrated by the British professional soldiers who were to fight them, these militia units were to become the cornerstone in securing the New World as a free colony. The militia were now used to combat the increasing problem of Indian attacks, some 1,000 being employed in 1675 to defeat the Wampanoag Indian chief known as Philip, who had led increasingly savage attacks on Massachusetts settlements, razing to the ground at least a dozen of them. This period became known as "The Killing Time," from the number of attacks launched by settlers on the Native American tribes who inhabited the east coast – Narragansetts, Wampanoags, and Nipmuk all suffered from the wrath of the Puritans, and this period was responsible for the near-total annihilation of most of the eastern tribes.

WEAPONS AND SUPPLY

Throughout the 17th century the weapons in use still varied widely, and some idea of the mixture of old and new in service can be gleaned from the description of a Boston muster in 1639:

> So there mustered on Boston common, then a mere pasture … cleared of cows, sheep and goats … some ten companies of stalwart militia. The Boston company is the largest numbering between one hundred and fifty and two hundred men. Its musketeers are ranged according to the length of their weapons, some carrying matchlock muskets six feet in length and strong, steel-shod rests, and holding between the fingers of the right hand doubled lengths of match ready for present use. Others have equally long, but smaller bored fowling pieces, with great powder horns and bags for bullets and "great shot"; but the most have "bastard" flintlock muskets or "snaphaunces" with

barrels four feet six inches in length, of smaller bore and destined soon to replace the clumsy matchlocks altogether.[6]

In practice, although the settlers were reasonably well supplied with muskets, they were scarcely capable of defending themselves in the face of any sustained Indian attacks, as almost everything they required was in short supply. Surprisingly, until 1666 there was no American manufactory for gunpowder and even by 1675 there were only two recorded makers in North America,[7] all supplies having to be imported, as was also the majority of the lead required for bullet casting. Casting was a normal fireside practice for most frontier families, with a mold, often homemade, being used to produce shot. Such was the value of lead that cast shot or lead ingot was often used as a means of trade in place of money. In 1630 a single musket ball was reckoned to be worth one farthing ($^1/_4$ penny),[8] which was no small amount, and all other components were just as difficult to procure. Iron was produced in small amounts, a modest foundry existing at Jamestown dating back to the first decade of the 17th century, but it was at Boston that the manufacture of iron began in quantity around 1646 with other foundries opening gradually. Despards Forge was established in Pembroke, Massachusetts, in 1702 but it was to be almost two decades before another, Christines or Reddings Forge, was built in 1720 in Chester County, Pennsylvania. After that, forges began to spring up like mushrooms in New England, some 86 appearing up to 1776, reflecting the rising demand for iron.[9] Until well into the 19th century ships arriving at the east coast ports used lead and iron as ballast, selling them off for a handsome profit and returning with timber in their place.

Meanwhile, by the latter quarter of the century gunmaking in Europe had become a far more organized and industrialized process. The old traditional methods that involved a skilled gunmaker and his apprentices manufacturing a firearm completely from scratch had all but died out, proving too labor intensive and expensive. The demand for guns, particularly from North America, was outstripping supply and the faster that weapons could be produced the better. A system of contracting-out had been in use in Europe for some years, whereby one supplier would provide finished locks, another complete barrels, and another stocks. The slow business of putting them together, or "fitting up" as it was known, fell to semi-skilled laborers who were not qualified gunsmiths, but were very competent in their own specialty. It was not quite production-line manufacture, but had many of the elements of what was eventually to become mass production. A single supplier might well be asked to provide a large order of completed muskets, and his responsibility was to ensure that they were fully functioning and had suitably proofed barrels. Unlike in America, proofing was required by law in most of Europe and demanded a barrel double-charged with powder and ball and test fired to ensure it would not burst.

The number of guns imported into the Americas brought about an interesting development in the use of firearms for purposes other than hunting or defense. Notwithstanding the shortages of powder and ball, many of the émigrés to the New World brought with them their passion for target shooting. The new flintlocks had not only radically improved the ability of shooters to hunt game, but also increased the popularity of the sport of target shooting, a pastime that was nothing new by any means. Archery and crossbow shooting had been hugely popular for centuries in Europe, and the first shooting matches using firearms appeared in central Europe around the mid-16th century. Indeed one of the first firearms clubs in existence had been formed in Switzerland in the mid-15th century. There has always been much misunderstanding about the exact capabilities of the early muskets in terms of achievable accuracy and it is usually quoted, quite correctly, that a musket was capable of hitting its target at no more than 50–90 yards, depending on the quality of gun. Probably the best contemporary comments concerning these weapons, the most common type used in North America until the introduction of the rifled musket, were the words penned by Colonel George Hanger, a professional British soldier and keen sports shooter, who wrote at the turn of the 18th century:

A soldier's musket, if not exceedingly ill-bored and very crooked, as many are, will strike the figure of a man at 80 yards; it may even at a hundred, but a man must be very unfortunate indeed who shall be wounded by a common musket at 150 yards, providing his antagonist aims at him; and as to firing at a man at 200 yards with a common musket, you may just as well fire at the moon, and have the same hopes of hitting your target. I do maintain, and will prove whenever called on, that no man was ever killed, at 200 yards by a common soldier's musket, by the person who aimed at him.[10]

These figures are borne out by empirical testing, but of course such comments relate to the use of *military* pattern muskets and, as has been shown, by the middle of the 17th century there were large numbers of commercial sporting muskets in use. These, in the hands of a skilled shot, were remarkably capable weapons, their long barrels, patched ball, and rudimentary but effective sights providing the shooter with a weapon capable of accurate shooting at 200+ yards. Indeed, a popular target was an iron pan, hanging in a tree at a distance of around 150 yards, for which the shooter had to allow for not only distance but also deflection as the target swung gently in the breeze; many men were capable of putting five shots consecutively into it.

POLITICS AND THE PEOPLE

It was not just problems with Indians that were occupying the minds of the colonists, for events in Europe were about to change the course of colonial history. Under King Louis XIV, France had at last begun to take a serious interest in events in the New World, and in 1663 the colony of New France was elevated to a royal province, with Québec becoming its capital. More importantly, Louis authorized the establishment of a barracks with 1,200 permanent regular soldiers in residence. The French had also established *compagnies franches* or "free companies" of militia, initially recruited exclusively from French colonists, but soon men from anywhere within the province were accepted; by 1688 these militiamen had replaced the regular army troops stationed there.

The British had also had their own problems, and despite the execution of King Charles I in 1649 the Civil War did not end until 1651. Oliver Cromwell's subsequent rise to power established a commonwealth government and was also to begin the slow process of the formation of the first standing, professional army in British history, the New Model Army. This was something Parliament, worried by the authority wielded by the king, had always fought shy of introducing but now, with Britain under new management, it acquiesced. The soldiers were to be equipped for the first time with standardized weapons, although these were still largely obsolete matchlocks or English lock muskets. The New Army had a relatively brief existence, though, for following the restoration of the monarchy in 1660 and Cromwell's death the new king, Charles II (1630–85), was forced to reduce the size of the King's Militia to 5,000 men. Nevertheless, Cromwell had established the concept of a regular army and under Charles' rule the American colonies were soon to be bolstered by British troops, although their actual use there was mainly left to the whims of their commanding officers. Had this situation continued then the history of the New World, indeed the entire world, might well have turned out very differently.

Alas for the New Englanders, in 1685 the repressive and dictatorial James II (1633–1701) acceded to the British throne. His heavy-handed actions and antipathy towards the colonists were not helped by his appointment of Sir Edmund Andros as Governor General in the colonies, whose attitude to the many problems besetting the New Englanders was, to say the least, unsympathetic. However, under James there were some significant changes made in the weapons issued to the army, which was finally following the French lead in starting to reequip with modern muskets. Some firearms historians have described the quarter century following on from 1675 as the start of a new age in British military firearms technology, although perhaps this is not entirely accurate. It would be more correct to say it was a period that heralded the beginnings of change. After all, the adoption of the fusil would not in itself radically alter the way warfare was conducted, nor would it give the army any overwhelming weapons superiority over any other professional army. Of course, the speed of reequipping was glacially slow, only two regular regiments having been furnished with fusils by 1689.[11] However, what was of greater importance for the future of the colonists was that under James the size of the army was dramatically increased to some 32,000 men. Existing contracts from the period give a good idea of the demands of the army for weapons from the Birmingham contractors, who by now were almost exclusively supplying the government. An order from the Master General of the Ordnance dated 1685 specified: "That the 2300 musket barrels last proved [proofed] be forthwith stocked and locked; that is all that are 3 feet or longer [in the barrel] to be stocked with walnut stocks and the locks to be double springs French locks with Kings cipher engraved."[12] The commonly used term of supplying something "lock, stock, and barrel" dates from this mid-17th century period, signifying that an item was to be supplied in complete and working form. There were also specifications drawn up for the standardization of firearms, six types being listed: matchlock and snaphaunce muskets, snaphaunce carbines, pistols, naval blunderbusses, and musketoons (carbines).[13] Only four years later, in 1689 James was deposed by William III (1650–1702) who was to continue with re-arming the army. He had been a professional soldier, fighting in the Dutch Wars, and under his command the new muskets were ordered to be supplied to line regiments as soon as possible. He also ordered that the old matchlocks be disposed of and he set about trying to ensure that the Board of Ordnance made the changes as rapidly as possible. His plans for swift reforms were to be somewhat thwarted by events occurring elsewhere.

THE FRENCH AND SPANISH WARS

The final years of the 17th century were to prove something of a watershed for European and North American politics, for in the year following James' deposition, events in the New World took a dramatic turn when a colonial congress met in New York and agreed to the conquest of Canada to wrest it from French influence. The New Englanders who embarked on this ambitious campaign were sadly doomed to fail, but in 1711 the uncomfortable peace with France was broken by the arrival of seven regiments of British infantry and nearly 1,000 marines at Boston. They were helped by some 5,500 locally raised troops. While the campaign was to be wrecked by natural causes, primarily storms causing several shipping disasters, it did see the start of the formation of an emerging professional fighting force. This force was to work well in the future American wars, comprising mixed regular and militia troops as well as locally raised native scouts. Of course the French also had alliances not only with native tribes but also with the Spanish, who were to support them against the British until the end of the Wars of Revolution. The English king was reliant upon his regular army troops stationed in the eastern colonies as well as locally raised militia units, the majority of whom were loyal to the Crown. However, there were to be more changes, for in 1714 the Hanoverian King George I acceded to the English throne, strongly allying Britain with the Hanoverian dynasty and its political machinations in Europe. George pursued the war against the French in the New World with new enthusiasm.

All these events usefully coincided with improvements in the manufacture and design of the service musket and the long-overdue introduction of a standard pattern British longarm, almost universally known now as the Brown Bess. How this name came about is the subject of much debate, as the original Long Land Pattern musket adopted in 1715 did not have browned but bright finished metalwork. Neither was the stock of dark walnut but a light yellow-brown color and the name did not actually appear in print until some 70 years after its introduction.[14] Nevertheless, it was not a radical design, being a traditional solidly made smoothbore flintlock musket, of .78 caliber with a 46in barrel. After experience in the field the barrel was subsequently reduced to 42in then 39in by the late 1770s. Its main claims to fame were its extraordinary longevity, as it stayed in service in slightly modified form for almost 130 years, and the fact that it was the first in a long series of military weapons to be assembled under Government Ordnance control at the Tower of London. Parts were supplied by contractors and assembly was done within the Tower by fitters-up.

Meanwhile, dissatisfied with its lingering quarrel with France, in 1739 Britain had also declared war on Spain in a conflict known as "The War of Jenkins Ear." This was to last for three years, concluding with a victory for the British at Saint Simon Colony in Georgia, effectively ending Spanish plans for expansion on the North American mainland. It cost Britain and her American and militia volunteers dearly, with some 10,000 casualties. Of the 500 Massachusetts men who embarked on the campaign, only 50 survived to return home.[15] The reason for such losses was partly the method of fighting that the European armies adopted, known as linear warfare. This involved lines of men, usually three deep, loading and firing volleys of muskets on command, at ranges often less than 20 yards. The net effect was for the bullets to cut huge swathes through the enemy's lines, which were immediately filled by the ranks closely packed behind. It was a test of both nerve and discipline and the French and British armies excelled at it. However, colonial militiamen were not used to disciplined fighting of this type and while many of them eventually adapted well to it others found it not at all to their liking. In particular, New Englanders with their accurate muskets could see little point to acting as standing targets for the enemy, when the obvious solution was to fire accurately from cover.

At this time, there is very little evidence that rifles were in use in any numbers. The vast majority of militiamen were still armed with a mix of commercial or military pattern smoothbore muskets, although there are a few unsubstantiated contemporary accounts of the use of rifles by the French. During the Braddock expedition against the French at Pittsburg in 1755, the author of a letter wrote that the French musket fire was different in that their bullets made a sound "like Poping [popping] shots, with little explosion, only a kind of whizzing noise," which is proof that the enemy's arms had rifled barrels.[16] This is an interesting little comment for a spinning rifle bullet made a sound distinct from that of a common musket ball as it passed by, different enough for an experienced soldier to note the difference. This does not, of course, provide any conclusive proof of the widespread use of rifles by the French, but it is certainly an indication that rifles may have been employed.

THE FIRST RANGERS

Barely had the New England militia been able to lick its wounds, when again war broke out against the French in a conflict known as King George's War (1744–48). In 1744 some 240 New Englanders were sent to Carolina to help protect it against expected French attacks, and in 1745 a large force of colonial militia, 3,200 from Massachusetts and 300 each from New Hampshire and Rhode Island, in company with ships of the Royal Navy, sailed to attack Cape Breton in Canada. To complicate matters further, a series of wars erupted between the French and Indians (1754–63). Within a couple of years the war had spread to involve both Britain and France, where it was to become known as The Seven Years War (1756–63).

The troops sent to battle against the French were successful in part because of the employment of some very irregular troops known locally as rangers. The use of rangers was to prove a very important factor in understanding how the American rifleman was eventually to develop and become the specialist soldier of the future. These locally raised units were originally Indian hunters who specialized in woodland fighting and skirmishing using Native American tactics. Their formation certainly predated the Revolutionary War period in which they came to fame. Rangers of this type existed during King Philip's War of the 1670s, and in 1709 a group of 14 men collectively known as Wright's Rangers had embarked on a marathon expedition up the Connecticut River deep into uncharted Indian territory. It is generally accepted that their formation came from the need for colonists to be constantly protected when working outside of the safety of their stockades; the rangers were men with sharp eyes and a steady aim whose job was to ensure the protection of their compatriots. Ranger units served their communities well during the Indian depredations in Massachusetts and New England, but their early employment as fighting troops under regular army command was something of a watershed, even though it could be perhaps described as something less than an unqualified success. Some of these veteran rangers were employed to train young recruits, including one youngster from Concord, Massachusetts, named Robert Rogers. However, their brief appearance during the French wars was merely a foretaste of greater things to come.

At the outset the rangers were, as one British diarist noted, "Of independent mind and spirit and took not easily to the discipline of an army." They acted as guards, scouts, and skirmishers and the provincial militia regiments raised to fight the French normally included one or two companies of rangers whose equipment and clothing differed substantially from that of the other militia soldiers. They dressed in the same hunting clothes that they habitually wore, outfits that bore no relationship to the formal military uniforms of the period. In the early years of ranger employment, many adopted and wore a mix of New and Old World clothing, wearing frontier-style shirts and short coats. Their trousers, or breech-clouts, featured leggings secured by thongs to protect against sharp undergrowth and the ruthless biting insects, which ranger Rufus Putnam described: "… having no blankets, and I had nothing but a shirt and Indian stockings, and no man can tell what an affliction those little animals were."[17] Hats were normally a mixture of knitted caps, loose woolen French-style berets, or round-crowned broad-brimmed slouch hats, a type commonly used in Britain during this period, as well as locally made leather and fur patterns for winter. European leather shoes or boots were found to be wanting in the harsh terrain and were difficult to mend, so rangers normally wore moccasins – comfortable, silent, and easy to repair or replace as required. An indispensable part of a ranger's dress was his shooting bag containing all he needed to ensure that his musket functioned. Early rangers tended to wear a mix of accoutrements, with a powder bottle or flask and priming powder flask slung round the shoulder and a small leather bullet pouch with knife and hatchet carried on a wide leather belt. A slung haversack served to hold clothes, food, and other necessary items. Above all else, though, there was one single object that defined the ranger, and that was his musket.

MUSKET AND RIFLE

The rangers' muskets were often different in form from those found in the fortified colonial settlements. Heavy matchlocks for defense were fine in their place, but the rangers, because their fighting method was characterized by constant movement and the need to carry everything they needed with them, invariably carried muskets that had evolved into something slimmer and lighter. As already stated, this trend was not new or unique; it had been occurring gradually in Europe from the mid-17th century. As the large military muskets had been changing so too had the commercial muskets, and the rangers and other settlers had begun to adopt their own distinctive styles. One significant form of musket was introduced in Europe that was to have a profound technological influence on the future of American gunsmithing and accurate shooting – the rifled musket.

As with so many mechanical innovations, the exact identity of the inventor of rifling is now lost in the mists of time; it may well have been the result of several individuals working independently of each other at a roughly similar time. In the 16th century the science of rifling, while it was certainly known, was imperfectly understood though rifled guns did exist. Indeed, matchlocks of the period with straight grooves in the bore are not unknown, showing at least a willingness to embrace new technology, even if the comprehension behind it was somewhat lacking; however, it is worth adding that straight-grooved barrels do have the benefit of helping to reduce fouling. For those who consider accurate rifle shooting to be a purely modern innovation, it might be surprising to learn that as early as 1547 in Mainz, Germany, one member of the flourishing Sharpshooters Guild was recorded as firing 20 shots at 200 yards with a rifled gun, scoring 19 bulls-eyes and placing one shot within 18in of it.[18]

What can be said of the invention of rifling is that it *may* have been developed as a result of the understanding bowmen had of the nature of the flight of their arrows. The fletching of an arrow when fitted to the shaft at a slight angle caused the arrow to spin in flight, providing greater stability and accuracy. Therefore, it did not take the brain of a genius to associate the flight of an arrow with that of a bullet. In the 16th century some rifled barrels were produced in Germany, albeit in tiny numbers. The spiral grooves cut into the bore formed what were known as lands and grooves, which performed the same task as angled fletching, causing the bullet to spin as it was propelled up the barrel and providing it with gyroscopic stability. From the viewpoint of the shooter, this innovation improved the accuracy of a musket beyond all imagination, enabling an aimed shot to be made to 200 yards, as opposed to the 80 yards of an ordinary musket.

These early German gunmakers deserve the credit for the eventual widespread adoption of the rifle, although as with any such inventions, its primary use was for sporting purposes. Hunting in Germany was an ancient tradition. Generations of young Germans had been initiated into the art of stalking and tracking in the dark, sunless woodlands, where shooting was often done at ranges well under 200 yards as the dense undergrowth usually made long-range shots impossible. A sure hit was required to ensure a potentially dangerous game animal went down, and stayed down. Certainly, the matchlock musket with its glowing matchcord had never been a good weapon for stalking in the confines of a forest and, while the invention of the wheellock had been a practical step forwards as a sporting weapon, it could prove fatally unreliable in the face of some of the more dangerous game (such as boar and bear) that inhabited German forests. By the turn of the 17th century, in response to practical demand, gunsmiths had begun to develop a shorter, heavy-barreled rifled musket known as the *Jaeger* rifle. They were materially aided in this project by improvements in manufacturing technology, with increased use of water power and improved methods of mechanical barrel-boring. Ignition had also evolved thanks to the introduction of the French flintlock. So successful was the rifle that by the mid-17th century the German hunting sportsmen, also known as Jaegers, had almost universally adopted this compact and powerful sporting rifle.

It took considerable time for the benefits of the rifle to come to the notice of the military. Boring barrels had hitherto been an exacting and very skilled task, both time-consuming and costly, which made such weapons too expensive for large-scale military issue. Yet so practical was the Jaeger design that in 1711 it was adopted for military use by the German states and was to remain almost unchanged for 150 years. A typical Jaeger was fitted with an octagonal barrel of 28–33in, with a heavy breech to withstand the large powder charges. Sighting was by means of a simple flip-up V rear sight and brass or iron blade foresight. The walnut stock was heavy and relatively straight to assist in transferring recoil straight into the shoulder, and the butt was made with a raised comb to provide a cheek rest. A distinctive patch-box was inlet into the right side of the butt, in either wood, brass, or a combination of the two, and the fore-end was capped either with brass or iron. These rifles typically weighed between 7 and 8lb, and the later models chambered a slightly smaller ball than the standard military musket, typically of between .52 and .65 caliber. In terms of accuracy, these rifles were not much inferior to modern weapons; tests carried out in 1953 between three short-range rifles showed that they were very capable indeed. The rifles tested comprised a wheellock target rifle, Jaeger rifle of *c.* 1730, and a brand new Winchester .30-30 carbine. It was soon established that the Jaeger was the most accurate at 100 yards, producing $2^3/4$in groups.[19] Later tests also showed it to be quite equal over longer ranges to later examples of Kentucky rifles.[20]

Despite the difficulties and relatively high cost of manufacturing rifled barrels, which had to be made with absolutely perfect consistency or they would prove useless, there was an ever-growing demand for them which ensured that by the mid-18th century rifles would become the predominant hunting weapons in Germany and much of central Europe. Neither should the contribution of the Swiss gunmakers be overlooked, for they were producing some of the finest and most accurate wheellock rifles in existence. While Switzerland was not generally involved in the periodic warfare that ebbed and flowed around Europe, its militia were exceedingly well armed and target shooting bordered on a national obsession. Many Swiss wheellock rifles of this period still exist, their quality a testament to the craftsmanship that went in to them; many were still in regular use well into the early 19th century, when wheellocks had long been eclipsed by flintlocks. The Swiss gunmakers and metalworkers who emigrated to the New World in the early 17th century took their skills with them and were to be fundamental in helping establish the American firearms industry.

The glory for inventing rifling must not go entirely to Germany, though, for the quiet innovation in 1635 of an English gunmaker called Arnold Rotispen has been an important factor in firearms development. In 1620 he invented and patented an improved "art, industrie, way, or means of making gonnes," referring probably to the mechanics of an improved barrel-boring machine. His later application for a more detailed patent specifically stated it to be: "To rifle, cutt out or screwe barrels as wyde or as close or as deepe or as shallowe as shal be required."[21] Of course, Rotispen was responsible for inventing the mechanical process of rifling, but his patent is significant because it showed that at this date there was a clear understanding of the technical and practical benefits of having rifling. Sadly there are few examples of English rifles existing from this date; doubtless many have succumbed to the ravages of time.

The 18th century was something of a watershed for American history, demography, and technology, with the country witnessing many profound changes. In 1710, in the space of two decades, the population in New England alone had grown from 251,000 to 360,000. By the early 1730s the colonists had formed a series of settlements along the eastern seaboard and cut a swathe 200 miles into the interior. Whatever weapons came over with them would have needed repair and modification and it was initially to the blacksmith that they turned. Over a period of time the increasing number of firearms in use demanded more specialisms, so it was inevitable that some blacksmiths turned more towards gunsmithing.

There were, of course, professional gunmakers within some communities, although they appear to have been very few in number. The earliest gunsmith recorded was working in New France in 1625, although Champlain's expedition of 1608 had the services of one Antoine Natel, a lockmaker, and he mentions another lockmaker working in French Québec in 1620.[22] Records from Jamestown show that an English blacksmith named James Read repaired firearms around 1607. There is little proof, however, that early settlements in New England had any professional gunsmiths working in them prior to 1630, when one named Pomeroy from Devon in England is recorded as establishing a small gunsmith's at Dorchester, Massachusetts.[23] The Pomeroy family actually continued to provide firearms to the frontier trade for some 219 years, becoming possibly the longest-surviving family firearms business in North America. The Dutch colonies could not boast a resident gunsmith until

1646, when the delightfully named Covert Barent was registered in New Amsterdam,[24] by which time a number of provincial gunsmiths had become well established in Massachusetts. The colonies were different from Europe, as there did not exist the rigidly controlled guild systems of professional artisans, so the gunmakers who arrived brought with them a broad mix of skills, styles, and specialisms which they were able to expand upon without interference. Unlike in Britain and Europe, no higher authority needed to be consulted before innovations could be introduced and no patents had to be applied for. Manufacture was on an "as required" basis, with modifications or alterations done where and when needed. By the middle of the 17th century there were a dozen established gunmakers in Boston and others in East and West New Jersey, New Haven, New York, and Pennsylvania, as well as the Carolinas and Kentucky. This was the dawn of a long and very fruitful period of gunmaking that would survive into the 20th century. While initially most of these men simply repaired broken weapons, it took little time before they were able to buy the raw materials needed to manufacture their own guns, and many began copying the styles with which they were familiar back in Europe. In particular a style of rifled musket was to emerge that would define the American rifleman of the 18th century, and is known now as the Kentucky.

THE EMERGENCE OF THE KENTUCKY

Like the name "Brown Bess," the origins of the term "Kentucky rifle" are a mystery, although it certainly appeared in a popular ballad of 1815 entitled "The Hunters of Kentucky" to commemorate the victory over the British in the Battle of New Orleans. Like its ancestor the arquebus, the actual type of longarm used was never specifically defined as a Kentucky, Pennsylvania, or any other type in print, but was invariably simply referred to as "a rifle," or, more often in contemporary writing, long gun. Pennsylvania was to be the traditional birthplace of the American rifle, although it should be pointed out from the beginning that in this evolutionary period from the start of the century to about 1750, there was really no such thing as an archetypical American rifle. The German immigrant gunsmiths in Pennsylvania worked with what they had and what they knew, so, while many early rifles such as the surviving example used by Pennsylvania pioneer Edward Marshall bear a very close resemblance to the Jaeger pattern, almost all rifles differed from each other in some or other respect. Barrels were octagonal but often much longer than standard Jaegers and the helical rifling varied between five and seven deep lands and grooves with varying degrees of twist. Twist, or pitch, is the rate of turn that the rifling spirals up the bore and had fairly recently been discovered to be an important factor in improving accuracy. It can be fast (one turn in 36in) or slow (one turn in 48in) and it affected the rate of spin of the bullet, although tests show that in practice neither barrel length nor twist actually radically alter the accuracy of these Kentucky rifles. The sights were simple, a V rear and blade front, both dovetailed into the barrel. Some rifles had butt-traps, some did not. From the late 1730s, however, a flat brass lidded box was becoming more evident and this was a purely American introduction. A fine contemporary account of the rifles then in use was written by Isaac Weld, an Englishman traveling through America in the latter part of the 18th century:

> The rifles barrel guns ... are nearly of a length of a musket and carry leaden balls from the size of thirty to sixty to the pound [between .53 and .42in]. Some hunters prefer those of a small bore ... others prefer such as have a wide bore, because the wound which they inflict is certainly more attended with death; the wound however, made by a ball discharged from one of these guns is always very dangerous. The inside of the barrel is fluted, and the grooves run in a spiral direction from one end of the barrel to the other, consequently when the ball comes out it has a whirling motion, and when it enters into the body of an animal it tears up the flesh in a dreadful manner.[25]

These rifles were not the exclusive property of the military, however, for the trappers and backwoodsmen who worked within the vast interior of eastern and central North America used their rifles to feed and defend themselves as well as earn a living. The financial importance of their work to the British and French governments should not be underestimated either.

By 1740 the value of furs exported to Britain from her colonies was a staggering £25,196 which equates approximately to £27 million ($50 million) in today's money, and the trade to France was of a similar value. It can therefore be understood why neither of the great powers was prepared to give an inch in its determination to acquire as much American real estate as possible. The New World was a hugely profitable business, to be exploited with relatively little risk to government, although what happened to the colonists was of course another matter and of little consequence to either Paris or London, provided it did not interrupt trade. While the Treaty of Paris in February 1763 ended the French and Indian Wars, leaving both sides free to lick their wounds, for the colonists there was to be no respite from battles with the Indians, who continued to make their lives a misery. One French settler who had suffered from a series of Iroquois attacks wrote:

[We] have no respite from these [attacks] … for they are most cunning and attack from concealment, using both with arrow and balls from their firelocks, taking captives and all they can carry … they will be gone before we can raise the alarum. They are a great trial and though we make haste to track them seldom do we find [any] trace.[26]

Despite the relatively little use the rifle saw during the wars, it had certainly made sufficient impact for a number to be sent to England for evaluation by the British Board of Ordnance, who were unsurprisingly unimpressed with them, considering the rifles to be too flimsy for military service, too slow to load and shoot, and far too expensive. Their tests were instructive, however:

Distance, yards	% of hits, musket	% of hits, rifle
100	74.5	94.5
200	42.5	80
300	16	55
400	9	52.5

At a time when a British musket cost 24 shillings ($10) a rifle of solid enough construction to act as a service arm was calculated to cost 75 shillings ($30). This cost, naturally enough, was something the Ordnance Corps could see no conceivable reason for agreeing to.[27] Actually, cost was not the prime reason for their reluctance to adopt the rifle, but its slowness of loading as compared to a smoothbore musket was a problem in linear warfare, as time would prove. The trials were the first of a series of representations to the Board for the acceptance of a rifle for British service use, but it was to be another 20 years before they grudgingly agreed the rifle might have some possible use in warfare. By that time, of course, the colonists had proved conclusively to the British that the rifle was a weapon to be taken very seriously indeed.

PART II
AMERICA AT WAR

Chapter 3

REVOLUTION

Despite the economic stranglehold the British Crown held over commerce in New England, and the apparent disdain in which London held the colonists, the coming of war in the New World was not necessarily an inevitable process. Somewhat to the surprise and ire of the British government, none of the restrictive measures they had introduced appeared to have any effect whatsoever on the American desire for continued exploration and settlement. The situation was further exacerbated by the colonists' irritating habit of regarding the payment of customs duties as an entirely voluntary act, which should be avoided at all costs. In June 1768 riots that broke out in Boston over the seized ship *Liberty* were symptomatic of this dissatisfaction.

Despite the majority of settlers still being loyal to the Crown, there arose through the 1760s an increasingly vocal and determined band of dissenters who, while not actually embarking upon resistance, were openly talking about rebellion. This talk was to turn into open defiance in the wake of events in Boston on March 5, 1770. The foolish and bloody repression by the 29th Regiment of Foot of a noisy but peaceful protest was to provide the more radical rebels with the excuse they needed. The "Boston Massacre," as it was soon known, was to become a catalyst for the events that were to follow, although the sum total of dead was small (seven, with six wounded). Perhaps if the population had remained at its earlier smaller levels the situation could have been controlled by the British forces, but by 1770 the Americas had some 2,148,000 inhabitants[1] dispersed over several hundred thousand square miles, including much of the territory formerly held in Spanish Florida, and of whom one in six residents was black, held in servitude.

In a vain attempt to forestall any future problems, British troops were dispatched to seize the powder stores and weapons held at Charlestown, Salem, Marshfield, and other towns with substantial reserves. In October 1774, King George III ordered Parliament to approve an embargo on all firearms, component parts, and gunpowder destined for America, and it was this issue that was to cause such widespread resentment. The reason for this was simply that there were no colonial gunpowder mills working in this pre-revolution time (the Everenden mill in Massachusetts had closed around 1770), and the question of how to manufacture powder was a vexing problem in the colonies. It was a fundamental issue, striking at the heart of the ability of the settlers to defend themselves. Charcoal was produced locally so its supply was not problematical and saltpeter was gathered from human urine and bird droppings; however, sulfur was always a problem to obtain and demand constantly outstripped supply. Some 80,000lb of powder[2] had been stockpiled by the patriots, but this was nowhere near enough. Determined efforts were made to capture or steal as much as possible, including some audacious raids on British magazines. For the duration of the Revolutionary War most gunpowder (some 1.5 million lb) had to be imported from the Netherlands, along with enough saltpeter and sulfur to manufacture another 700,000lb,[3] but even so the quantities manufactured were barely adequate.

The Crown's measures to limit access to firearms and accessories were, in a quite unintended way, to have the effect of boosting the emerging American firearms industry, helping lay the foundations for the huge enterprise that it was to become. In view of the enduring problems with Native Americans that the frontiersmen were facing and the escalating aggression on the part of the Crown's army, these restrictions were seen as little more than an attempt to leave the settlements defenseless. In reaction the Continental Congress in Philadelphia was to announce a Declaration of Rights followed by a decision to suspend all further trade with England.[4] Inevitably, relations between the Crown and colonies continued to deteriorate and the Provincial Congress of Massachusetts preempted war by forming companies of militia "to be every fourth man, aged twenty five years or under ... to be ready ... at a minute's notice."[5] They were soon to become known as Minutemen. There has grown up an enduring myth that all of these men were active sharpshooters, picked for their deadly expertise with a rifle, but this is not supported by facts. The main criteria for their selection were that they could be called upon at short notice and were capable of providing their own weapons and ammunition when needed. Few militiamen had ever owned or used a rifle and many did not actually own a firearm at all. Captain Johnson of the New Hampshire Militia informed Congress that he had "only one pound of powder to twenty men" and furthermore, less than half of his men actually *possessed* a firearm of any sort.[6]

While there were undoubtedly some rifles and competent shots amongst the men, they were by no means predominant, the majority of the militia owning varying patterns of smoothbore musket. Moreover, few of these men had any military experience, a fact that was to prove extremely costly for them in the near future. On June 14, 1775, an act of Congress voted to raise a standing army. Although it was to be raised and equipped along the traditional lines of all 18th-century armies, it did have provision for ten companies of riflemen – six from Pennsylvania and two each from Maryland and Virginia. The first of these companies, under the command of one Daniel Morgan, joined George Washington at Cambridge, Massachusetts, in July 1776. They had already missed the first brief clashes of the war, for on April 19, 1775, some 700 British regulars under the command of Lieutenant-Colonel Francis Smith had advanced towards the small town of Concord, Massachusetts. After a brief exchange of shots with militiamen, they set to burning the town. The militia drawn up to meet them were largely armed with muskets, and the militiamen, unused to the discipline of linear warfare, waited nervously in loose ranks as the redcoats formed rank and fired. Eight militiamen were killed and ten wounded, and their commander Captain Parker ordered them to disperse. One man wrote later, "There was ... not a gun fired by any of Captain Parker's company within my knowledge."[7] Reinforced by more men, the militia regrouped and began to shoot back, driving the British from the vital bridge while killing three and wounding eight others, including four officers. It was the first real test of both nerve and shooting for the colonists and they eventually acquitted themselves well. The British ordered a withdrawal, then began to face an unaccustomed tactical scenario. If fighting face-to-face was an uncomfortable form of warfare for the Minutemen, then stalking the British was second nature. It was a manner of fighting totally alien to British soldiers, one with which they were to become terribly familiar over the next few years. As they withdrew, one of their officers later wrote that:

> The country was an amazing strong one, full of hills, woods, stone walls etc which the rebels did not fail to take advantage of, for they were all lined with people who kept an incessant fire upon us ... for they were so concealed there was hardly any seeing them. In this way, we marched ... their numbers increasing while ours [were] reducing by deaths wounds and fatigue and we were surrounded by such an incessant fire as it's impossible to conceive.[8]

Many of the guns used by the militiamen were ordinary British or French military-pattern muskets, in calibers typically between .75 and .78in. Some were already family heirlooms from earlier fighting which served a dual purpose, being employed both as hunting guns and for militia use, for which many were modified. Usually this meant their wooden fore-end would be cut back and a stud added to the top of the muzzle (often misinterpreted today as a foresight) to permit the fitment of a bayonet. There was an eclectic mix of weapons to be found – one observer of a militia unit at Valley Forge noted that "muskets, carbines, fowling pieces and rifles were found in the same company."[9] There were also problems with ammunition supply, for, as the Pennsylvania Council reported in 1776, they required seven different calibers to be issued.[10]

While the resident gunmakers struggled to cope with demand in the face of shortages of materials and labor and escalating prices (the cost of blacksmith's files doubled in six months), the various local Committees of Safety, formed to organize the scattered communities and help provide protection, decided on adopting a series of muskets to be manufactured to predetermined specifications. These were to be standard military-pattern flintlocks, iron furnished of between .65 and .78 caliber with barrels of between 41 and 46in. They were supplied with maple or walnut stocks, had brass fittings, and were between 9 and 10lb in weight. These were to become generally known as Committee of Safety muskets and they were produced in their thousands, although they were never manufactured in the numbers required to meet demand. There is also some evidence that a quantity of rifles was also supplied, although the exact number is not known. As happened in the Civil War a century later, large quantities of weapons had to be imported illegally through the British naval blockade, many supplied by the French who were only too delighted to help the rebels fight the British. Some 102,000 firearms were purchased in this manner,[11] the bulk of which were French Charleville muskets of varied patterns.

REVOLUTION AND RIFLEMEN

Up to the Revolutionary period, the use of the rifle had been minimal. Those most familiar with rifles were the trappers, woodsmen, and mountain men from Pennsylvania and the territory stretching south along the Appalachians, who all knew and respected the rifle. Many of them heeded the call to join the patriot army, and to the New Englanders they presented a strange and exotic group, with their long guns and curious dress. Of course, their clothes were entirely suited to the frontier lives they led, but to contemporary eyes they looked more than a little out of the ordinary. Although required to wear the uniform of their fellow soldiers, the obdurate frontiersmen rarely had time for such niceties, and a contemporary account describes a typical rifleman as follows:

... the dress of the men was partly Indian and partly that of civilised nations. The hunting shirt was universally worn. This was a kind of loose frock reaching halfway down the thighs with long sleeves ... and so wide as to lap a foot or more when belted ... the hunting shirt was sometimes made of linsey [wool], sometimes of coarse linen and a few of dressed deerskins. These last were very cold and uncomfortable in wet weather. The shirt and jacket were of common fashion. A pair of drawers or breeches and leggings, were the dress of the thighs and legs, a pair of moccasins answered for their feet much better than shoes ... the cape was large and handsomely fringed. The belt, which was always tied behind answered several purposes, besides that of holding the dress together. In cold weather the mittens and sometimes the bullet bag occupied the front part of it. To the right side were suspended the tomahawk and to the left the scalping knife in its leather sheath.[12]

It was in its way a uniform of sorts, which had changed little from that worn during the Indian Wars of the previous century, for it was utterly practical for the fighting in which they were engaged. Many of the men spent their time demonstrating their shooting skills to an admiring audience, and many accounts exist of the abilities of riflemen to achieve impressive results. Typical shooting ranges were between 50 and 80 yards, and there were many accounts of the prowess of the riflemen. J. R. Bright noted that "One marksman from Virginia put eight successive shots through a board 5 x 7 inches at 60 yards."[13] When compared to the inability of a standard military musket to achieve a body shot at this range, then it was excellent shooting indeed, particularly as shooting was done freehand, standing upright. There are also accounts of similar feats being achieved at more respectable distances, up to 250 yards. However not everyone was impressed with them, one observer commenting: "To be sure, there was never a more mutinous and undisciplined set of villains that bred disturbance in any camp." Neither was he particularly impressed with their marksmanship: "the army is now universally convinced that the continual firing which they kept up by the week and month together has had no effect other than to waste their ammunition and convince the King's troops that they are not really so formidable."[14] How objective an observation this was is debatable but there is doubtless some truth in the opinion that not all riflemen were the dead-eyed shots that they wished to appear to be.

Their guns, known generically as long rifles, had through the mid- to late 18th century begun to acquire the characteristics that evolved into the form that is most commonly recognized today. Over a period of some half a century, the heavy military-type stock with its club-like butt and straight wrist had changed to a far more graceful and curved pattern, with the highly distinctive droop at the wrist providing the rifle with a unique visual characteristic that makes for instantaneous identification, although this was by no means a universal feature. A graceful swan- or goose-necked cock sat on a flat-faced lockplate that was slightly curved, so it could be accommodated within the curve of the stock. The stock profile was greatly reduced down compared to the heavy dimensions of the British military musket, giving the rifle a slimmer and far more graceful line. The barrel length was generally shortened from the military norm of 46in to a more manageable 40in or so. More significantly, experience had taught the gunmakers that the large, heavy ball of about .76 caliber used in military muskets was merely a waste of good lead. By the late 1770s, American rifles were mostly manufactured in calibers of between .50 and .60in and rifling took the form of seven or eight grooves. All of these factors, however, varied greatly depending on the gunmaker and the specific requirements and depth of pocket of the purchaser. The trigger-guard invariably incorporated a raised finger grip, adopted from the traditional style found on the Jaeger rifle, as was the patch-box inlet into the right side of the stock. This description could be applied to the majority of rifles used during the Revolutionary War, although it must be stressed that they represented only a relatively small number of weapons when compared to the total in service of the American forces during the conflict.

There has, over the last century or so, probably been more misinformation relating to the employment of riflemen during the Revolutionary War than any other single issue, so perhaps some facts should be placed in context. The rifle per se was to have very little impact on the eventual military outcome of the war, or even on the manner in which it was conducted. Battles were still linear, using orthodox infantry tactics and smoothbore muskets to provide volley fire as quickly as it could be delivered. It took nerve to fight in this manner, as Amos Barrett wrote after meeting British regulars for the first time:

> We were all ordered to load and had strict orders not to fire till they fired, then to fire as fast as we could. Their musket balls whistled well. We then was all ordered to fire ... it is strange that there weren't no more killed but they fired too high ... we soon drove them from the bridge.[15]

As was the case with the employment of snipers two centuries later, for the first few months of the war few commanders possessed the understanding of how to use their riflemen in the correct tactical manner. There were some exceptions, for when employed by commanders who understood their fighting abilities, such as generals Daniel Morgan and Nathaniel Greene, the use of riflemen as scouts and skirmishers ensured they were a force to be reckoned with. However, properly employed they could help turn the tide of a battle. The 12 companies of riflemen initially employed were quickly singled out to act as light infantrymen whose purpose revolved around their ability to observe, harass, and confuse the enemy, often from the relative protection of the woodland and thick brush to which they were inured. John Adams recalled that these men proved "an excellent species of light infantry. They use a peculiar kind of musket, called a rifle. It has a circular bore – or grooves, within the barrel and carries a ball with great exactness to great distances."[16] The ranges at which these rifled muskets were capable of shooting have also been the subject of some debate. Empirical tests have been undertaken to prove or disprove some of the many theories put forward over the capabilities of the rifles of the period. Bearing in mind that a smoothbore musket, firing a *properly patched ball*, was probably capable of hitting a target roughly the size of a human head at 150 yards, then claims for a rifleman to be able to achieve a hit on a human body at 300 or 400 yards seem quite reasonable.

One of the most frequently cited accounts of being on the receiving end of a rifleman's bullet is that by Major [later Colonel] George Hanger, a British officer and also a very capable shot. His account is often quoted to prove the abilities of the American rifleman. Some pertinent parts are rarely quoted, however, which is a shame as he was an expert rifleman himself who, having been captured during the war, had the chance to talk with many colonial riflemen about their guns, powder, and bullets. Lastly, he was able to obtain examples of Pennsylvania and Kentucky rifles with which he experimented to see which loads and rifles performed best and what they were capable of in terms of accuracy. His opinions, therefore, are based on sound experience. One of his more pertinent comments was regarding the crudity of the sights on American rifles:

> I can assure you … that the American riflemen have but one sight behind to their guns I mean by this that they have no rising [adjustable] sight, by which to give their guns a greater degree of elevation; and that one sight is not above two sixteenths of an inch in height. I do believe that, if he shot at a man standing still at four hundred yards, by only aiming at the man's head, that he would drop the ball into the man's breast, not lower or go so near him as to alarm him devilishly.

In other words, a good rifleman should be able to make a body hit at 400 yards. Hanger's later experience of being a target is proof positive of this:

> … to mention but one instance, as a proof of most excellent skill of an American rifleman. Colonel, now General Tarleton, and myself were standing a few yards out of a wood … there was a rivulet in the enemy's front and a mill on it, to which we stood directly with our horses' heads fronting, observing their [the enemy's] motions. Our orderly-bugle stood behind us, about three yards, but with his horse's side to our horses' tails. A rifleman passed over the milldam, evidently observing the two officers, and laid himself down on his belly. He took a deliberate and cool shot at my friend and me, and the bugle-horn man. It was the month of August, and

not a breath of wind was stirring. Colonel Tarleton's horse and mine, I am certain, were not anything like two feet apart. A rifle ball passed between him and me: looking directly at the mill, I evidently observed the flash of powder ... the bugle-horn man, directly behind us ... jumped off his horse and said, "Sir, my horse is shot." The horse staggered, fell down and died. I have passed several times over this ground; and I can positively assert that the distance he fired from, at us, was fully four hundred yards. Now ... speaking of the rifleman's shooting ... he had much in his favour. First there was not one breath of wind, secondly that atmosphere is so much clearer than ours, that he can take a more perfect aim.[17]

There are also some interesting contemporary accounts of the use of a black-powder rifle at far greater ranges than one would normally expect. Between April and May 1813 General Proctor and his British infantry, with a large number of Indians led by Tecumseh, laid siege to Fort Meigs on the east bank of the Ohio River. One Indian climbed a tree and began shooting at foraging parties that had to leave the fort to collect water from the river. He was the subject of much laughter and banter, as he was in excess of 600 yards away. The joking stopped when he began to inflict casualties, wounding two soldiers. Private Elijah Kirk of Boswell's Regiment, Kentucky Militia, asked for permission to retaliate but was told it was not worth the waste of powder. After suffering more casualties, the officers relented and Kirk found a suitable observation point to watch the smoke from the discharge. This gave him clear evidence not only of the sharpshooter's position, but the wind strength and direction. Loading his rifle, Kirk took careful aim and fired, while onlookers waited with hushed expectancy. First a musket, then the Indian dropped from the tree, to the amazement of the spectators.[18] Recent tests on a man-sized target using 75 grains of powder and a carefully patched .53-caliber Kentucky rifle resulted in hits with four out of ten shots at 600 yards with the misses being reported as "very close" to the target. Kirk's shot was perhaps exceptional, but it does indicate that perhaps the riflemen of the time were more accomplished than we give them credit for. Hanger's subsequent conversations with likeminded shooters were also instructive:

I have many times asked the American backwoodsmen what was the most their best marksmen could do; they have constantly told me than an expert rifleman … can hit the head of a man at 200 yards. I am certain that provided an American rifleman was to get a perfect aim at 300 yards at me standing still, he most undoubtedly would hit me, unless it was a very windy day.[19]

Being a deliberate target for a sharpshooter was not something infantrymen were used to, which is evidenced in the following account from a British officer during the Battle of New Orleans:

… what attracted our attention most, was the figure of a tall man standing on the breastworks, dressed in linsey-woolsey, with buckskin leggings, and a broad brimmed [felt] hat that fell around his face almost concealing his features. The body rested on the left leg … the right arm was extended, the hand grasping the rifle near the muzzle, the butt of which was rested near the toe of his right foot; he seemed fixed and motionless as a statue. At last he moved, threw back his hat rim … raised his rifle and took aim at our group. Our eyes were riveted upon him; at whom had he levelled his piece? But the distance was so great we looked at each other and smiled. We saw the rifle flash. My right-hand companion, as noble a fellow as ever rode … fell from his saddle. The hunter paused for a few moments without moving the gun from his shoulders. Then he reloaded and resumed his former attitude. Once more the hat rim was thrown back and the gun raised to his shoulder. This time we did not smile [but cast glances at each other] to see which of us must die. When again the rifle flashed, another of our party dropped to the earth. There was something most awful in marching to this certain death. The cannon and thousands of musket balls playing upon our ranks, we cared not for; for there was a chance of escaping them … but to know that every time that rifle was levelled towards us … one of us must surely fall; to see it rest, motionless as if poised on a rack, and know when the hammer came down … that the messenger of death drove unerringly to its goal, to know this and still march on was awful.[20]

Still, under the prevailing battle conditions, when they were placed in an infantry role the riflemen often suffered badly, as recounted by George Hanger:

> When Morgan's riflemen came down from Pennsylvania ... they marched to attack our light infantry under Colonel Abercrombie. The moment they appeared before him he ordered his troops to charge them with the bayonet; not one in four [riflemen] had time to fire and those that did had no time to reload again; the infantry not only dispersed them, but drove them for miles over the country.[21]

The continual vulnerability of the riflemen to bayonet-equipped regulars was difficult to overcome unless they were very carefully employed, for unlike the regulation military musket the rifle was normally incapable of having a bayonet fitted to it. This shortcoming was an early example of a lesson that was soon to be learned by commanders who used specialist troops, sharpshooters, and scouts, for employing them in roles for which they were not trained or equipped frequently led to unnecessary losses.

As the Revolutionary War continued new tactics were adopted that particularly suited the mixed employment of riflemen and ordinary troops, of which General Nathaniel Greene became a master. Although he employed the traditional three ranks of infantry, he placed his riflemen in the front rank, state troops and militia in the second, and seasoned professional soldiers in the rear. As the British advanced the rifles took a steady toll of officers, NCOs, and men, then were withdrawn to the rear leaving the second and third ranks to volley fire, by which time the British were frequently in disorder and beginning to falter. The experienced third line would advance with fixed bayonets to encourage the enemy's flight, but if called upon the riflemen would again move forwards between the two front ranks and pour deadly fire into the retreating troops. This tactical arrangement not only made the most of the shooting abilities of the men, but gave them the protection they needed from the enemy, whom they could not engage on equal terms in close fighting. Even admirers of the rifle such as Major Hanger openly admitted that: "Riflemen ... are a very feeble foe and not to be trusted alone any distance from camp; and at the outposts they must ever be supported by regulars, or they will constantly be beaten in and forced to retire."[22] They were still able to provide deadly assistance when required, though. During the naval battle for Lake Erie in September 1813 Commander Perry employed 100 Kentucky riflemen to keep the decks of the Royal Navy ships clear of Royal Marines, which they did with great effectiveness, ensuring eventual victory.

As the fighting ebbed and flowed the use of the rifle became more commonplace on the battlefield, although it remained at the fringe of 18th-century military requirement. There is evidence that even Congress was not overwhelmed by the performance of the riflemen:

> If musketts were given them instead of rifles the service would be more benefitted, as there is a superabundance of riflemen in the army. Were it in the power of Congress to supply muskets they would speedily reduce the number of rifles and replace them ... as they are more easily kept in order, can be fired oftener and have the advantage of bayonets.[23]

Neither should it be forgotten that a significant body of colonists were loyal to and fought for the Crown, and certainly some of them were armed with rifled muskets manufactured in Britain. There still exists a number of contracts showing that several well-established Birmingham gunmakers such as Barker, Grice, Ketland, and Wilets were paid to manufacture and supply 500 rifles to the loyal colonists. Most of these rifles were finished and shipped to North America prior to the contract being canceled by the government in April 1776. Exactly where they ended up is not known, but doubtless many were issued to loyal riflemen and they perhaps provided the wherewithal for sharpshooters to indulge in what was to later become known as counter-sniping. Specific accounts of the sharpshooters' effectiveness in combat do not appear to exist, but a comment by an American rifleman after the Battle of King's Mountain in October 1778 is telling, as he recalled that many of the American dead appeared to have been shot through the head by other riflemen, being found slumped over their weapons "with one eye opened in the manner of marksmen when levelling at their subjects."[24] The American sharpshooters were able to exact a steady toll on the redcoats, targeting officers and NCOs in particular, a practice that was abhorred by the British as opposed to the civilized rules of warfare. The methods used to deal with any riflemen who were captured also had little to do with the civilized rules of warfare, for many sharpshooters were executed on the spot, a practice that endures to the present day. Many dead found after the Battle of Brandywine had their arms and displayed bayonet or sword wounds. One British officer even went so far as to voice his displeasure in print, writing in an English journal in 1776 that "It frequently happens that they find themselves run through the body by the push of a bayonet, as a rifleman is not entitled to any quarter."[25]

While there is little evidence that riflemen actually altered the course of history, they did sometimes help to reshape it. For on occasion an individual rifleman could make a palpable difference to the outcome of events, such as at Saratoga when Private Timothy Murphy, a Pennsylvania rifleman under Colonel Daniel Morgan, shot General Simon Fraser of the 71st Highlanders. Fraser's death caused such confusion that it halted the British counterattack. Neither were the British blind to the advantages of the rifle, for some 4,000 Hessian Jaeger auxiliaries were employed in North America by King George III, equipped with the military version of the popular Jaeger hunting rifle. At a relatively late stage in the war Britain even adopted its own rifle, the sophisticated Ferguson breech-loader. It is ironic that at one stage its inventor, Major Patrick Ferguson, had in his sights two mounted American officers. He later wrote that "it was not pleasant to fire at the back of an unoffending individual who was acquitting himself very coolly of his duty, so I let him alone."[26] Had he done so, then without a doubt his rifle bullet would have changed the course of history, as one of the officers in question was almost certainly George Washington. Under the command of its brilliant inventor, the Ferguson rifle saw limited use during the Battle of Brandywine, where it proved very successful. Alas for future firearms development, Ferguson was killed at the Battle of King's Mountain and his rifles soon faded from history. Of the 100 or so manufactured hardly any have resurfaced over the intervening years, despite a number being known to have been captured at the Battle of Stoney Point, New York, in May 1779. The whereabouts of the missing Ferguson rifles is still an enduring mystery.[27]

As the war continued, understanding of how best to utilize the sharpshooter on the battlefield increased among commanders. Perhaps the apogee of the use of sharpshooters was reached in the closing stages of the Revolutionary War during the Battle of New Orleans in January 1815. A vastly superior force of British regulars attacked a force of colonists, among whom were some 2,000 riflemen. When the smoke had cleared, British losses amounted to over 1,500 for the loss of 60 Americans, most of whom had been killed by cannon fire, the majority of redcoats having died before they could even advance within musket range. It was doubly unfortunate for the men killed that by the time of the battle the Treaty of Ghent had already been signed (on December 24, 1814) and the war was officially over. By the time the fighting had reached its final stage in the early 19th century the rifle had at last emerged from the backwoods to become an accepted item of the military armory and before very long it was to become the dominant weapon on the battlefield.

Chapter 4

HEADING WEST

Although a fledgling American firearms industry was established to cope with the demands of the Revolutionary War, the uneasy peace that followed the cessation of hostilities did not lead to any slowing down in the demand for firearms. If anything quite the opposite was happening, for large numbers of men who had been unsettled by the rigors of war began to look for new excitement and challenges. For the easterners who had borne the brunt of the war, heading west appeared to offer an ideal solution. There were financial lures too, for a good fur trapper could earn upwards of $2,000 a year at a time when a skilled carpenter in the east might expect to earn $550. The Louisiana Purchase of 1800[1] had secured for the United States a vast area of former French territory in the Midwest, which encouraged many hundreds of people to venture west from the staging post city of St Louis, Missouri. They followed either the Missouri River north or the Platte River westwards to cross the Rockies into Oregon Country.

The first decade of the 19th century was an incredibly fruitful time for exploration. Merriwether Lewis and William Clark traversed the northwest between 1804 and 1806. Zebulon Pike's exploration of 1806–07 went south to El Paso, spearheading the opening of the southern route to the Spanish possessions of what were to become Arizona, New Mexico, and Texas. But these early settlers were by no means the first: for many years solitary trappers, hunters, and backwoodsmen had trodden a fine line between the old and new country, spending their lives in the vastness of the woods, prairies, and mountains. The one thing above all else that these men depended upon for their livelihoods was their rifles. A white man in such territory with no firearm was as good as dead, for few possessed the inherent ability of the Native Americans to live off the land. Washington Irving commented of the trappers that "In such dangerous times, the experienced mountaineer is never without his rifle. [It] is his constant friend and protector."[2] Their lives were dangerous indeed for, apart from wild animals, Indian attack was a constant possibility. Most of these men hailed from eastern or central states such as Tennessee, Virginia, Carolina, or Pennsylvania and their preferred firearms were invariably locally made rifles. These guns, until now often frustratingly identified by contemporary writers only as "long guns," were, depending on their place of manufacture and style, more often specifically referred to as either "Tennessee" or "Kentucky" rifles. They were to form the basis for a whole new generation of rifled muskets.

These guns varied somewhat in style and form depending on their place of origin. While every generalization about these weapons appears to have an exception, it is fair to say that the Tennessee was of a slightly heavier construction than the Kentucky, with iron rather than brass fittings, and their calibers also differed, with the lighter Kentucky being between .40 and .45in and the Tennessee .45in or larger. The demand for rifles also ensured that Midwestern gunmakers began to establish a very firm niche for themselves. During and after the war a number of gunmakers had established themselves in the valleys of Philadelphia and Pennsylvania, where rivers were available to provide the necessary water power. These makers had risen in numbers from a pre-Revolutionary War handful to several dozen. While many were to fade into obscurity some would continue to the very forefront of the rifle manufacturing industry. Creamer, Goertz, Dickert, Gill, Gumpf, and Deringer were but a few who produced good rifles for the adventurer, hunter, or traveler.

During the 1820s the types of rifles produced slowly began to change as demand and use reshaped the requirements of the weapons. In terms of accuracy and lethality, the new rifles were certainly an improvement over those of a previous generation, although these improvements were to be incremental rather than made in any single quantum leap. In the 21st century, where change happens daily and technology has all but replaced skill, we tend to be dismissive of past technology, believing that the improvements brought about by modern science and engineering make us infinitely superior to our forebears. To a certain extent, for example in the case of medicine, this is quite undeniable, but almost all modern men and women would struggle to survive in the environment in which most Americans lived during the early 19th century. While modern firearms have benefited enormously from improved components and manufacturing, to dismiss the flintlock rifles of that period is to ignore the fundamental point that shooters of that period made up with knowledge and ability what technology has largely replaced today.

Neither were the rifles lacking in accuracy, for while the old military musket when hurriedly loaded with no bullet patch was indeed a woeful weapon, a carefully loaded and patched rifle was a different matter altogether. The popular Tennessee rifles had become increasingly accurate – one observer noted that in a backwoods shooting match the contestants, shooting offhand at a distance of 30 paces (roughly 35 yards) had to place five of their shots into a target that was a rifle barrel pointing directly towards them. Most achieved between two and four hits.[3] Tests undertaken in *American Rifleman* magazine in the 1950s found that an original rifle loaded with a .45-caliber ball produced an astonishing muzzle velocity of 2,410fps, comparing well to modern centerfire ammunition such as the US .30-caliber M2 ball round, which reached 2,500fps at the muzzle.[4] Lesser charges still produced respectable velocities of around 1,700fps, the ball being capable of smashing through a $1/4$in wooden plank at 300 yards. As this board is roughly the same thickness as a human skull, the test indicates how the rifle was a potent weapon in the hands of a competent shooter. The test rifles could produce a group of 2–3in (2–3 Minutes of Angle or MoA) at 100 yards, which in practical terms meant that a head shot at 300 yards was perfectly feasible, thus confirming Colonel Hanger's early comments.

The big disadvantage of the rifle for shooters was still the limitations of the propellant, for the burn rate of black powder did not generate high pressures and bullets lost velocity very quickly. Therein lay the issue that faced all rifle shooters whose lives depended on their guns, for the fundamental problems with any bullet revolved around ballistic efficiency and weight. There had long been an argument in favor of the use of heavier bullets whose mass provided greater killing power, although this was often at the expense of accuracy. Here is a fundamental argument that still exists today. The light Appalachian-made rifles were good for small game in open country or light woodland, but the mountain men required something heavier. Facing an aggressive bear or buffalo with a .36-caliber rifle was not a guarantee of longevity, a contemporary writer, Alexander Ross, noting that "Observing the effect by guns of different calibers, it was found that the rifles of a small bore [.40 to .43 caliber] very frequently do not kill although might hit; while rifles from [.49 to .54 caliber] seldom missed killing on the spot."[5] The reason for this was fairly straightforward, for a .70-caliber ball round weighed 730 grains and a .54in bullet only 370 grains. The big dilemma for the frontiersmen was in finding a happy compromise. To a certain extent the solution was simple in that the weapon chosen had to suit the precise requirements of the individual; thus a buffalo hunter seldom purchased a .32-caliber squirrel rifle. In the Midwest and Rockies there had begun a gradual displacement of the traditional lighter rifles in favor of a new form of longarm, the resulting weapon being known as the Rocky Mountain or Plains rifle (although "new" is a relative term here for these owed much to that earlier favorite, the Jaeger rifle). Many makers produced them, the names of most now lost to posterity, but foremost among them were the fine rifles made by the Hawken brothers, Samuel and Jacob, whose weapons soon became a byword for accuracy and durability. The style of these rifles also reflected a new purpose for the rifle and a contemporary description by an Englishman, George Ruxton, makes interesting reading:

> He first of all visited the gun store of Hawken, whose rifles are renown[ed] in the mountains, and exchanged his own piece which was of very small bore,

for a regular mountain rifle. This was of very heavy metal, carrying about thirty-two balls to the pound [.53 caliber] stocked to the muzzle and mounted with brass, its only ornament being a buffalo bull, looking exceedingly ferocious, which was not very artistically engraved upon the trap of the stock.[6]

The thick-walled octagonal barrels of these rifles provided them with an inherent advantage in accuracy over the old longer-barreled, thinner-walled rifles, a factor not lost on target shooters for whom accuracy rather than power was paramount. As ever, it was from the sport shooting fraternity that many of the first practical sharpshooter's rifles were to spring. Such innovation must be kept in context though, for in this period the rifles made by various gunmakers could, and did, vary greatly. Functioning had also been greatly improved with the wider introduction of double-set triggers and flintlock mechanisms being fitted with rollers on their bearing surfaces to smooth and speed up the ignition process. Furthermore, the range of rifles available was ever increasing. In St Louis alone there were 18 registered gunmakers by 1840 producing a wide range of types that met the needs of the new breed of frontiersmen.

MILITARY RIFLES

By the turn of the 19th century great moves had been made towards the standardization of military firearms. While the Army was traditionally light years behind the commercial world in regards to adopting new weapons, even they could not continue for much longer to ignore the importance of the rifle in the hands of the Minutemen and rifle companies of the American forces during the Revolutionary War. It was therefore not surprising that in 1803 the US Army sanctioned the manufacture of its first service rifle. Produced at Harper's Ferry, it was an iron-mounted flintlock of fairly standard pattern but with a comparatively short 33in half-round/octagonal barrel with seven-groove rifling. Of specific interest was the caliber of .54in, which by the accepted standard of the day for military longarms was almost miniscule. It had a raised cheek piece to provide the shooter with a comfortable rest for his face and a brass patch-box on the right side of the butt. It was less than coincidental that the rifle was extremely similar in appearance to the British Baker rifle produced in 1800 which itself was copied more or less from the venerable Jaeger. Despite being manufactured to a standard pattern they were still hand-finished on an individual basis, and they suffered accordingly from difficulties when replacement parts were required.

Several pioneering military expeditions were armed with the M1803 rifles, the use of which appear to have been of mixed blessing. Major Zebulon Pike's men were armed with them, upon which he commented: "We bursted one of our rifles, which was a great loss, as it made three guns which had bursted … one of my men was now armed but with my sword and pistols."[7] The M1803 was carried by Lewis and Clark and also caused trouble, as Lewis wrote: "But for our precaution in bringing extra locks and duplicate parts of the locks, most of our guns would now be useless."[8] The Army continued to develop rifles for military service and between 1803 and the War of 1812 the Ordnance Department had adopted three new patterns. The Pattern of 1803 had its barrel length increased to 36in (some 15,000 were manufactured), but probably of greater importance was the manufacture of an M1814 Deringer rifle. This weapon was one of the first military rifles made that attempted to address the problems of standardization by ensuring that all component parts were uniformly manufactured, the contract stipulating "That a sufficient number of pattern muskets and rifles be made … for the purpose of insuring practical uniformity; no deviations from those patterns to be tolerated after the work now in hand shall have been finished off."[9] An improved M1817 Harper's Ferry rifle was also ordered, but this was to be chambered for a .525in patched ball (the barrel was nominally .54in) and over 30,000 were supplied, although many did not reach government arsenals until the late 1840s where they remained stored, many being issued for the first time during the Civil War.

If the Department of Ordnance was thought radical for adopting rifles for military service, it excelled itself in 1819 by providing a contract to one John H. Hall of Maine for a unique breech-loading rifle. The 1811 patent for this rifle shows an ingenious system employing a tilting breech-block in the receiver, that when unlatched enabled powder and ball to be loaded from the front. Once charged, pushing the front of the block down seated and locked it and enabled the rifle to be fired. Usefully, the entire chamber, trigger, and lock could be removed for cleaning and at least one US Dragoon, Sam Chamberlain, used his as a makeshift pistol to keep guerrillas at bay when cornered in a bar during the Mexican Wars. Crucially for its success, the component parts of the Hall were totally interchangeable and it was also tolerably accurate. Testing at the time showed it to be capable of 7in groups at 50 yards and 16in groups at 100 yards, fired offhand and with a sustainable ability to hit a man-sized target at 400 yards. Dragoon Chamberlain recalled his troop officer spotting a Mexican soldier prior to the Battle of Buena Vista: "Captain Steen, getting impatient at seeing a Mexican officer watching us through a glass, took our best shot [Tennessee Jim] with him … At a distance of four hundred yards he fired with a Hall's long range rifle and brought the officer to the ground."[10]

The Hall was by no means perfect, though. Some examples suffered from gas leakage at the breech with a consequent loss of velocity, although this was to prove a common problem in all early breech-loaders. It resulted in a loss of power: a 70-grain charge in a standard rifle musket produced 1,755fps, whereas the Hall managed only 1,490fps. Unfortunately, increasing the charge merely raised the chances of the breech-block blowing or the stock splitting. Nevertheless in 1817 an initial contract for 100 Halls was issued at $25 apiece, to be followed by almost 3,000 more before the gun was declared obsolete. Once issued with rifles, many soldiers found shooting matches to be a great pastime. The journal of the Yellowstone expedition of 1819 noted:

> May 6th. The troops were classed and commenced shooting at targets with ball cartridges … those who hit a circul [sic] of three inches diameter off hand at fifty yards three times in six were raised from the awkward squad to the 2nd class. Those who could hit the same mark one hundred yards three times in six are raised to the first class. They make rapid improvement. There are but a few who are not in the first class.[11]

In reality, any form of marksmanship training was rare at this time. Line infantry armed with muskets were provided with only the most basic instruction in loading and firing, with no shooting qualification demanded or expected. This is not altogether surprising if one looks at the capabilities of their issue muskets, which had improved little over the years. The flintlock .69-caliber M1808 musket in the hands of a competent shot could group five shots in $12^3/_4$in at 50 yards. At 100 yards it could group at 42in but was pretty well incapable of actually hitting a target at 400 yards, providing a level of performance that would have been entirely acceptable to the soldiers of the 18th century.[12] However, things were to change in a fairly radical way, for the old flintlock mechanism was about to become redundant, at a speed that was almost indecent. The age of percussion was just around the corner.

THE PERCUSSION SYSTEM

If any one man could be said to be responsible for the most innovative and far-reaching technological advance in firearms over the past 400 years, then the Reverend James Forsyth would probably be the most unlikely candidate. Born in 1768 in Belhevie, Aberdeenshire, Scotland, he was a dour but brilliant Scot with a flair for science, an abiding passion for firearms, and a singular dedication to hunting. Naturally curious, he was interested in all popular forms of science, in particular the early experiments with new but dangerous forms of propellant called fulminating compounds. He was by no means the first to be interested in attempts to harness the violent power of these chemicals, for diarist Samuel Pepys recorded in November 1663:

> At noon to the Coffee-house, where, with Dr Allen, some good discourse about physick and chymistry. And among other things ... he telling me that something made of gold, *Aurum Fulminans*, a grain I think he said, of it put in a silver spoon and fired [i.e. struck] will give a blow like a musquett, and strike a hole through the silver spoon downward, without the least force upwards.[13]

86

Of all of the fulminates, mercury was deemed the most powerful and dangerous, and experiments showed it could be ignited by friction, electric current, or a blow from a hard object. In fact almost anything could set it off, as several gunmakers and chemists had found to their cost, the net result invariably being fatal and very messy. Forsyth had dabbled for years with improved propellants for his flintlock fowling guns and had published his own paper in the journal of the Royal Society, to which the meaningful addendum had been added "The force of this powder is too great for firearms."[14] If fulminates were too powerful to use as propellants, Forsyth reasoned that using it in tiny quantities as a priming compound might be beneficial. The lure of improving the ignition efficiency of the flintlock was strong, for it possessed many disadvantages. When hunting the flash of the priming charge alerted every bird and animal for miles and the explosion of the primer in the face of the shooter was potentially very dangerous. Flintlocks were also notoriously unreliable to use in bad weather and protective hoods of leather or tin were constructed to try to protect the locks and help conceal the priming flash. Some English gunmakers such as Knock and Jover even went so far as to make guns with totally enclosed locks.[15] Exactly when Forsyth struck upon the idea of using fulminates for priming rather than propelling is not known, but by 1805 he had invented a simple bottle-shaped powder magazine that screwed to the touch-hole in the breech. Turning it once deposited a tiny charge of fulminate into a chamber under a pin striker. Rotating the magazine back again placed the striker under the hammer of the musket, which was then cocked and fired. The process was then repeated until the magazine was empty.

The British government was interested enough to employ Forsyth at the Tower of London, but after considerable difficulties over manufacture and money, the Board of Ordnance canceled Forsyth's contract. Undeterred he went on to take out a patent in April 1811 and his invention found a ready and enthusiastic market with sportsmen. His patent effectively blocked any further development of detonating locks for the next 14 years. However, in the interim Joseph Manton, the famous London gunmaker, had also produced his own version of a percussion lock, using a thin copper tube filled with fulminate. Other inventors packaged the fulminate in pills, balls, and all manner of tubes, as well as small copper and brass caps.

If the situation were not confused enough, an English artist from Lincolnshire named Joshua Shaw claimed that in 1815 he had actually produced the fully evolved percussion cap. Shaw had emigrated to America in 1823 and took out a patent the following year. The tiny hollow copper cap had a fulminate compound inside its top, protected from the elements by a coat of varnish, and was known from its shape as a "top-hat cap." It required no revolving magazine or fiddly tubes, but was simply placed on a hollow steel nipple that was screwed directly into the breech of the gun. When the hammer struck it, the tiny priming charge was invisibly and silently ignited and the weapon fired.[16] It was certainly an astute creation on his part, for in 1847 the American government awarded him the huge sum of $18,000 following their adoption of the percussion system. One lingering problem for shooters was that all of these early fulminates were very corrosive and it was left to one Frederick Joyce, a London chemist, to produce an "anti-corrosive percussion powder." This clearly was what the shooting public had been waiting for, as by 1827 demand was such that he ceased to be listed in the London trade directory as "Operative Chemist" but became "Percussion Powder Manufacturer."[17] And what became of Forsyth? Having, as it were, set the musket ball rolling, he returned to Scotland to continue writing scientific treatises and to hunt on his beloved moors, but to his dying day he bore a grudge against the British government for depriving him of what he saw as his rightful fortune.

Thanks primarily to Shaw the percussion system was very quickly adopted into use across the eastern coast of America, the *American Shooter* magazine noting in 1827 that "Most eastern sportsmen now exclusively employ the percussion system in shotguns." Within a decade the same could be applied not only to shotguns, but to muskets, rifles, and pistols. However, the east was a long way, both geographically and figuratively, from the land being explored in the west, and while many percussion guns were certainly finding their way there, their popularity was by no means universal. This was due in part to the conversion cost if a flintlock mechanism was to be replaced, but of more fundamental importance to shooters was the purely practical use of flintlocks when compared to percussion ignition. Flint and powder were two items available almost universally where there were firearms, whereas percussion locks required specially made caps. Available only from limited sources, the caps were both easy to lose and fiddly to use with wet or cold hands. Balanced against this was the fact that they were impervious to the climate and generally provided more reliable ignition in wet or windy weather, neither of which was in short supply. A hunter based near Fort Snelling in 1839 had a very definite opinion on the matter of flintlocks, which he aired:

> When I raised and levelled my piece, [the bear] was not six feet from the muzzle. Snap! went the flint, but no explosion followed ... Snap! snap! snap! was all I could get out of the infernal rifle, which no persuasion could induce to go off ... Now my opinion ... is, that any man calling himself a sportsman who will not use a percussion, when he can procure one, in lieu of a flintlock gun, should be ... furnished with a straight-jacket at the public expense.[18]

If sportsmen quickly found the percussion system to their liking, the military powers of Europe and America were less enthusiastic. While it is easy to be critical of their glacially slow decision-making when it came to adopting new technology, this must be weighed against the fact that the supply of any new weapon on a wholesale basis was hugely expensive, complex, and fraught with logistical difficulties. There was always the possibility that a decision taken in haste might well prove to be a costly mistake, particularly bearing in mind that the bulk of US Army soldiers were stationed in far-flung places and shipping anything at all to them was a laborious and slow business. Whatever system the governments of Britain, America, or France adopted had to be proven, effective, and soldier-proof, requirements that still exist today. While the British Army eventually adopted the percussion system in the early 1840s circumstances across the Atlantic were very different from those of Europe.

THE MILITARY RIFLED MUSKET

The US government armories, scattered widely over a vast area in the Midwest, held large stocks of weapons, many of which were obsolete and in poor condition. An audit carried out by the US Ordnance Department in 1834 showed some 73,000 flintlock muskets on hand, most of which had been shipped west by regular army regiments that had no use for them once more modern muskets had become available.[19] Of that total only 5,000 were recorded as being rifled muskets, the bulk of them being older smoothbore Harper's Ferry models. However, while the Ordnance Department was keen to improve the quality of longarms issued, it still had reservations about the rifle. The issue was not accuracy, but speed of firing in battle. In linear warfare, accuracy was not a requirement but speed was. As had been demonstrated during the Revolutionary War, companies of riflemen were at the mercy of infantry or cavalry once they had discharged their weapons, as they were unable to reload before they were overwhelmed. The Army conducted tests in 1826 to determine how effective riflemen were in comparison to musket-armed infantry, and they found that a company of infantry could fire 845 shots in ten minutes, almost double the 494 fired by riflemen.[20] However, in the increasingly frequent clashes between Indian tribes in the Midwest the most commonplace form of warfare encountered was hit-and-run raids that usually left the soldiers reeling, unable to respond quickly or accurately enough with their inaccurate smoothbore weapons. Besides, using a flintlock musket to hit a mounted Indian on a fast pony was well nigh impossible for most soldiers.

One response to this problem was the Ordnance Department's decision to issue buckshot or "buck and ball" ammunition to the troops. This measure was an effective enough solution to the problems of actually hitting something with a musket at relatively close ranges. It comprised a standard .64-caliber paper cartridge filled with either 12 to 15 small lead bullets or three small bullets on top of a standard size ball. It certainly worked, as tests showed 16 out of 20 buckshot bullets would hit a target at 80 yards. Indeed, between 1835 and 1840 the regular army was issued with 2,700,000 buck and ball cartridges compared to 950,000 ball cartridges. It did something to address the woeful inaccuracy of the average infantryman's musket, but it was only a partial solution.

Faced with the monumental logistical problems of having a very large number of different muskets in service, many of which were old, poorly maintained and spread over an entire continent in the hands of badly trained soldiers, the US Ordnance Department's decision not to try to arm the Army wholesale with rifles was understandable. At least by 1822 they had finally adopted a well-designed and properly manufactured flintlock musket, the M1822 Springfield. In this they were aided to a great extent by improvements in manufacturing techniques, using early forms of machine mass production to make stocks and to stamp metal parts from blanks. Much of this pioneering work had been done by makers such as Eli Whitney in the first decade of the 19th century, who invented and adapted machines to cut stock blanks, bore barrels, and generally simplify and speed up the manufacture of gun parts. The importance of this early machine production cannot be overemphasized, for it was to pave the way directly towards the modern age of mechanical mass production without which much of our modern society could not exist. Some 415,000 M1822 muskets were produced between 1823 and 1839, but the Ordnance Department was unable to ignore the wind of change blowing around the firearms industry in the form of percussion ignition.

The final incarnation of the old Springfield was the M1840 flintlock musket, whose manufacture was sanctioned simultaneously with the monumental decision by the Ordnance Department to switch to percussion ignition, creating the bizarre situation of having a new musket in production that was technically obsolete before it was issued. The subsequent trials and tribulations of the Ordnance Department's tests to find an acceptable pattern of musket for percussion conversion were long and convoluted, but it was almost inevitable that it was the M1840 that was selected, thus becoming the M1842 percussion musket. Although still smoothbore, its credentials were actually very good, for not only was it was made with fully interchangeable parts but it had a heavier barrel than previous models and was the ideal candidate for conversion to rifled musket. However, the decision to convert it to a rifle was a long way from actually producing one and the Ordnance Department were still concerned about how to address the problem of issuing it to a standing army whose woefully uninformed soldiery had to be taught to use it properly. Perhaps the most pithy contemporary comments on the subject at the time were made by an American engineer named Bosworth, himself a rifle-shot of considerable expertise, whose treatise on rifle shooting was many years ahead of his contemporaries. He succinctly summed up the problem of issuing military rifles:

> The [rifle] in the hands of one who has studied its properties, will throw a ball with an accuracy that would surprise a large portion of those who are in the habit of using it. What we seriously want is more knowledge among the soldiery, both of guns and gunpowder."[21]

Alas, the Army had no formal rifle regiments at all until 1846 and the rifles in store were only issued at the discretion of the post commanders, often being used exclusively for hunting purposes. At Fort Atkinson, 37 rifles were issued in 1820 solely to help contribute to the cooking pot. If the military demand for rifles during the Revolutionary War had been minimal, by the mid-19th century there had arisen a considerable defiant attitude among the commanders of the western outposts, where huge distances, violent weather, and non-conventional forms of warfare provided considerable justification for their demands for the issue of modern rifled percussion weapons. Clearly the Ordnance Department needed to move with the times, but in the wake of deciding to manufacture the M1840 and then modify it, it needed an interim rifle that could be easily produced.

The answer was found in the shape of the US M1841 rifle. The gun was initially made at Harper's Ferry, but other manufacturers were soon contracted to produce them, among them Eli Whitney and Robbins, Kendall, and Lawrence. The M1841s were referred to by contemporary writers by a number of names: the Windsor, Whitney, or Mississippi, although it is the last of these by which they are now most commonly known. These rifles saw considerable service across the frontier and in the Mexican Wars, and proved devastating when used against massed infantry: "The unerring aim of our Mississippi rifles, acting in concert, cast terror and dismay among the cowardly and unprincipled foe."[22] Its use in the Mexican Wars was an ominous portent of what was to come when the Civil War broke out in 1861, but at the time its military advantages were largely ignored. It was certainly regarded as a successful design, however, as can be gleaned from the fact that some 7,500 were issued to the regular army, which at the time amounted to no more than 10,000 men and up to 1855 the Harper's Ferry armory alone produced some 18,000 rifles.

EARLY OPTICS: AN IMPERFECT SCIENCE

The study of optical science was an ancient one, certainly dating back to Roman times, the Emperor Nero having been recorded as watching games using a *smaragdus*, which historians believe to have been a simple form of telescope. Generally, Galileo Galilei (1564–1642) is accredited with perfecting the modern telescope with which he viewed objects in the heavens. His simple device used a large convex objective (front) lens and small concave ocular (rear) lens, with a sliding tube in between to allow focusing.

The name of the first person to put an optical sight on a firearm will never be known. There is some anecdotal evidence that they were in use in shooting matches in Switzerland and the German states by the late 1820s, though their effectiveness must have been limited. The power of magnification of the early tube scopes was small, about 2x, and their lenses were made of quartz, a liquefied silicon dioxide. When cooled and polished into a lens this gave a magnified but imperfect image with a sharp center but fuzzy edges, and the small tube diameter of the scopes provided a very limited field of view, typically about 3°.

There had been an unexpected benefit to the use of scopes with the adoption of percussion ignition, enabling shooters quite easily to mount optical sights to their rifles. Hitherto it had been near-impossible with a flintlock mechanism, whereas percussion lent itself perfectly to the fitment of a simple telescope that could be mounted over the barrel to assist aiming.

The idea had quickly been taken up by target shooters, for whom the use of open iron sights for long-range shooting had always posed difficulties. Notwithstanding possible Swiss use, exactly where the concept of fitting optics to sporting rifles arose is difficult to ascertain. Certainly Colonel D. Davidson, Crimean War veteran and an experienced long-range shooter, wrote in an article in 1864 that "I … had introduced it to India some thirty years ago" and that there were "gentlemen now at home and in India, who have used the same rifles to which I fitted telescopes, for more than fifteen years, without their getting out of order."[23] If accurate, this would place the practical date of introduction for telescopic sights to the early 1830s, which is not at all improbable although their use would have been limited by both cost and practicality. The making of lenses was a slow, exacting, and expensive process; the result was a costly instrument beyond the pockets of the ordinary shooter. Nevertheless, the concept was a sound one and during the 30 years that had elapsed since the first rifle scopes appeared, considerable advances in optical science and technology had been made.

It was actually the American optical industry that was to take the lead in the manufacture of telescopic sights for shooting, in part due to the explosion of interest in long-range target-shooting. From the 1830s, a new form of heavy bull-barreled target rifle had become the darling of the target-shooting fraternity and there are mentions by contemporary writers of primitive optical sights being used on some of these weapons by about 1835. One man primarily responsible for the wide use of these scopes was an expatriate Englishman named John Ratcliffe Chapman. Contemporary optical sights were normally brass bodied and most were soldered into position, with only the dovetail of the rear or foresight providing any lateral adjustment. Placing any strain on the body often sheared it and the stress of recoil could also break the mounts. Chapman disliked their flimsy design and poor fixing methods and he wrote:

> I am aware that telescopes have been in use for some time, but to the best of my knowledge they never perform so well … until made and used as described. The tube in which the lenses are fixed is three feet one inch long,

$5/_8$th inch in diameter … weighing 10 ozs. It can be made very good and true out of sheet iron. To the front end a saddle of steel is firmly fitted and brazed … the object to be attained being stiffness for when fixed on the rifle, a discharge has the tendency to pitch it forward and break out the dovetail. A carriage is made to slide through the bead sight [front sight] dovetail, through which two screws pass into the saddle, serving as axis or pivot pins of elevation and depression. The back movement for elevating and depressing without taking out the telescope is designed to adapt itself to all ranges.[24]

His saddle design was simple, effective, and has never really been improved on, being in common use still in the late 20th century. Aside from providing a firm mount for the brackets it solved one of the biggest problems in using optical sights, namely how to adjust them for elevation (trajectory) and windage (lateral) movement. Using the saddle brackets and their screw adjusters meant that either the front or rear of the scope could be fine adjusted independently, providing almost limitless control for zeroing. This invention also happily coincided with improvements in the manufacture of optical glass, helped to no small degree by Alavan Clark.

Born in Massachusetts in 1832 Clark became an optical glass grinder, specializing in mirrors for large observation telescopes. (It was he who found and identified the star Sirius B.) As a sideline he made beautiful lenses for small telescopes, each of which was ground precisely to match the vision of the user. Chapman's scopes, which by the late 1840s were being made under license by Morgan James of Utica, New York, provided excellent bodies into which Clark's or other lenses could be fitted, and they were available for almost two decades, from 1845 to the end of the Civil War. Around 1855, another expatriate engineer, Scottish-born William Malcolm, began to make scopes in his Syracuse workshop that differed from all earlier patterns. The bodies of Malcolm scopes were of cold-drawn steel, providing a very strong, solderless tube that enabled much finer tolerances to be used when fitting lenses and mounts. They were also the first to be fully *achromatic*, the lenses being free of any chromatic aberrations caused by poor glass. For the shooter this provided a sharper image and wider field of view with none of the fuzzy-colored fringes of the older lenses. Power could be up to 20x and using the Chapman-James mounts provided the shooter with a reliable and very effective telescopic sight. And all of this happened, fortuitously, just in time for the Civil War.

LANDMARK: THE MINIÉ RIFLE

Although the Indian Wars have been largely popularized as having occurred mostly during the latter part of the 19th century, fighting on the frontier pre-Civil War was the single greatest drain on resources for the US Army and reached a peak in the 1850s. Apache, Sioux, Navaho, Ute, and Comanche attacked forts, Army and civilian wagon trains, and isolated settlements with a monotonous regularity. Despite frequent defeats inflicted by the Army (although defeat was a relative term when dealing with native tribes), little headway could be made in subduing them. Everyone, from the President downwards, agreed that the size of the Army needed to be increased significantly, and in 1855 two new line regiments (9th and 10th) and two cavalry regiments (1st and 2nd) were authorized. Equipping them was another matter, but in that curiously coincidental way that seems to pepper history, they were to be aided by an advance in weapons technology from a wholly unexpected source.

Since its part in the development of the perfected flintlock mechanism in the early 18th century, France had contributed little to weapons technology, Napoleon being rather more concerned with European domination. However, her gunsmiths had not been idle and some small but significant inventions appeared in the decades between the 1820s and the 1840s. In the early 1820s, Captain Henri-Gustav Delvigne had invented a hollow-based conical bullet which was itself a very significant development, but it did not entirely solve the problem of how to load a tight-fitting bullet into a rifle bore without it becoming jammed through fouling. In 1846 Captain Louis-Etienne de Thouvenin, an artillery officer, improved upon this situation by inserting a steel spigot in the center of the breech plug. When the bullet was rammed onto it, its hollow base simply expanded to fit the available space in the breech, albeit at some cost to long-range accuracy. The system enabled a rifle to be loaded and fired as fast as a musket and it was quickly adopted by France, Belgium, and Austria, where it was known as the "tige" or "stem" system. These tige rifles were to see considerable use in the years to come, but all suffered from being extremely difficult to clean. French ballistic ingenuity did not end there, however. Captain Claude Etienne Minié, who had been closely following the development of the new rifles, correctly reasoned that the weaknesses of the tige system were in the fragility of the spigot itself, the problems caused by fouling and the deformation of the bullet during loading. His solution was to simplify the entire process, and consequently he redesigned the hollow bullet and placed a thin steel cup inside the base. When fired, the gas drove the cup into the bullet's interior, forcing the skirt hard against the bore.

The US Ordnance at Harper's Ferry, already interested in the tige system, had obtained a number of minié bullets and molds and began testing. It wasn't a perfect system, though, and their report outlined one of the major drawbacks in the early design of the bullets. "An objection has been found to exist in the use of this cup [or plug], on account of its liability to be driven through the hollow part of the ball, leaving a ring of lead firmly adhering to the sides of the bore."[25]

Nevertheless, their overall impression was favorable, for the benefits of the rifle over the musket were now so obvious that there were few in the Army who could justifiably make a case for the retention of the old system:

> Arms constructed on … these plans have been found capable of making close shooting at a distance of 500 yards, and to be effective in firing … at 1,000 yards. The choice between them is, therefore, to be determined chiefly by reference to the facility and convenience of loading and using the arm.[26]

The slight problem of the bullet remaining welded to the bore by the exiting iron cup was neatly solved by James H. Burton of Harper's Ferry, who simply widened and deepened the cavity in the base of the bullet, eliminating the iron cup entirely. Deep grooves on the outside of the bullet held lubricating grease, easing even further the task of loading so that by the 1850s there were few drawbacks in using rifles, for all of the old problems concerning speed of firing and accuracy had been effectively solved by the minié system. A rifled musket could be loaded and fired just as fast as a soldier could manage. An added benefit was that the minié bullet could be used in all existing rifles, such as the M1842 Mississippi and smoothbore muskets. In one year alone, Allegheny Arsenal supplied 450,000 cartridges and 930,000 bullets of the minié type.[27]

A new Springfield rifle musket, the M1855, soon began to emerge from the armory production lines. Its speed of manufacture was directly related to even greater improvements in manufacturing processes. Machine tolerances were reduced, to the extent that factory inspectors would only pass for service barrels that did not deviate by more than .0025in from factory specification, a practice that during the Civil War had eventually had to be relaxed. Simultaneously, the Ordnance Department embarked on a major program of refurbishment of the thousands of old muskets held in Army arsenals, some 20,000 Models 1832 and 1842 being rebarreled and converted to percussion ignition. It was reported that when issued these proved to be very serviceable weapons:

> There seems no doubt that all serviceable flint-lock muskets may, by rifling and percussioning, be converted into good and efficient long-range arms such as are commonly called "minié rifles" … The improved ammunition … has been issued to all troops bearing grooved arms, and in use in actual service has fully realised all the advantages that were anticipated.[28]

One useful side effect of the new rifles was that *in extremis*, buck and ball loads that produced a useful spread of shot could still be used. The new arms quickly began to be issued to the frontier-based regiments, who sorely needed them. By the fall of 1855 some were already seeing action, as recounted by Captain John Todd of the 6th Infantry, whose men were faced with a Sioux war party in South Dakota:

A warrior dashed out from the crowd and approaching us, rode down the line at full speed parallel to it and distant about 300 yards. Poor fellow! What hope of escape ... from the hundred Minnies levelled upon him. Did he die? *Quien Sabe !* ... we poured a plunging fire upon the Indians with our long-range rifles.[29]

Many of these muskets were also manufactured to take the Maynard tape-primer system, a roll of priming caps similar to those used on modern toy pistols which was inserted into a small cavity on the side of the lockplate. Each time the hammer was cocked, an actuating arm pushed a new cap forwards on to the nipple. It was a good system in theory and in tests had proved reliable enough but was found wanting in service where poor weather conditions, bad handling of the fragile tapes, and the erratic feeding of the caps onto the nipples made it more trouble than it was worth. In 1859 the Ordnance Department decreed that the Maynard system was to be abandoned in favor of the simple and reliable copper percussion cap.

While the Army was finally getting its house in order, the civilian shooting fraternity was enjoying the start of a golden age of firearms improvement, covering every sphere of shooting – mechanical, ballistic, and optical. The muzzle-loading rifles of Dimick, Henry, Hawken, and a plethora of others were selling as fast as they could. Most older muskets were now converted to percussion ignition and many fine commercial rifles were purchased by Army officers en route to their western postings. Manufacturers were not slow in recognizing this demand and began producing variants of the service rifled muskets, advertised as "Officer's models" with fine-quality checkered stocks, special sights, and silver or German silver (nickled steel) fittings. How many found their way west is incalculable, but it set an early precedent for the carrying and use of commercial rifles that would linger in the military for generations to come and would have interesting implications in future wars. The commercial weapons generally provided greater accuracy and reliability than the service arms, at the small cost of sometimes requiring non-issue ammunition. Lieutenant D. Maury of the Mounted Rifles recounted his use of just such a rifle about 1857:

One day I surprised him [the wagon master] by cutting down an antelope at a great distance. I told him to step it off, because his legs were long and would leave no occasion for cavail at short measure. He paced four hundred and seventy-five paces to the antelope.[30]

From the late 1850s there was also emerging in the commercial marketplace a new type of rifle that had none of the problems traditionally associated with muzzle-loaders. These were eventually to supplant totally the rifled muskets, for the age of the breech-loaders was about to begin.

Chapter 5

THE SHARPSHOOTER'S WAR

From the early 1840s there had been a steady increase in the use of percussion ignition throughout the armies of Europe and the United States. Most countries initially modified their old smoothbore flintlock martial arms, then gradually turned towards reequipping with newly designed rifled percussion muskets. Britain, Austria, France, the German states, Sweden, and Italy all began to produce similar weapons. One in particular was to stand out, however, and its manufacture was to have considerable impact on the future war between the Northern and Southern states of America.

The Pattern 1853 Enfield began its life, as did so many similar weapons, as a simple percussion conversion of the old Flintlock Brown Bess muskets that had served the British Army so well. The first model of 1838 was a Land Pattern musket converted by the addition of a percussion lock, but this soon progressed through the patterns of 1839 and 1842 to the Pattern 1851 Minié rifle. This initially fired the original minié bullet, with its problematic steel cupped base, but the Board of Ordnance in Britain was also unhappy with it and it was eventually modified to use a boxwood plug instead, which worked very effectively. The rifle went into production in 1852 and was first issued to line infantry in January 1853, barely in time to see limited use during the Crimean War. Its rifled barrel, .70-caliber bullet, and much improved range (the rear sight was graduated to 900 yards) came as an unpleasant surprise to the Russian troops, who were initially mystified as to the manner of projectiles landing among them, as an artillery officer wrote:

> We dismounted from our horses and watched with curiosity these strange things, little appreciating the new danger we faced. [These bullets] were aimed at our artillery's cartridge boxes but were in no way meant for us … we looked death right in the eyes. But after a few seconds we learned from experience the significance of these "thimbles."[1]

Neither was the accuracy of these rifles lost on the British troops who soon began to preempt the war of 1914 by setting up impromptu "sniper" posts in the trenches at Sevastopol. This novel form of warfare had been watched by Lieutenant-Colonel D. Davidson of the City of Edinburgh Rifles, a keen prewar promoter of the use of optical sights on rifles:

> One soldier was observed lying with his rifle carefully pointed at a distant embrasure, and with his finger on the trigger, ready to pull, while by his side lay another with a telescope directed at the same object … watching the moment when the [Russian] gunner should show himself, in order he may give the order to fire.[2]

Another officer, Lieutenant Green, took it upon himself to force a Russian gun team to retire after shooting at them from 800 yards with a Jacob double rifle. It was a new and radical form of warfare and was watched with interest by the many European and American military personnel who gathered as campaign observers. When in late 1854 the new .577in Pattern 1853 Enfield rifle was introduced for all branches of the British Army, its significance as a new tool of warfare was yet to be understood, but it was soon to prove a benchmark in firearms design and manufacture.

THE BLUE AND THE GRAY

The outbreak of war between Northern and Southern states began in mid-April 1861 with an artillery bombardment by Confederate forces on Fort

Sumter, South Carolina, and it was an inauspicious beginning to the greatest conflict America was to witness. The war would embroil virtually every state in the country, eventually claiming 600,000 lives; a greater total than the United States lost in the two world wars and Vietnam combined. At the beginning of hostilities the Federal army of the North was still armed with a mix of muskets and rifles of varying manufacture and patterns, mostly in the .58 caliber that was by then the universally accepted standard for US military longarms. The M1855 rifle had been modified and simplified; its Maynard priming mechanism was eliminated but its basic specifications remained unchanged. Harper's Ferry, along with some 16,000 stored muskets, had been burned to the ground to prevent the Virginian militia from capturing it, thus effectively putting a stop to the production of the old M1855 rifled musket. This placed the Ordnance Department in a quandary, as clearly the Springfield factory alone was incapable of producing sufficient rifles to equip a new and large volunteer army. Its solution was to place contracts with commercial gunmakers to supply the new M1861 rifles to the pattern supplied by Springfield, and these went to factories such as Colt in Hartford who were capable of setting up the machinery and providing sufficient workmen to meet the demands of the contract. Interestingly, the Colt-produced rifles were not fully interchangeable with Springfield, resulting in much frustration on the part of unit armorers. However, no factory was able to arrange instantaneous production of a new model on demand and production delays were inevitable, sometimes stretching into many months. This meant that many of the regiments comprising the Army of Virginia had to enter into the war equipped with a motley collection of weapons. In fact, so desperate was the Union government for muskets and rifles that thousands were purchased from almost anywhere they could be sourced; it made little difference if they were new models or obsolete. An Ordnance report of 1862 provides a detailed glimpse of some of the weapons that had been purchased for service:

8,999   English Tower muskets
116,740   Enfield rifles
6,409   Prussian rifles

105,140   Prussian muskets
135,755   Austrian rifles
34,500   Austrian muskets
23,994   Belgian rifles
33,200   Belgian muskets
48,108   French rifles
4,850   French muskets
5,179   Minié rifles
203,831   other foreign rifles[3]

It is clear that uniformity of longarms was not initially a prerequisite of the Federal army and through the duration of the war this was to remain the case. The M1861 rifle was never to be uniformly issued to all units and it was redesigned to reduce production time, becoming the M1863. Some 794,000 of these models were manufactured by the Springfield Armory alone during the war. There remained in service a huge number of disparate types, with the consequential problems involved in the issue of ammunition and parts. While this confusion was not an entirely satisfactory state of affairs, it was the best the Ordnance could do to equip its dozens of newly raised line infantry regiments. The use of the new rifle muskets in the field at once began to introduce a new element in the manner that warfare was fought, albeit one that went unnoticed for some time. Prior to the issue of these rifles, the rules of linear warfare applied: muskets were fired, the men moved forwards in serried ranks until the enemy broke. Allowing for the short ranges of the average musket, armies might close to within 20 or 30 yards of each other, eventually allowing a bayonet charge that would force one side or the other from the field. The use of rifles quickly turned this accepted military tactic on its head. Defenders could open accurate fire at 500 yards or more and decimate attackers before they could get anywhere near a range at which they could pause and return fire. This was painfully evidenced during the Battle of Gettysburg, when accurate Federal rifle fire literally stopped a Confederate charge led by Major-General George Pickett in its tracks. Although the defending soldiers waited until the Confederates were within 200 yards, as they closed on the Union lines some 1,700 Union rifles suddenly opened fire. As one eyewitness wrote:

> The lines underwent an instantaneous transformation. They were at once enveloped in a dense cloud of dust. Arms, heads, blankets, guns and knapsacks were tossed into the clear air. A moan went up from the field distinctly to be heard amid the storm of battle.[4]

Although it took time and considerable organization, the Union army would eventually become well armed and supplied, perhaps unsurprisingly considering the bulk of America's industrial capacity was in the North and its population of some 23 million dwarfed the nine million of the predominantly rural South. If the Union was to lead the way in arms design and production, it also became the very first to raise a dedicated sharpshooter regiment.

THE 1ST REGIMENT OF SHARPSHOOTERS

Hiram Berdan was, on the face of it, the ideal candidate to lead a newly raised regiment to glory on the battlefield. He was wealthy, famous, mechanically brilliant, and a naturally gifted rifle shot. While undoubtedly an extremely clever engineer he had some serious character flaws, being a supreme egoist and an obsessive self-publicist, and he appeared on many occasions extremely reluctant to actually place himself in any physical danger. It has long been accepted that it was entirely Berdan's idea to form a sharpshooter regiment, generally because it was Berdan who had said this was the case. However, there is a good argument in favor of a colleague and fellow shooter, Caspar Trepp, as the one who first mooted the idea.[5] A New Yorker of Swiss birth, Trepp was also an excellent shot and it is quite probable that sometime in early 1861 he suggested to Berdan the idea of forming a specially trained sharpshooter unit. After all, the Swiss had a long and honorable tradition of shooting and Trepp was of the opinion that he could raise at least a company or more of volunteers to serve the Union army. However, he had no political connections or funds behind him, both of which Berdan possessed. If it was Trepp's idea that was taken to Washington by Berdan, it proved to be a popular one. It was materially assisted by the fact that Berdan assured Washington that he would assume responsibility for the cost of raising the regiment. Naturally, such a generous offer was considered to be "of great value" by Secretary of War Simon Cameron[6] and on June 15, 1861, Berdan was duly given authority to raise a regiment within 90 days, to be armed and equipped "without expense to the government."[7]

Three months seems an extraordinarily short period to raise, train, and equip a specialist regiment, but the idea of an elite rifle regiment proved highly popular and the unit was over-subscribed from the start. Of course, the concept of such a unit was not entirely new, for irregular riflemen had served in the Revolutionary War and light infantry units had been widely employed on all sides during the Napoleonic Wars – the British had raised the highly successful 60th and 95th Rifles for just such a task. Their use as scouts, sharpshooters, and ambush parties proved a constant source of irritation to the French, who had promised no quarter on any men captured. However, unlike the concept behind the sharpshooters, they had been used in the same manner as line infantry, taking their place in the firing line when required. It is worth pointing out that the term "sharpshooter" was even at this date an old one, dating at least from the 17th century where it was commonly used in Germany and Switzerland to describe a good shot. A *Scharfschutze* was quite literally a sharp-eyed shooter and the word had certainly been adopted into the English language by the early 19th century.

Berdan's use of the term was possibly taken from its commonplace use by the German speaking Swiss or the Englishmen in his command and it owed nothing to his regiment's eventual adoption of the Sharps rifle. Berdan's suggestion was radical in many ways, for he wanted his men to work independently of the Army command, being an entirely separate unit within the Army structure. In both the North and South, regiments were raised around their home states and these units once formed would, for example, become the 1st Michigan or 2nd Illinois, etc. with their ranks filled primarily by local men.

The sharpshooters were to be different in accepting volunteers from any state in the Union; thus the first five companies were formed from men living in Maine, Michigan, Minnesota, New York, Pennsylvania, New Hampshire, Wisconsin, and Vermont. There were also many men from outside of America, with volunteers from countries including Germany, Great Britain, Ireland, Switzerland, and Austria. All of the recruits had to meet exacting requirements to be able to enter the ranks of the sharpshooters. This meant passing a shooting test in which ten consecutive shots had to be fired offhand into the bull at 200 yards making a string no larger than 5in. While many men could easily improve on this requirement, a large percentage were found incapable of achieving it. The *New York Times* commented on this, unconsciously stating a fact that was to become better understood during the large-scale employment of snipers in the World War I: "About two-thirds were found unfitted, and indeed the general average of incompetent applicants is more than that. The American riflemen prove superior, *especially the hunters of New England and the West* [author's italics]."[8] Such results were early evidence that accepting men who could shoot well did not necessarily make them ideal candidates for sharpshooting or sniping, but it was a lesson that was to be learned slowly in the future. In fact, from the large numbers of men who applied to Berdan's regiment there was never any shortage of men who met the standards required and eventually two regiments were formed, the 1st and 2nd United States Sharpshooters (USSS). They were not, however, the sole regiments of marksmen to be raised in the Federal army, for nine other units were formed who would serve in the Army of the Potomac and also in the western theater of war. They comprised the 66th Illinois (1861), 1st and 2nd Massachusetts Companies (1861), Birge's Missouri Regiment (1861), 1st New York Battalion (1862), 1st Michigan Battalion (1863), 1st and 10th Ohio Companies (1861–64), and 1st Maine Battalion (1864).[9]

TRAINING

Initially levels of training for the USSS fell well below that expected of the regular army. The recruits believed from the outset that they were an elite, which was to an extent quite true, and that their shooting abilities would provide them with all the training they needed, which was not. This was proven during their first taste of battle at Yorktown on April 4, 1861, which was to be a sharp lesson for them, losing two men dead and several wounded. Rudolph Aschmann, a close friend of Caspar Trepp and by then a captain in the sharpshooters, wrote subsequently: "This experiment showed very clearly that courage alone does not make a soldier and that competent elementary training is a necessary preparation for active service."[10] As a result not only were normal training methods enforced, but also more specialized forms of instruction were devised, allowing for the unusual role that the USSS would perform. While the primary function was for its troops to operate independently as observers, pickets, skirmishers, and sharpshooters, they would also be needed at times to serve alongside the line infantry so their training was evolved to cover close drill, battalion and company field movements, target practice (still almost unknown in the regular army) skirmishing, and patrolling, as well as the more mundane guard and camp duties. Probably the most vital function for the fledgling sharpshooters to master was skirmishing, for it was vital to their role, and while it is often mentioned it is seldom explained. Skirmishing required steady nerve and good discipline as was clearly outlined by a serving sergeant in the 2nd USSS, Wyman White:

> It is an open order drill. Men form line in two ranks then at the order ... deploying to the distance of five paces apart until the whole company or regiment was a single line five paces apart. Thus deployed, three hundred and fifty men would make a line about a mile long. We took our orders from calls of the bugle ... to advance, commence firing, cease firing ... lay down, rise, halt and retreat ... Every man knew his place.[11]

Unlike line regiments, who stood in serried ranks to fight, the sharpshooters took a far more practical line. On spotting the Confederates, their line would suddenly break, as one private wrote: "When the order to halt is given we ... run for the nearest tree and if there is none, lay down flat on our bellies so to get out the reach of the enemy's fire."[12] Captain C. A.

Stevens, serving with the 1st USSS wrote that after training the men "were soon able to execute the most difficult regimental drills and were probably unexcelled … in skirmishing, a service they were destined to perform at the front, in all the great battles of the Army."[13] As skirmishers they moved forward across enemy ground, each man watching for his own target (often enemy pickets) and relying on those either side to protect him. The maneuver required nerve, discipline, and common sense, particularly when fighting in dense woodland. When threatened by cavalry the men would be grouped in fours and could watch and shoot at each other's flank.[14]

Picket duty was if anything more demanding and it was a task at which the sharpshooters of both sides would excel. It was, as one Union officer, John D. Young, wrote "[a duty] that above all others … requires most individual intelligence in the soldiers."[15] Picket duty consisted of both guarding and scouting, and was comprised of a series of outposts of up to six men, in front of whom were concealed sentries watching for enemy movement. "If attacked the pickets would use their accurate fire to hold the enemy until reserves, usually camped close by, could be summoned."[16] Young also commented that "A picket line, judiciously posted, in woods or swamps, will oppose a formidable resistance, even to the line of battle."[17] Pickets were often the first to spot enemy formations and could halt advancing troops by shooting officers and NCOs, but it took a steady eye and good nerves to stand and face an advancing enemy unsupported by any infantry. Aside from military drills, sharpshooter training also involved sports, as officers understood that only fit men could march and fight effectively, especially as much of the work the sharpshooters were to undertake required them to move over long distances and crawl stealthily on all fours to places of concealment, or to get within firing range. The usual sports – football, athletics, and boxing – were employed as well as some custom-designed sessions to improve hand-to-eye coordination, like bayonet fighting and fencing.

The sharpshooters were probably the first and only military unit of the Civil War to be schooled in such a wide range of tactics, many of which would be adopted by later generations of sniper instructors. While the training helped to instil order and foster the attitude that they were indeed an elite, it did little to solve the tricky problem of discipline. The men who enlisted were of non-military backgrounds, well educated by the standards of the day, and mostly all of independent spirit. In fact, the profile of an average 1st USSS was a man of $24^1/_2$ years of age, 5ft 6in tall, weighing 140lb, and from a professional background. Almost without exception they resented military discipline and in their six-month sojourn while training in Washington DC they earned a reputation for being somewhat cavalier in their attitude to regulations, not unlike many special forces troops today. At one stage when an irate Brigadier-General J. H. Ward threatened to shoot an insubordinate sharpshooter, every man in camp raised and cocked his rifle. "He heard the 'click-click' and rode off, swearing hard at us."[18] Some who joined disliked Colonel Berdan's overbearing attitude so much that they preferred to enlist in other sharpshooter units, and a few even deserted to rejoin different regiments under assumed names. The majority, however, were proud to belong to such a specialized unit and they began slowly to form into a more or less cohesive fighting force. This development was helped in no small part by the issue of uniform and weapons, although the subject of the latter was nearly to cause wholesale mutiny and lose Berdan command of his regiment.

UNIFORM AND WEAPONS

The issue uniform for the Union army was a dark-blue woolen sack coat and sky-blue trousers, which as one recruit commented "fitted only where it touched."[19] It was hardly the stuff that would enable a man to blend seamlessly with his surroundings; while at the time it served well enough for line infantry it was clearly not good enough for the sharpshooters. Considerable thought had been given to the uniform by Berdan, Trepp, and other officers and it was clear from the outset that men employed as skirmishers and intelligence gatherers would not be able to perform their duties if they were instantly visible to the casual observer. It was therefore decided that a similar uniform to that of the British rifle regiments should be adopted, a dark-green summer uniform coat, trousers, and kepi, while for autumn and winter a gray uniform coat was suggested. As with the British uniform, the buttons were black and non-reflective. Leather leggings made from goatskin were also supplied to protect the legs from thorns and snakes.

Typically, Berdan capitalized on the fame of his unit by writing to the governor of New York, asking that the state fund the cost of uniforms and explaining:

> My reasons for selecting this uniform are that the men will not consent to wear the common US uniform; and as they will be skirmishers, they should not be conspicuously dressed – the green will harmonize with the leaves of summer while the gray overcoat will accord with surrounding objects in fall & winter.[20]

His argument was flawless, but in reality the desired issue of uniforms did not go quite as planned, as the trousers failed to materialize and standard sky-blue ones were issued instead. Once in combat some problems became apparent with regard to the gray coats and gray "Havelock" caps. As Captain Stevens commented:

> We wore for a time a gray round hat ... good enough around Washington far within the lines but after our first appearance before the enemy the following spring they were discarded as endangering a fire from the rear. Certain gray felt, seamless overcoats were likewise abandoned.[21]

Looking like an enemy soldier had hitherto never been a problem, as linear warfare enabled the lines to differentiate between each other with relative ease. In hand-to-hand combat the difference between uniforms was apparent enough to prevent much confusion. However, the sharpshooter's war required different parameters and clearly any uniform that gave the men the appearance of Confederate soldiers and attracted fire from their own side had to be abandoned. Uniquely, too, the USSS regimental officers clothed themselves in the same manner as their men, Captain Aschmann noting that:

The officer's uniforms ... were not much different from those of the soldiers and just as simple by comparison. The insignia were no glittering epaulettes, only a narrow band edged with gold braid and fastened on the shoulder. For daily use ... we had a blue flannel jacket which was worn in the field even by officers.[22]

However noble the intentions of their colonel in clothing the men in new uniforms, it soon became clear that in the field sharpshooters would wear only what they believed to be the most suitable clothing for the purposes. Initially the green coats worked well enough, but the high, formal collar was not comfortable in hot weather or when lying down, digging into the neck and restricting movement. Trousers became a mixed pattern of green, blue, or even civilian types, and the peaked forage cap, often decried as the most useless piece of military headgear ever devised, was usually replaced by a practical broad-brimmed slouch hat in black or other dark color. Equipment normally included a waist-belt with cartridge and cap pouches, and a good all-purpose knife. The socket bayonet issued with the rifles was more often than not "lost" on campaign as few sharpshooters had any use for it. When inspected by a staff officer in late 1862, the 1st USSS were castigated as being "perfect slouches and slovens in appearance and of whom it can be said that hardly any two are uniformed alike."[23] As a result strenuous efforts were made to ensure some uniformity of dress, with the renewed issue of the green coat foremost among the requirements. The efforts appear to have had some result, for early the next year a private wrote home that "This is the best dressed regiment I have seen." The change was also partly engendered by demands from the Army command that the men behave more in keeping with regulations, with more training, drill, and harsher discipline. This policy only worked up to a point, however, for the sharpshooters had by then gained an everlasting reputation for being uncompromising in their attitude to Army bureaucracy, poor-quality officers, delayed pay, and inadequate rations or equipment. It was an early indication that the Army could not always have its cake and eat it, for in employing men of intelligence, resource, and determination it was laying itself open to their criticism (usually quite justified) of its inadequacies and operational shortcomings from men who were quite different from the usual mold of Army recruits. As one man wrote, "It appears ... [the sharpshooters] are hated by all that have to deal with us."[24] In a way this comment has been echoed over the decades by other sharpshooter and sniper units, who always appeared to be blessed with a love/hate relationship between themselves and their own armies.

Nowhere was this attitude more visible than in the vexing problems surrounding the issue of rifles to the 1st USSS. Many of the men enlisting to form the first companies of sharpshooters did so carrying their own rifles, most of which were heavy target weapons, some equipped with optical sights. These guns were certainly the apogee of their day for target shooting, with their massive bull-barrels, set triggers, and fine-adjustable target sights, but despite Berdan's own exhortation that "All who have favourite guns of their own which they wish to bring are at liberty to do so,"[25] their weight (anywhere between 15 and 28lb) made them manifestly unsuitable for carrying any distance on campaign. In addition, their small calibers, typically from .30 to .40in, meant that they were not necessarily deadly at longer ranges, and by Berdan's own admission by late 1861 he had "About two hundred heavy target rifles, which is as many as I care to have of these heavy guns."[26] While a number of these guns were always to be at hand, normally carried in the supply wagons, the men waited expectantly for the issue of their service rifles. Initially these were to have been the standard M1861 Springfield rifle, a pattern that Berdan had endorsed in July 1861 as the most suitable then available, and these rifles were quickly supplied to the Washington arsenal by the Chief of Ordnance, Brigadier-General James Ripley. However, Berdan, always reaching for the next star before he had grasped the first, had turned his attentions to the new breech-loading rifles that were beginning to appear; in fact what he specifically wanted were M1859 Sharps rifles.

Christian Sharps' rifle had its origins in a design of 1848, and was a simple falling-block rifle that had been adopted by the US Navy as the M1855. Sharps had continued to improve its design and his new model, the M1859, incorporated the Lawrence pellet priming system, which was not dissimilar in function to that of the Maynard. There was some merit in this change of heart for there were of course many shortcomings with muzzle-loading weapons. The most serious problem in combat was the fact that a soldier who had fired his rifle was inevitably forced to stand upright to reload it, thus making him an easy and helpless rifleman's target in the time it took to recharge the weapon. While sharpshooters were taught to reload lying down, it was an awkward procedure. At a stroke breech-loading solved this and most other problems. Loading was simple: a hinged or sliding breech-block was opened and a cartridge inserted, the breech closed, the hammer cocked, and the rifle was ready to fire. Unlike loading the musket, the breech-loading procedure could be carried out easily by a soldier lying prone. In addition, the bullet could be made a perfect fit for the bore, totally eliminating windage and improving accuracy and velocity. Usefully, too, each subsequent shot cleared much of the fouling residue left by the previous shot. The Sharps rifles wanted by Berdan were not standard issue, however, being special-order weapons with double-set triggers and no sword bayonet lug, although they could accept a socket bayonet. The guns weighed $12^1/_2$lb with 30in barrels and they were uniformly chambered for the Sharps .52-caliber combustible cartridges. As a result, Berdan wrote to Simon Cameron, Secretary of War in the fall of 1861, baldly stating that "any of the ordinary weapons would make my men little better than the common infantry & as my men are getting very good drill no time should be lost in arming & sending them forward."[27]

The snag as far as the Ordnance Department was concerned was that the Sharps were $43 each, compared to $13 for an M1861 Springfield or $25 for an Enfield. Additionally, the government had already contracted Sharps to supply carbines for the cavalry, and their production capability would be compromised if the new rifles had to be manufactured. Whether Hiram Berdan actually expected General Ripley to endorse this request is a moot point; perhaps not, for Ripley was deeply and fundamentally opposed to the issue of any non-standard weapons to the Army. Neither was he a particular advocate of Hiram Berdan or his theories on breech-loading, so it seemed that the likelihood of the USSS receiving their Sharps rifles was fairly slim. In view of this, within a month Berdan had changed tack again and was frantically chasing Colt for supplies of their M1855 revolving rifle. This choice on the part of a good and experienced shot like Berdan is puzzling in the extreme, but probably owes much to his playing at politics. Berdan's friends and allies were Colonel R. B. Marcy, Chief of Staff of the Army of the Potomac and a close personal friend of both Samuel Colt and General George B. McClellan, the Army's commander.

In January 1862, after intervention by no less a person than President Lincoln, Ripley was forced to give consent for the supply of 1,000 Colt rifles. The Colts were basically long-barreled .56-caliber side-hammer variants of their famous revolvers. As revolvers they certainly worked very well, but when used as longarms they proved deficient in almost every respect, two shortcomings proving particularly dangerous. On firing there would be a sideways spray of tiny lead particles from the chamber, but probably more serious was their propensity to chain fire (ignite several chambers simultaneously), which was deeply unfortunate for the firer if he was supporting the weapon in his left hand, a normal position for shooting a rifle. Private T. Preston, Company B, 2nd USSS, wrote home of the Colts that:

> I have often seen the boys picking out these pieces of lead from one another's necks and faces. Not long ago a fellow on Co.G was firing when three barrels went off at once, cutting away his forefinger and thumb. The Major was firing one not long ago when it burst. But still they say it is a safe gun ... if the Sharps is poorer, we want it.[28]

The operational faults might have been forgiven if the Colts had proved to be particularly accurate, powerful, or reliable, but they were not. Some sharpshooters issued with them commented, "While pretty to look at ... [the Colts] were inaccurate and unreliable, prone to get out of order and even dangerous to the user." Another said that the new rifles were "As much work to take care of ... as it would be to keep two pairs of horses."[29] Clearly the Colts had proved to be a poor choice on the part of Berdan, but he had not lost all in his gamble to override the Ordnance Department, and he may simply have seen the Colts as a means to an end. He had, after all, finally defeated Ripley on the matter of non-standard arms and he continued to badger Washington for his Sharps rifles.

On January 27 Ripley was finally overruled, being forced to acquiesce and allow an initial supply of 1,000 Sharps rifles to the sharpshooters, followed on February 6 by an order for 1,000 more. Although the men were very keen to have the Sharps rifles, so many promises about their issue had been made and broken that they were becoming angered at the delays. The dissatisfaction was compounded by the temporary issue of the Colts, which were only grudgingly accepted as one man put it, "until we get the Sharps."[30] But their patience was wearing thin and the matter came to a head on March 6, 1862, when the regiment was warned to prepare for the battlefront with its detested Colts. Representatives of the soldiers met with Colonel Berdan to demand the issue of their promised rifles, or they would simply refuse to leave camp. Berdan was left frantically lobbying the Ordnance Department for delivery of his Sharps rifles. On April 21, 1862, the first shipment of 500 left the factory followed by further shipments of 500 on May 2, May 14, and May 24. At last, the sharpshooters had the rifles they wanted, arguably the best breech-loader then in existence, as well as the uniform and equipment they required. What they now needed was to find out just what sort of opposition the Confederate forces would offer.

SHARPSHOOTERS OF THE CONFEDERACY

If neither side was particularly well prepared for the conflict that began in 1861, on balance the South was the worse off. Its regular army consisted of a mere 16,080 officers and men on a frontier that stretched from the Canadian border to Mexico, and the sudden requirement to raise a huge new citizen army faced the Confederacy with an even bigger set of problems than the Union. How could it train, equip, and arm the large number of volunteers required to a standard sufficient to enable them to fight against overwhelming odds on two fronts, without the benefits of the industrial economy enjoyed by the North? Confederate regiments were also raised on a state-by-state basis and went to battle, certainly for the first year of the war, employing the traditional methods of linear warfare. While they had some rifled arms, until late in the war the vast majority of Confederate soldiers in the field fought with smoothbore muskets. These admirably suited the tactics then employed, of course, for few army commanders recognized the powerful abilities of the new rifled arms, assuming that the old method of closing with the enemy and defeating him in a spirited charge would serve as well as it had always done. This attitude was well reinforced by an unnamed officer of the Alabama Brigade who was interviewed in early 1864 and asked by the journalist about the efficiency of the new rifles and their long-range capabilities:

> [he] disagreed entirely with me in regard to the utility of long-range muskets. In practice [he said] these long-range weapons had been found of little or no use, inferior in every way … especially in warfare against the Yankees, who had been whipped by Lee's army always by bold charges and firing at close quarters, never by shots from long taw [range].[31]

There was no doubt that the South was going to be quickly disabused of this opinion and it was soon realized by the many forward-thinking Confederate commanders that the use of rifles and sharpshooters was going to prove vital in what was increasingly looking to be a long drawn-out war. After much lobbying by senior officers such as Generals Earl Van Dorn, Robert E. Rhodes, and Cadmus Wilcox (some of whose men had already suffered at the hands of the USSS), in April 1862 the Confederate Congress passed an act to permit the raising of several battalions of sharpshooters consisting of "Not less than three nor more than six companies [per regiment] to be composed of men selected … and armed with long-range muskets or rifles." Initially at least supplies of the required weapons were going to prove a problem and the act went on to add that:

> The government has not at its command a sufficient number of approved long-range rifles of muskets wherewith to arm the said corps. Requisitions will be made upon the Ordnance Department for the arms … and until such

requisitions can be filled … such exchanges and transfers of long-range muskets and rifles to be made as may be necessary to arm said battalions, returning surplus arms when such requirements are filled to the Ordnance Department.[32]

In simple language, there were no rifles available to equip the sharpshooters, so they had official sanction to beg, borrow, but not actually steal the weapons they required to enable them to function.

RECRUITMENT AND TRAINING

In total 16 Confederate sharpshooter battalions were raised, these being: 17th, 23rd Alabama; 1st, 12th Arkansas; 1st, 2nd, 3rd, 4th Georgia; 14th Louisiana; 1st, 9th, 15th Mississippi; 9th Missouri; 1st North Carolina; 2nd South Carolina; 1st Texas.[33] In many respects the men recruited were superior to those of the Federal sharpshooters, for they had already been serving as line infantry and were battle hardened. Their farming backgrounds usually meant that they were markedly better at using their weapons. Lieutenant William Ripley (no relation to the Ordnance general), in his contemporary history of the 1st USSS, wrote of the Confederate troops that their predominantly rural backgrounds allied to skills at hunting and tracking meant that they were often to prove better than the Federal sharpshooters. "It became painfully apparent that, however inferior … the Confederate armies were in point of education and general intelligence to the men … of the Union … man for man they were the superiors of their northern antagonists in the use of arms." He further reasoned, quite correctly that "their armies were composed mainly of men who had been trained to the skilful use of the rifle [in] that most perfect of schools, the field and forest."[34]

The Southern army thus began to try to organize its sharpshooter battalions on a more formal basis and this usefully coincided with a massive shake-up of the entire Confederate military establishment. No single regiment could provide sufficient men who had the skills required for sharpshooting, so units were raised through their own state regiments from the selection of men serving as regular line infantry. This system provided the material to form sharpshooter battalions, and some were raised very quickly indeed. The 17th Alabama and 9th Missouri sharpshooters were serving in the field by April 28, 1862. Unlike Berdan's units, though, there was considerable reluctance to join Southern sharpshooter battalions from among men who had already made close friends and fought together. Their state regiments were their homes, and the sharpshooter units were an unknown quantity staffed by strangers. While some were extremely keen to join the new units (Sergeant Benson recalled that his friend, a lance corporal, willingly gave up his stripes to join a new unit as a private soldier[35]), many commanding officers had to detail men to join the sharpshooter battalions, as Colonel John Pressley of the 25th Carolina Regiment wrote: "Every regiment in the department was invaded and where volunteers could not be obtained [and very few were found willing to go] compulsory details were required."[36] As a result the inept, lame, and in some cases even partially sighted were found to have been transferred into sharpshooter units. Much time and effort had to be spent in weeding them out, reinforcing the concept that such specialist units could only be properly manned by volunteers, a fact that still holds true today.

By the fall of 1863 a training manual for the men had been drawn up by Major Calhoun Benham and a manual of arms had also been produced by Major-General Cadmus Wilcox. Between them, the two men covered all of the necessary skills, although for the Confederacy the training of their men was simplified to a great extent by their familiarity with their rifles and previous military experience. The disciplines of picketing, skirmishing, and very-long-range shooting, however, all had to be learned. Then, as now, estimating of ranges was always a difficult skill to teach and master, and one officer of Mahone's Brigade wrote of their training that:

the spring of that year [1864] was spent in perfecting ourselves in the skirmish drill by signals and in rifle-target practice at different ranges – from 50 to 1,000 yards – and so proficient did the men become in estimating distances that [check-measuring the distance] was finally discontinued as being unnecessary.[37]

Targets were invariably pine planks, of 1in thickness, placed at varying distances from 100 to 1,000 yards, the long-range target being a modest 6ft x 6ft, and shooting drill was often practiced for six hours a day until the men were totally proficient. Major Eugenel Blackford of the 5th Alabama, placed in command of the Corps of Sharpshooters, may have been the pioneer of the now universally accepted method of target marking. Frustrated at the slowness of having one man shoot then having to check his target, he placed men as target markers in trenches dug underneath the target boards and gave each one a paddle painted white one side and black the other. White side was a bull, black side a miss. As he later said, "The record was kept with perfect accuracy, yet firing was as rapid as ordinary file firing."[38]

At the end of their training, the majority of men were capable of hitting a man-sized target with their first shot at ranges of up to 800 yards, given good weather conditions. Those who were not able to meet the exacting standards were soon returned to their units as there was no room for slackers. There were compensations, though, for like their Northern counterparts these units were exempt from normal fatigue duties, it being understood that the demands of their profession were heavy enough without adding the irksome and often unnecessary routines of infantry life. Drill was also a daily routine and gradually the enthusiastic, reluctant, or dubious recruits were molded into very effective fighting units, with their own *esprit de corps*, convinced that theirs was, without question, the finest battalion of sharpshooters in the Confederate army.

UNIFORM AND WEAPONS

Unlike their Union counterparts, the men who joined the Southern sharpshooter units were already clothed and equipped in standard Confederate uniform and rarely was any attempt made to furnish them with any specialist clothing. The tunic and trousers were a gray or butternut brown color with similar colored kepi, although felt slouch hats were widely worn. These colors were actually very practical for field use and were chosen partly as a result of tests undertaken by the British Army during the Napoleonic Wars, where targets of red, green, and gray were set up and fired at, the gray proving a far more difficult color upon which to estimate range and subsequently to hit. (Nevertheless the British had obstinately continued to issue red uniforms for line infantry, although green was subsequently adopted for light infantry and rifle regiments.)

If the Confederates had one major problem, it was in preventing their own sharpshooters from being arrested as deserters or spies when working in the front lines away from their units. To prevent confusion, the sharpshooter units devised and issued a series of special badges made locally of red felt and these took many forms, examples being a red cross or red diamond worn on the left forearm or a red band running diagonally across the left elbow. They served to identify the men as sharpshooters and were unique in providing them with a distinction that was instantly recognizable, although from some viewpoints this was not always a good idea, particularly if they were captured.

The rifles required by the men came from anywhere they could be sourced; regiments were combed for rifled muskets, shipments of foreign arms were sorted through with good rifles being put aside and, of course, as with the Federal sharpshooters, many men carried their personal rifles. Because of the huge range of home-produced and foreign weapons in use in the Confederate army there was a bewildering number of calibers and supply was always a problem, but having sharpshooters carry non-standard rifles did not overly concern quartermasters. This was in part because most men who had their own weapons invariably carried bullet molds and could cast and manufacture their own ammunition as long as a supply of lead was available. Generally speaking, a shortage of lead on the battlefields was the least of their problems. There were a number of Springfield-type rifled muskets being manufactured by Confederate factories; the story of the production and supply of these arms is both interesting and complex. Suffice it to say that for the regimental sharpshooters, there existed certain rifles which were held as superior to all others, these being the British Pattern 1853 Enfield and Whitworth long-range target rifle, US M1861 Springfield, and Sharps long rifle (as opposed to the Sharps carbine, which, as one veteran rifleman said, "served no purpose but to frighten horses and scare folk"). Except where they had acquired Sharps rifles through capture the Southern sharpshooters primarily used rifled muskets, generally preferring the Enfield above all others. Although no less well made than the Springfield, Enfields had a well-deserved reputation for accuracy at extreme ranges and they had been extensively tested by officers and men of the Sharpshooter Brigade. In his interesting account of life in a Confederate sharpshooter unit, Major W. S. Dunlop wrote of the Enfield:

> The Minnie rifle, the Enfield, the Austrian, Belgium, Springfield, and Mississippi rifles were put to the test, and while each of them proved accurate and effective at short range, the superiority of the Enfield rifle for service at long range, from 600 to 900 yards, was clearly demonstrated ... while other rifles could only be relied on at a distance of 500 yards.[39]

The biggest problem for the South was in obtaining enough of these rifles, for the Federal naval blockade dramatically pushed up the prices for any weapons smuggled into the South. This meant that a $25 Enfield could cost the Confederate government over double that price as the rates charged to run the blockade were high. Some 117,000 Enfields were imported along with tens of thousands of Belgian copies, and the Confederate armory also made good copies. It should be stressed, though, that none of these Enfields were British military issue rifles, despite many opinions to the contrary. Regardless of which side was supplied by Britain (who very fairly sold rifles to both North and South), all of the rifles purchased were commercial contract weapons, for at no time did the British government ever sanction official sales to either the Federal or Confederate governments. Some Kerr rifles were also purchased from England and were highly prized, so much so that General John Breckinridge, commander of the Kentucky brigade, presented 11 to men who had proved themselves particularly adept shots, sensibly warning them to use their rifles to target Federal artillery from 400 yards behind their lines, so as not to put themselves and their precious rifles in unnecessary danger.

Of all the rifles supplied by Britain, without a doubt those most highly sought after were the Whitworths. Probably more folklore has sprung up around these rifles than any other used in the war, but their scarcity and cost certainly made them very rare and exotic beasts even by contemporary standards. A Whitworth at first glance looked similar to a contemporary Enfield, but on closer inspection the resemblance ended, for they were chambered for a .45-caliber bullet and had a hexagonal bore and polygonal-grooved rifling.[40] The Whitworth Company of Manchester, England, had mastered the art of manufacturing the finest possible quality target rifles. Their skill lay in absolutely precise quality control, fine workmanship, and ammunition produced so that each bullet would perform nearly identically to the previous one. Whitworth clearly understood that no matter how good a rifle might be and how adept the shooter, poor-quality ammunition would produce mediocre results. It was a lesson that was not entirely appreciated by the military until well into World War II. The combination of fine engineering and high-quality ammunition produced incredibly accurate rifles. They were also materially assisted by the use of optical sights, although the number of weapons so equipped was very small, possibly fewer than 50 out of a total of around 250 Whitworths purchased. The match-quality ammunition was unique, and every cartridge supplied was manufactured to the highest possible specifications, as one sharpshooter recalled:

> The cartridge was made with great care, the bullets of compressed lead, $1^1/_2$ inches long, and of precisely uniform weight; the charges of powder precisely of the same weight ... of uniform size, finely glazed; the cartridge wrapped in parchment and coated with paraffine.[41]

The rifles were also frighteningly expensive, with a standard Whitworth costing $600, a cased one with 1,000 rounds of ammunition $1,000, and a cased one with optical sight $1,200. The issue of these rifles was split between the two armies, in the North and West, and in both locations they gave excellent service. The rifles were normally awarded to the best company shots after stiff competition. Private Sam Watkins of the 1st Tennessee explained how his sharpshooter battalion decided on who would get a Whitworth. Soldiers who wanted the guns shot three rounds at a small marker board 500 yards away and "Every shot that was fired hit the board, but there was one man who came a little closer to the spot than any other one and the Whitworth was awarded to him."[42]

SHARPSHOOTERS IN COMBAT

Despite the legends that have grown up of the individual prowess of the sharpshooters, much of their combat was undertaken in company order with perhaps one or two specially positioned companies of sharpshooters on the battlefront. At times their advanced shooting skills were barely required, as an account by a Federal sharpshooter at the Battle of Gaines Mill showed:

> The "Ninth" [Massachusetts Regiment] were drawn in ... back half way up the hill ... where we took cover behind trees and stumps. Then a brisk firing commenced on our right and scattered along until it come opposite of me. We fought pretty much on our own hook the officers being far to the right, and the human voice was of no account. The rebels rushed down the hill in line of battle, but it wasn't quite so easy rushing across a swamp, waist deep in thick mud, and as they tried it we tried Sharps rifles at eight rods [approximately 45 yards], firing as fast as we could put in cartridges, the distance being so short that aim was unnecessary. The bullets came like hair, and the trees looked like nutmeg graters, but our cover was pretty good and their aim was feet too high so our company lost only one man killed and three wounded.[43]

His rifle actually became so hot he had to cease firing to allow it to cool, but his account is interesting for it underlines a number of factors that were important in understanding the distinction between the trained rifleman and ordinary soldier. The Confederates, shooting across a valley at men concealed up a slope, did what most untrained shooters do: they overestimated the range, shooting far too high. The sharpshooters were also well concealed, making them a difficult target at the best of times, and the rate of fire of the new breech-loading rifles was overwhelming compared to that of muskets. Once his gun discharged, it was well nigh impossible for a running man to reload a musket quickly without stopping, instantly making him a perfect target. Unfortunately this was not a unique event, for time and again the sharpshooters of both sides proved the superiority of their weapons and training. After the Battle of Antietam in September 1862, some 200 Confederate dead were piled into a mass grave in front of the Berdan sharpshooters' lines and at Chancellorsville in May 1863 the sharpshooters decimated the 23rd Georgia Regiment with sheer volume of fire.

Yet it was the occasional, albeit less public, long-range shooting for which sharpshooters were mostly remembered, the tales of their prowess retold over campfires by the Union and Confederate armies. The experience they gained established the ground-rules for the use of snipers on the battlefield and enemy officers, NCOs, and artillery teams were favored targets. Private George Chase of the 1st USSS took up a commanding position overlooking a rebel field gun battery and succeeded in preventing the gunners from using their guns for two days.[44] The Sharps was perfectly capable of registering 1,000-yard hits in competent hands. One famed exponent of its capabilities was Truman Head, universally known as California Joe. He was, at 52, already old by Army standards and it was rumored, actually with some truth, that it was Joe's love of the Sharps (which he had used prewar for bear hunting) that had strongly influenced Hiram Berdan in his quest for the best rifle for his regiment. One of Joe's favorite pastimes was killing enemy artillery gunners at ranges of up to 800 yards, yet despite contrary reports from newspapers he showed none of the characteristics that men expected from such a skilled marksman. He was "the gentlest of men … entirely free from brag and bluster and unassuming."[45] In fact, he exhibited almost all of the traits that are still found in the best and most effective military sharpshooters: calmness, near saintly patience, and very acute vision. Neither was he alone, for there were many others in both armies of a similar mold. One sharpshooter, annoyed at being spied upon from a tree by a Confederate armed with field glasses, decided to remove him. However, the range, of about 1,400 yards, was greater than the Sharps' rear sight could be adjusted to. He set about cutting a makeshift rear sight from cardboard that he then attached to his rifle, eventually accounting for the Confederate with his second shot. Humor was never far away from army life and the sharpshooters were no exception. As in the war of 1914–18, occasional truces were common along the battlefront to allow dead to be collected, washing to be done, food to be prepared, or simply because no one felt like killing anyone else. The yell of "time up" or a single shot fired into the air was normally sufficient warning to send men scurrying back to their posts. At Petersburg in 1864 one rebel ignored the call and sat sipping his cup of coffee and chewing a hard-tack biscuit. A sharpshooter called, "I say Johnny, time is up, get into your hole," to which the response "all right" was made, but the man did not move. The rifleman responded, "Just hold that cup still, and I will show you whether it is alright or not." A second later the cup was smashed by a bullet, sending the Confederate diving for his trenches, to the jeers and laughter of others who witnessed the event.[46]

For their part, the Confederate sharpshooters were also to give a good account of themselves. Although their employment was more often in the traditional role of line infantry, they were normally the first troops in action during an engagement. They were usually on picket duty and were expected to establish skirmish lines well ahead of their main lines to occupy the Union forces. This use of their skills, while understandable, was not the best method of employment, and as a result their casualty rates were to be far higher during the course of the war than those of infantry units. "The proportion of killed and wounded in the sharpshooters was exceedingly large, probably without a parallel. The battalion went into the fight with 104 men and officers, and of these ninety-four men and officers were killed or wounded." So wrote Major George Bernard, then commanding a sharpshooter unit during the Battle for the Craters during the siege of Petersburg in 1864–65.[47] The fighting was not all one-sided, though, for during the siege of Chattanooga, Confederate marksmen of General Longstreet's brigade were ordered to prevent a Federal supply column from crossing the river some 12 miles into enemy lines. Equipped with scoped Whitworths, according to an eyewitness they managed to leave behind a "road … left choked with dead and dying men and mules, and overturned wagons."[48]

One of the most enduring stories of the prowess of the Confederate sharpshooters is that of the shooting of Union major-general John Sedgewick, who is sadly remembered to posterity not for his thoughtful compassion towards his men (he was universally known as Uncle John), but for his unfortunate comment a few seconds before he was shot that the Confederate riflemen "couldn't hit an elephant at this distance." Lieutenant-Colonel Martin McMahon, standing next to Sedgewick, wrote of the events:

> For the third time, the same shrill whistle [of a bullet] closing with a dull heavy stroke, interrupted our talk ... as I was about to resume, the general's face turned slowly to me, the blood spurting from his left cheek under the eye in a steady stream. He fell in my direction, I was so close to him ... that I fell with him.[49]

Usually cited as the candidate for firing this shot is Confederate sharpshooter Private Ben Powell, at the time equipped with a scoped Whitworth in the rebel lines some 800 yards away. However, Powell's company officer, Berry Benson, recalled Powell saying that he had shot a *mounted* officer from his horse, and Sedgewick was on foot at the time. Powell had probably accounted for General Morris, shot earlier in the day. It is unlikely that anyone will ever know who the sharpshooter really was, but, alas for General Sedgewick, it was very fine shooting.

THE PSYCHOLOGY OF SHARPSHOOTING

One of the more curious aspects of the increasing use of sharpshooters on the battlefront was the manner in which both their own and the enemy's infantry regarded them. As had already been noted, riflemen in the Revolutionary War were frequently given no quarter when overrun or captured, as the loss of comrades through deliberate, aimed shooting frequently enraged infantrymen. After Sedgewick's death, angry Union troops turned a cannon, loaded with grapeshot, onto the Confederate treeline to dislodge several snipers, a tactic that was to be revived in later wars. Some sharpshooters, threatened with capture, deliberately hid their rifles. A Tennessee cavalryman, J. W. Minnich, found an unusual-looking rifle concealed in heavy underbrush during the Battle for Campbell's Station in November 1863. It was very heavy and "more deeply grooved [rifled] than any gun I had ever seen, of smaller caliber than any of our guns."[50] At this point the owner, one of General Longstreet's sharpshooters, returned, explaining that it was a Whitworth rifle and he had stashed it during the Yankee advance. When captured, men of Berdan's command were frequently badly treated or simply killed, as the downside of having such a distinctive uniform was an inability to blend in with ordinary infantryman. The adoption of normal combat clothing, with no distinctive badges, was not to become commonplace until early in the 20th century.

As the war progressed and the quality of men conscripted decreased, there was a marked change in the attitude of the armies, with brutality and callousness becoming more evident. This manifested itself in many ways, by the robbing of dead, for example, which had been a rare occurrence at the start of the war but was an accepted practice by 1864. There was also an increased antipathy towards sharpshooters of both sides as newly conscripted, less professional soldiers regarded them as little better than murderers. If captured, they could no longer expect to be treated like ordinary prisoners. A Federal officer, Major Stevens, recalled the relief of a number of Confederate sharpshooters taken at Devil's Den, Gettysburg, when they realized that they had been captured by their counterparts, the 1st USSS, as they "fully expected to be hung as snipers."[51] This attitude was of course a clear double standard, for although men were always pleased to have the services on hand of their own snipers, they treated them with a mixture of awe, disdain, and frequent contempt. It was an attitude that was not to change much over the next 150 years.

So what did the sharpshooters achieve on the battlefields of Virginia, Tennessee, and elsewhere? It is well-nigh impossible to ascertain exactly how effective they were, nor how many casualties fell to their rifles. Perhaps one statistic from the Union troops encamped opposite Charlestown sheds a tiny glimmer of light on the subject, as it specifically mentions casualties at the rate of ten per day from Confederate rifle fire. One Army engineer wrote that "the least exposure above the crest of the parapet will draw the fire of his telescopic Whitworths which cannot be dodged. Several of our men were wounded by these rifles at a distance of 1,300 yards."[52] While this shooting is specifically attributed to Whitworths, bearing in mind there were so few in the Confederate army it is perfectly likely they were fired from Enfields (over 281,000 of which were supplied to the South during the war) or even Springfields. Whatever the means, the end result must have been inconsiderable nervousness and unease among troops who believed they were safe from enemy fire, the psychological impact of which was clearly not understood at the time.

For the sharpshooters the sport of war (sport being a word often used in contemporary accounts), soon became a far grimmer struggle as men hardened themselves to killing. All sharpshooters who subsequently wrote of their experiences went through several very distinct phases; initial excitement followed within weeks or months by a realization of the deadly nature of their profession, and eventually a sense of fatalism over their ability to survive. Normally this latter phase was the most dangerous mental state for a sharpshooter to be in, as he would begin to become careless. Perhaps the best contemporary summing up of the effect of their lonely profession was by Colonel William Ripley, who later wrote:

> Service of this independent nature has a peculiar fascination for these men. In fact sharpshooting is the squirrel hunting of war; it is wonderful to see how self-forgetful the marksman grows … with what coolness and accuracy he brings it [his target] down. At the moment he grows utterly indifferent to the human life or human suffering and seems intent only on cruelty and destruction; to make a good shot and hit his man, brings for the time being a feeling of intense satisfaction.[53]

This is an early and interesting description of what later snipers have referred to as "being in the bubble" or the "mind-set" where intense concentration blots out all extraneous stimuli. Yet there were strange anomalies in this attitude, for as Ripley pointed out, while "Few however, care to recall afterwards the look of the dying enemy … there are none who do not risk as much to aid the wounded victim of their skill as they did to inflict the wound."[54] These are attitudes that have not altered at all in the 21st century. The sharpshooters certainly provided considerable tactical benefit to their respective armies, but with the cessation of hostilities they were quickly mustered out of service and their rifles put into store. Their use, it was believed, had merely been a necessary response to a peculiar set of circumstances, and there was to be little gained in retaining them or their rifles. It was unfortunately an attitude that was to cost the US Army dearly over the coming years.

PART III
A WORLD AT WAR

Chapter 6

GLOBAL WAR

At the end of the Civil War in 1865, sharpshooters were mustered out of service as quickly as possible and more than a few of them contrived to take their rifles with them. For many men across whose home states the war had raged, what little they had owned had now gone and there were few reasons to go back to their old lives. Although they had learned a great deal about killing, most were sick of war and all that it entailed, and the desire to start a new life and try to wipe the slate clean was a strong one. While the war had primarily been waged in the east, there had been much fighting in the west and southwest as well, but the level of destruction here was not so marked across such a huge expanse, and feelings did not run so high in the immediate antebellum years. There were thus many compelling reasons to head west, in particular to California, Oregon, or Texas, where land was plentiful and easy to buy, in some cases even being offered free to settlers.

The postwar period saw the trickle of emigrants heading west become a flood over the next decade. In need of feeding and protecting, these pioneer families used many a Sharps, Enfield, and doubtless the occasional Whitworth to fend off Native American attacks and provide meat for the wagon parties, with many ex-soldiers becoming professional guides and hunters. Their services were sorely needed too, for as the white people encroached more frequently into Indian lands there were renewed and savage attacks made upon them. The experience many of these men had with their rifles held them in good stead in defending both themselves and their charges. With the demands of war behind them the gunmakers in the east had to find a new market for their weapons and the pioneers were the perfect customers. As well as new weapons, there were also tens of thousands of surplus firearms for sale, which had a ready market. Ex-Berdan Sharps rifles could be had for $25 a piece and Enfield rifles were $11, while a Springfield could be had for $8. Other, lesser muskets could be purchased for as little as $2 each. However, the war had taught everyone – the Army, firearms manufacturers, and soldiers – a great deal about the practicality of their weapons and the one thing that all were agreed upon was that the days of the large-caliber, muzzle-loading rifle were already numbered.

As if proof was required, within a year of the war's end the US Department of Ordnance had 5,000 M1865 Springfields converted to the new Allin breech-loading system. In Britain a similar modification, the Snider, was being used to upgrade the old Enfields. These conversions were designed to provide practical stop-gap measures between the old and the new technology, without costing their respective governments too much for what were essentially converted but obsolete rifles. Like all compromises, this worked well enough, but the new breech-loaders had their limitations. While the single-shot rifles were accurate enough up to 500 yards, they were comparatively slow to load and fire and they still held only one cartridge at a time. Breech-loading rimfire rifles, which had appeared during the war, had gained a considerable following, but by the late 1860s they had already reached the zenith of their development due to limitations in cartridge manufacture and their relative lack of power.

As usual it was the commercial sporting market that was to lead the way in design and manufacture of the new technology. The importance of this market had been clearly evident during the war with the introduction of many new breech-loading rifles, all of which had come from commercial manufacturers: the Sharps, Spencer, Hall, Greene, Ballard, and Henry (destined to evolve into the famous Winchester). The Spencer's rimfire design incorporated a useful tube magazine that enabled up to seven rounds of ammunition to be fed one after another into the chamber and fired as quickly as the action could be worked. It suffered from underpowered ammunition, though, and was not a good long-range rifle. Yet its mechanical design was both clever and strong and the magazine capacity gave it a level of firepower that was almost unique. The Henry also initially used underpowered rimfire cartridges, but its weakness lay in its lever-action mechanism, which could not cope with the increasingly powerful ammunition that was being developed. Though it was limited as an accurate long-range rifle, in its subsequent guise as the Winchester it gained a huge following as a shorter-range hunting rifle. Most single-shot breech-loaders suffered from extraction problems due to their primitive cartridges and this was because postwar gunmakers were predominantly reliant on the newly introduced Berdan or Boxer primed cartridges. These predecessors of the modern brass cartridge used a separate metal base with primer inserted in the center, riveted to a foil-wrapped case in which was contained the powder charge. They were not particularly durable and they suffered problems from verdigris in moist climates, which would effectively cement the fired case into the hot breech. Worse, the poorly attached bases often ripped off when the breech was opened, leaving the frustrated shooter frantically digging with a knife blade in an attempt to extract the remains of the cartridge. It would be a decade before the advent of the brass-cased, centerfire cartridge. When this appeared, however, it would herald a tremendous advance in shooting technology.

THE NEW BOLT ACTION

The problem with all of the weapons described above was that somewhere in their design they had serious shortcomings – single-shot capacity, low-powered ammunition, combustion gas leakage, difficult loading or extraction, and so on. The gunmaking industry knew what was needed, of course: a rifle that was simple to operate, robust, and able to chamber a powerful cartridge then shoot the bullet accurately out to long ranges. This was the Holy Grail for cartridge firearms, in the same manner that solving the problems of accuracy and windage had been for muskets. Experiments began in 1872 when the Ordnance Department began to purchase and test a new type of rifle that had become increasingly popular in Europe, but had yet to make any real impact in the United States. This was termed a "bolt-action" rifle and its use had been pioneered by the Prussians in 1841 when they adopted the radical Dreyse system. Although still a single-shot weapon, at the time it had a 3:1 advantage in firepower over contemporary muskets and in 1866 France followed suit when it issued the Chassepot rifle. The effectiveness of these guns was well exhibited during the Franco-Prussian War of 1870–71, when their rate of fire resulted in such massive casualties that one pundit commented, in a *London Times* article, that they "Would witness the end of civilized warfare." Switzerland, Germany, France, and Russia had adopted bolt-action rifles by the late 1870s, Russia ironically using the Hiram Berdan-designed Berdan M1870 rifle in which the US government had shown no interest, producing over 3.5 million up to 1891. All of these weapons used a rotating locking-bolt system operated by a handle, the bolt body having lugs that engaged in machined slots in the receiver, ensuring it was locked solid once closed. The conservative Ordnance Department decided to examine all of the best American designs then available – Burgess, Chaffee-Reese, Remington-Keene, Ward-Burton, Winchester-Hotchkiss, Colt-Franklin, Sharps-Vetterli, and Lee – before making any rash decisions; the tests they undertook seemingly continued endlessly. They were still being conducted in 1887 and had proved little, other than what was already well understood, which was that single-shot, large-caliber rifles of *any* type were outdated for military use. Just as it began to look as though no decision at all would be forthcoming, the development of the rifle was materially assisted from some unexpected sources. In this instance the catalyst was an invention by a Swiss major named Rubin allied to the results of experiments in chemical combustion undertaken by a small laboratory in France.

A serving soldier, Major Rubin had reasoned that the old solid lead bullets were both inefficient and too heavy. Manufacturing technology had by the 1870s finally solved the problems of being able to manufacture brass that could be spun or lathe-turned to produce cartridge cases that were strong, durable, and reusable. The increasingly powerful charges often resulted in such high velocities being generated that lead bullets stripped themselves as they moved up the bore, being unable to grip the rifling. Rubin developed a lead-cored bullet that could be made in a much smaller caliber than normal (at this period typically .45in or 11mm caliber) with a thin but hard copper jacket that enabled the bullet to grip the rifling. The bullet allowed higher velocities and thus greater range and accuracy. It happened to be a very timely invention, for a French chemist by the name of Marcel Vielle had been experimenting for some time with new chemical propellants, in particular one called nitro-cellulose. He had found that a mix of 58 percent nitro-glycerine, 37 percent nitro-cellulose, and 5 percent mineral jelly produced a virtually smokeless propellant that generated far higher pressures than black powder. Vielle had perfected it by 1885 and so impressed was the French government that in 1886 it ordered the wholesale adoption of a new rifle, the 8mm Lebel, to replace its old service rifles. In their own unique way the French solved the problem of patents relating to copper-jacketed bullets by producing solid copper ones.

France's adoption of the new rifle rapidly forced all of Europe to reassess their infantry rifles as these new-generation smokeless powder weapons were in every respect so much more efficient that their acquisition became a matter of political and military expediency to ensure no one was lagging behind in the arms race. Indeed, some historians have argued that, in adopting the Lebel, France actually steered Europe on an inevitable course for war. By 1888 most countries of any military significance had adopted magazine-fed, bolt-action rifles in the new caliber, which averaged around .30in (8mm) and almost all were modified to fire the new ammunition. In practice, the new powder was initially quite unstable and several French military magazines were damaged by explosions, but such minor problems were soon solved and "nitro" was to become the predominant propellant for all subsequent small arms.

It is not quite true to say that every country had adopted the bolt-action rifle, for the United States was still prevaricating. In 1890 the military had begun yet another exhaustive series of tests that were to last two years, covering rapid-fire ability, accuracy, reliability, ease of maintenance, rust resistance, and high-pressure ammunition testing, at the end of which only three rifles, the Lee, Mauser, and Danish Krag-Jorgensen, were left. Surprising some ordnance men, it was the Krag that was chosen, in part because it had a side-mounted box magazine that could be isolated from the chamber. The board was particularly concerned about the likelihood of troops wantonly squandering government ammunition by rapid fire and the Krag's magazine was a design feature that appealed strongly to it. The fact that the locking lugs on the Krag's bolt were only just strong enough for its not overly powerful .30-40 cartridge did not seem to concern them unduly. In 1892 it was adopted into service, but it was not to remain so for long for improvements in ammunition design meant that it was unable to make use of the more powerful cartridges that had been developed, and in 1898 the hunt for a new rifle began all over again.

Not all of the lessons of the Civil War had been lost on the Army, however, and while there was general disagreement over the actual weapon the Army should adopt, it had been widely agreed that marksmen should be issued with a suitable rifle, preferably equipped with an optical sight. Krags used by the Norwegian Army had already been successfully fitted with side-mounted telescopic sights, and when they were adopted for US service an example was acquired from Norway for evaluation. The results appeared to surprise the Ordnance Department:

> As a result of this test the Board is of the opinion that the use of this telescopic sight appears to be of especial value in hazy or foggy weather and at long ranges. In either case the target can be seen with remarkable clearness, and the marksman can be absolutely sure he is aiming at the proper object. This would be of especial importance to sharpshooters acting independently.[1]

Testing was taken to extreme ranges of 2,000 yards, at which distance the Department commented "With a telescopic sight a man could be distinguished easily."[2] The result was the production, on June 8, 1900, of the US Army's first ever bolt-action sniper's rifle. It had a tube scope manufactured by the Cataract Tool and Optical Company of Buffalo, New York, and followed quite closely the method of mounting used by the Norwegian rifle, which was in practice little different from some side-mounted scopes in use during the Civil War. Yet, oddly, nothing further appears to have been done about equipping any more service rifles with optical sights. Possibly this was due to the short service life of the Krag, for tests were already well underway to find a replacement and the new rifle was to come from none other than Springfield Armory.

THE MODEL 1903

The "United States Magazine Rifle, Model of 1903" was officially approved for service on June 19, 1903. Although it was to become the most iconic and longest-serving rifle in US military history, it owed much of its design to the Mauser. In fact, somewhat paradoxically for a weapon soon to be used against Germany, the US government had to pay royalties to the Mauser Company for the use of their bolt and locking mechanism design and the clip-loading arrangement. The original Springfield design had been created in 1900 with a 30in barrel chambering a cartridge similar to the old .30-40 Krag. However, tests soon proved the ammunition to be underpowered and the barrel too long, so it was shortened to 24in, enabling it to be used by infantry and cavalry alike. It was re-chambered for a more powerful .30-03 cartridge that produced more useful velocities of around 2,400fps.

Production commenced at the Springfield Armory in mid-1903 at the rate of 225 rifles per day. A significant later modification was the introduction in October 1906 of a new standard cartridge, the .30-06. This had been hurriedly brought about by the adoption in Germany the previous year of a radical new design of pointed (as opposed to round-nosed) bullet called the *Spitzer*. This new bullet was streamlined, providing it with greater range and improved stability, and it was to set a new world standard when it was introduced by Germany. Used in the Springfield, the new .30-06 increased the maximum range from 2,400 to 2,850 yards and provided a higher velocity of 2,675fps. As far as the Department of Ordnance was concerned, the M1903 was the very best that could be provided for its army and it was indeed to prove to be an enduring and reliable weapon. While the adoption of the Springfield rifle was not in itself such a remarkable event, the Ordnance Department actually still considered it a necessary requirement to furnish some designated marksmen with an optically equipped rifle, something no other army in the world was doing. In view of their lack of enthusiasm for sniping *per se*, this was indeed a forward-thinking decision. Even in Germany, long the bastion of expert riflemen and scope-equipped hunting rifles, there had been no consideration given to equipping soldiers with anything other than the Mauser Gew98 rifle, adopted as standard in 1898. The Department's immediate problem in deciding on a suitable optical sight was to become a perennial one.

SCOPE DEVELOPMENTS

By the 1900s there were a large number of telescopic sights available commercially in Europe. Manufacturers had benefited from still more advances in optical technology, in particular improvements in glass manufacture that had originated around 1884 at the Glastechnisches Laboratory in Jena, Austria. A method of mass-producing near perfect optical glass had been patented, and the company (later named Schott Glasswerke) began to provide most of the raw material for optical sights around the world. At this period in the United States there was still a shortage of both good scopes and scope manufacturers, although within 20 years the availability of both would have increased dramatically with the appearance of makers such as Stevens, Fecker, Winchester, and many others. In 1903 there was a fallow period, though, and the Ordnance Department was limited to one suitable scope. The Warner & Swasey Model of 1903 was a 6x prismatic pattern manufactured in Cleveland and based on similar types of artillery optical sight also being manufactured by the company, but its price was a then prohibitive $80. Recommendations by the Department that a simplified pattern be developed were taken seriously and in 1908 a new scope, "The Telescopic Musket Sight, Model of 1908," was submitted for trials. Reports from the Chief of Ordnance indicate it was mechanically and optically satisfactory with the exception that its very short eye relief of $1\frac{1}{2}$in caused problems for the firer: "Recommendations were received that the sight be moved forwards on the rifle to prevent the eyepiece striking the eye upon recoil; also that the rubber eyepiece be made of softer rubber."[3] At least one sniper who was to use the Springfield/Warner combination recalled that shooting it could "make a flincher out of a cigar store Indian."[4] Men were taught to adjust their shooting positions and allow for the recoil accordingly, not pressing their eye too hard against the eyecup. Those who did found that it had suctioned itself to their eye socket, whereupon one veteran noted dryly that "It took three strong men to pull you loose from the fool telescope."[5] Later production eyecups sensibly had holes in them to prevent this.

The scopes were equipped with range and elevation drums, the ranges being marked up to 2,000 yards. In addition, the horizontal stadia lines on the reticles were placed so that they spanned the height of an average man (5ft 8in) at a distance of 100 yards, giving the shooter some ability to estimate range by height comparison. Concerns about the ingress of water, the fragile mounting system, and the power of the scopes caused a number of revisions to be suggested by the Department, which were duly adopted by Warner & Swasey into their final pattern, the M1913. This had its power reduced slightly to 5.2x, a more secure fitting for the eyepiece, and a locking nut for the range drum (prone to working loose under recoil), and it was to be the final variant adopted into service. At $58 apiece, they were still expensive and by the time they were to be used in combat there already existed a plethora of better alternatives.

Springfield rifles to be mated to these scopes were specially selected for quality of manufacture and the barrels in particular were examined for uniformity of rifling. Quite literally every inch was checked to ensure the lands and grooves fell exactly within design tolerance and that the barrels were perfectly straight. Those deemed satisfactory were star-gauged, with a small star stamped onto the crown of the barrel at the muzzle. All parts were checked for flaws and the rifles test fired. Each scope was fitted and numbered to its rifle and every designated marksman was issued with a leather rifle sling, the Pattern 1907, a brilliant design that doubled as a carrying sling but also as a shooting support, being quickly adjustable to enable it to be looped around the left hand, helping take the weight of the rifle and providing a steady rest. So good was the design that it was to remain in first-line service until well after the Vietnam War and many can still be seen on military sniping rifles being used in the current Iraqi conflict.

THE GREAT WAR

Although it is generally believed that the inaugural use of the Springfield/ Warner combination was in the trenches of France in 1917, in practice they first saw limited service in 1916 as US troops chased Pancho Villa into Mexico. One unit, Lingler's Sharpshooters, was equipped with scoped Springfields, and there is evidence that a small number were even fitted with silencers. These, based on a 1911 design patented by Hiram Maxim and manufactured by the Maxim Company, probably made the use of such weapons a double first in the history of military sniping. There appear to be no surviving records of the efficiency or otherwise of these scoped rifles, and the Mexican campaign was halted when in 1917 American relationships with Germany deteriorated to the point that war had become unavoidable.

As it became clear that it was only a matter of time before the United States became involved in the European conflict, the Army took stock of its resources. Of the total of 5,700 Warner scopes purchased up to the end of 1918, only 1,530 were actually fitted to rifles. Most of these had been acquired prior to 1913 and in the three subsequent years up to 1916 only 30 new scopes were delivered by the factory to Springfield.[6] Indeed, of the total purchased most were stored, and it is one of the reasons that the Warner telescope is found with relative ease in today's collector's marketplace. To a great extent, the reluctance of the army to issue them was due to the increasing number of problems with them being reported from the Western Front. Their practical use in France is quite difficult to document today as few records remain of the use of these sniping rifles.

When the American Expeditionary Force (AEF) arrived in France their entry into the trenches was to be a shocking baptism of fire for many. For four years German snipers had been honing their skills and by 1917 they were very adept indeed.[7] It was estimated that only three seconds of exposure of any part of the body was sufficient for a sniper's bullet to be the net result and many curious American soldiers paid the ultimate price for taking a quick peek over the parapet of their new homes, as one soldier reported: "We lost three men today as a result of sniping. One, a tall fellow, simply forgot himself and stood upright in a shallow portion of trench. The bullet struck his helmet and penetrated it, killing him instantaneously."[8] The US troops were eager to give the Germans a taste of their own medicine. There were certainly many excellent shots in the Army, but by 1917 sniping had become a science and failure to learn the rules properly would result in its having a very brief service career. US marksmen were therefore detailed to attend British sniper schools on a ten-day course where all of the basics were taught. Major E. Penberthy, an instructor and commander of a sniper school, was impressed by the quality of American recruits:

A large number of officers and men passed through our schools and were distinguished by their passionate desire to learn all they could, in order, as more than one man said to me, "to make up for lost time." They started schools of their own, modelled on ours ... they even borrowed some of our officers to go to America and give instructions at the training camps."[9]

All snipers were introduced to the ghillie suit, named after the eponymous Scottish highland guides and deer-stalkers who had invented it in the 19th century. There was no set pattern for these suits, each man making his own, but it basically consisted of a robe made of several pieces of loose dark-colored material, covered with strips of cloth in varying shades of brown and green. The camouflage varied according to the terrain and the requirement of the sniper, and the trainees were expected to produce effective suits and then use them to learn how to move from one location to another under the eagle eyes of their instructors without being spotted. For most of the neophyte snipers the actual mechanics of shooting posed few problems, for most were expert riflemen who understood range, elevation, and windage estimation. They had also mastered smooth trigger operation and the need to hold a part-lungful of air to cushion the chest and steady the heartbeat. However, few of them had ever seen a telescopic sight before and learning to master its many intricacies required some patience on the part of the instructors. A scope had to be zeroed with its rifle to ensure the point of impact of the bullet coincided exactly with the aiming point of the crosshairs; moreover different batches of ammunition had varying ballistic characteristics and the students were urged to find a reliable batch and keep as much of it as possible solely for use in their own rifles. Failure to do so would mean re-zeroing their rifles. Other broader lessons had to be understood as well, and a leaflet supplied to American snipers who attended the British First Army School of Sniping listed the following three primary headings: Observation, Shooting, and Cover and Concealment, with the duties of a sniper being:

1. To dominate the enemy snipers, thereby saving the lives of soldiers and causing casualties to the enemy.
2. To hit a small mark at a known range, but without the advantage of a sighting shot.
3. To keep the enemy's line under continual observation and to assist the Intelligence of his unit by accurate and correct reports with map references.
4. To build up and keep in repair his loopholes and major and minor sniping posts.[10]

Neither was the reason for employing snipers simply to kill enemy soldiers. At lectures provided for NCO sniper instructors at the British Second Army School of Sniping in France, the primary reasons for their employment were listed as:

1. To shake the enemy's morale.
2. To cause him casualties.
3. To stop him working.
4. To retaliate against his snipers.[11]

In practice this was not so different from the employment of sharpshooters during the Civil War, although the psychological impact of sniping had now been recognized to a far greater degree. By 1918, by which time the majority of US troops were engaged in frontline combat, the rules had changed somewhat, as the methods they had been taught relating to trench sniping had largely been usurped in the wake of a more mobile form of warfare. In open country, it was realized that the scouting and observation skills of the snipers were worth considerably more than their sheer shooting ability, and it is from the battles of very late 1917 and 1918 that there began to be a shift in the focus of the employment of snipers. An update sent to scouting officers of all corps on the Western Front dated mid-1917 explains why:

> In view of the more open nature of fighting which is now taking place, scouting and observation have become of increased importance, as opposed to sniping and the use of telescopic sights of trench warfare. It is considered that teaching in the two last mentioned subjects should, therefore, take a subsidiary place.[12]

By this date soldiers of the AEF had access to their own locally set up sniping schools, albeit these were often assisted by British NCOs. Despite the training, the number of US snipers killed in their first months of the war was disproportionately high. It was not until late in 1918 that the US troops began to gain the upper hand when facing such a cunning and experienced foe as the Germans, and they slowly mastered the lessons taught to them. Generally it was believed that a sniper who survived his first two weeks in the trenches had a reasonable life expectancy.

It was not only the US Army that was engaged in the sniping war, for wherever there was fighting, the US Marine Corps was never far away. Never a Corps to follow Army dictates, pre-World War I the Marines had not accepted the Warner as their operational optical sight. Their decision was materially assisted by the Winchester Company's introduction of a new telescopic sight, the Model A5 (Model A, 5x). It would not have been unfamiliar to a sharpshooter of the Civil War, being a tube scope, mounted

Handgunners, Alesia, 1533. As the design of the stock made aimed shooting from the shoulder impossible, musketeers fired their early matchlock muskets from the waist, the butts braced against the stomach. Their powder horns are clearly visible. (Alte Pinakothek Museum, Munich)

A Pennsylvania long rifle dating to around 1760, maker unknown. It is in .45 caliber and while it still retains a slightly martial form, its slim stock and patch-box show a distinct evolution away from the heavy military musket. (Courtesy Trustees of the Royal Armouries)

An early English sporting gun of 1790. These fowlers were commonly found in New England and served as both sporting and militia guns. Their general shape and dimensions are very similar to those of the British Land Pattern muskets of the period. (Courtesy Trustees of the Royal Armouries)

Above:

A representation of an English musketeer of c. 1600. His clothing and long musket typify those carried to the east coast of America by the first colonists. In his left hand is the forked rest necessary to take the weight of the heavy matchlock. (Jeffery Mayton photo)

Right:

Two German-manufactured Jaeger rifles, with typical octagonal barrels, straight stocks, scrolled trigger-guards, and sliding patch-boxes. Many were carried by German and Dutch settlers to the New World. The similarity between these and the later Mississippi-pattern rifles is self-evident. (Courtesy Trustees of the Royal Armouries)

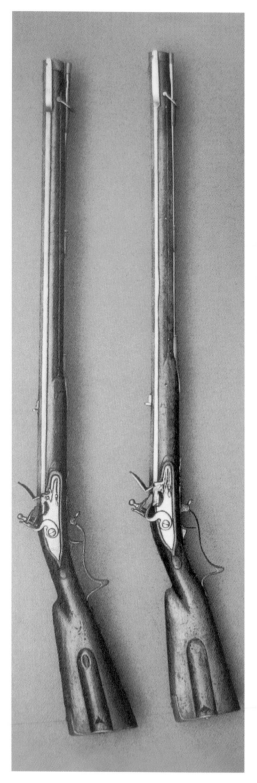

The weapon and accessories carried by a matchlock musketeer of the late 16th and early 17th centuries. Long musket, slow match, rest, powder bottles, and ball were all required, and carrying this weight over any distance was punishing. (Courtesy Trustees of the Royal Armouries)

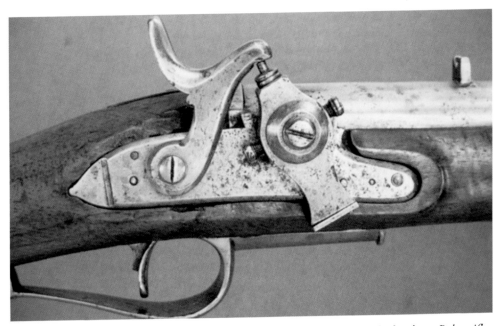

The first practical percussion priming system developed by the Reverend Forsyth, fitted to a Baker rifle of 1810. Swiveling the bottle deposited a priming charge under the hammer. (Courtesy Trustees of the Royal Armouries)

A contemporary painting of Davy Crockett (1786–1836). It serves as an excellent guide to the weapons and equipment carried in the early frontier period of c. 1800, showing him wearing a typical loose jacket, deerskin leggings, and moccasins, and holding a slouch hat. His shooting bag, skinning knife, powder horn, and octagonal-barreled long gun are clearly shown.

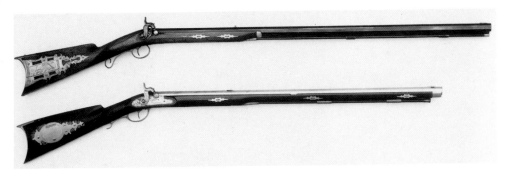

Two percussion rifles. The top, by Cooper, is converted from a flintlock around 1840 and it retains its original long .54-caliber octagonal barrel. The lower rifle is an improvised Hawken pattern plains rifle, with no maker's name. Its original long barrel has been cut down and the fore-end shortened. Such modifications were commonplace on the frontier. (Courtesy Trustees of the Royal Armouries)

Although thousands of Enfield Pattern 1853 rifles were supplied by Great Britain, many hundreds were also made by American manufacturers. This .58-caliber example is a good-quality copy by Ezra Millward. (Courtesy Trustees of the Royal Armouries)

The breech of the Hall unlatched for loading. Powder and ball were inserted from the front; the breech-block was then pushed down to lock it into place, and the pan primed. It was much quicker than loading from the muzzle and could be done either standing or lying down. (Author's photo)

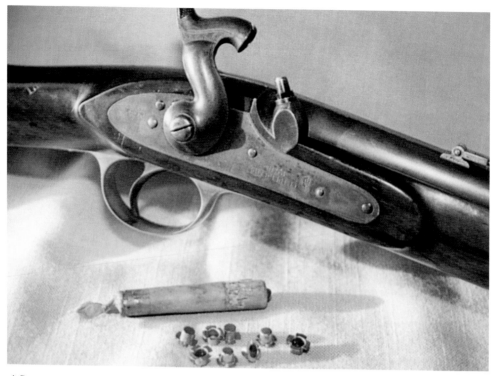

A Pattern 1853 Enfield rifled musket, with an original paper-wrapped cartridge and Joyce "top hat" percussion caps. The simplicity of the percussion system over the earlier flintlock is easily seen. (Author's collection)

A .45-caliber bull-barreled target rifle by Marshall Tidd of Woburn, Massachusetts, carried by a Federal sharpshooter during the Civil War. The fragile scope mounts are all too visible, and, while they were adequate enough for target shooting, they were not durable enough for sustained campaign use. (Roy Jinks collection)

The Maynard tape priming system on an early slant-breech Sharps rifle. The hinged cover is just visible at the bottom of the picture. (Author's collection)

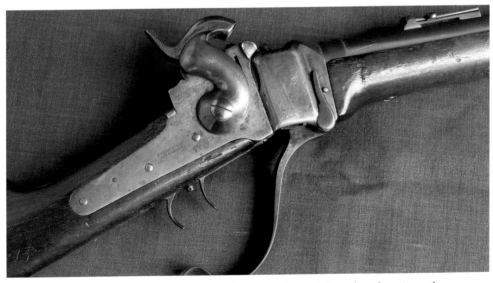

A Berdan Sharps rifle, showing the distinctive double-set triggers. The cocking lever is partly unlatched, permitting the breech-block to drop. This example has considerable wear on the underside of the fore-end as a result of being carried by resting across the pommel of a saddle. It may well have been one of hundreds that found their way west after the war. (Author's collection)

The mounts designed by John Chapman revolutionized the fitting of telescopic sights. Here is an early example fitted to an unnamed American percussion long rifle converted from a flintlock. (Author's collection)

Hiram Berdan poses for the camera in September 1862 with Truman Head, alias "California Joe," who holds his Sharps rifle. The two set triggers with which all Berdan rifles were equipped are just visible. (Vermont Historical Society)

An M1851 Mississippi rifle made by Robbins and Lawrence. (Courtesy Trustees of the Royal Armouries)

An American soldier holds up his Warner & Swasey equipped Springfield for the camera. Note that the stock on the rifle has been camouflage painted. (US Army)

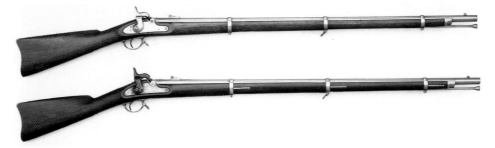

Two Colt-manufactured rifled muskets, M1861 and M1863. Both were chambered for the standard .58-caliber cartridge. (Courtesy Trustees of the Royal Armouries)

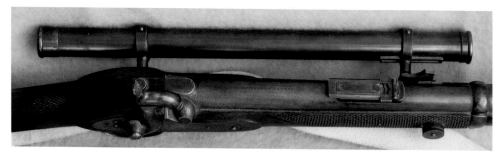

A Whitworth rifle and scope of the type supplied to Confederate sharpshooters. The scope is an English Davidson pattern. The small thumb-wheel at the lower right of the stock is the locking nut for the elevation adjustment plate of the scope, which is visible just above it. (Danny Pizzini collection)

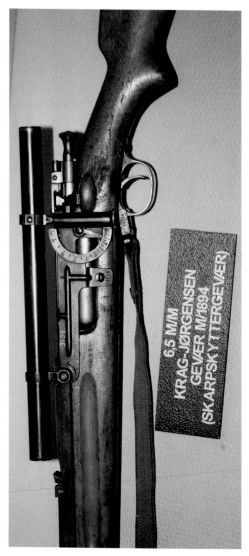

Above:
A British-made .58in minié bullet, showing the wooden plug in the base and in the nose. The wound it inflicted was devastating. (Author's collection)

Right:
An original Krag–Jorgensen sniping rifle, developed in 1894 for the Norwegian Army. The scope and mount system was loosely copied by the Cataract Tool Company for the US Army. (The Norwegian Army Museum, Oslo)

A close-up of the Warner Model 1913 on a Springfield M1903. The air hole in the eye cup is clearly visible, as is the rather vulnerable mounting arm and its range and elevation drums. (Springfield Armory collection)

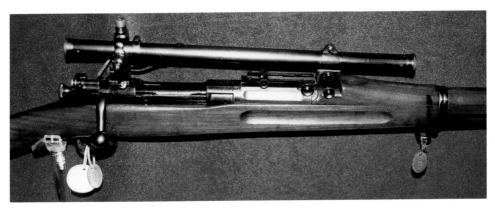

A Marine Corps Springfield with Winchester A5 scope. (Springfield Armory collection)

A Marine Corps Springfield M1903 with its Unertl scope (serial 1479). The length of the scope is clearly visible here: it is obvious why the Corps decided it was too vulnerable to be an issue telescopic sight. (Springfield Armory collection)

An Army sniper cleans his M1904A4. The small size of the scope and lack of iron sights are very clear in this photo. Like most snipers, he has camouflaged his helmet and packed its cover to soften the shape. (US Army)

US Army snipers in ghillie suits somewhere in France, 1918. They have M1903 Springfield rifles, but no scopes are fitted, probably to avoid damage while training. (US Army)

US Marines land on Guadalcanal. The incredibly dense nature of the vegetation, which often reached to the shore line, is visible here. A Japanese sniper could lurk only yards away and still remain utterly invisible. (US Army)

Although the rifle is still cocked, the Unertl scope is actually in the forward recoil position, which would make a shot impossible until the scope had been manually pulled back "into battery." (US Marine Corps)

Chajang-ni, Korea, 1953. A 5th Marines sniper sights a Garand M1C fitted with a commercial 2.5x Lyman Alaskan scope. Note his flak jacket, which had become standard issue by this time. (US Marine Corps)

A Winchester-manufactured XM21 with a very early Redfield 3 x 9 scope. This example has a five-round magazine and also a bipod. (Author's collection)

Surprising rifles sometimes turned up in the hands of the Vietcong. This rare sniping variant of a 1940-dated Soviet SVT38 was captured by the 1st Air Cavalry Regiment at Lang Vei on April 10, 1968. (Author's collection)

Winchester Model 70, with Lyman Targetspot scope. This is one of the Van Orden contract rifles, of which many were to see service in Vietnam. (Author's collection)

Remington M40A1 With McMillan fiberglass stock and non-standard ART1 scope. This scope normally resides on the author's XM21 but was swapped with the Redfield to enable him to enter a long-range sniper shooting match, alas with little success ... (Author's collection)

Boxes of Lake City match ammunition in both 7.62mm and .30 caliber issued during the Vietnam War. (Author's collection)

A trainee Marine sniper is instructed in aiming techniques by Master Gunnery Sergeant Boitnott. The rifle is the iconic Springfield/Unertl combination. (US Marine Corps)

The buddy system at work. A sniper with a Springfield takes aim as a BAR gunner cuts loose during street fighting in Seoul. In the background a radioman relays information to other teams working the area. (US Marine Corps)

A soldier wearing the bulky battery pack and carrying an M1 mounted Sniperscope poses for the photographer. (US Army)

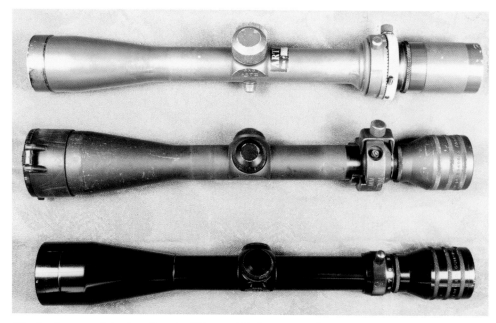

The development of the Auto Ranging Telescope. The lower example is a commercial Redfield 3 x 9; the center is an ARTI of late 1960s to mid-1970s; and the top is an ARTII, which remained in use on the Army's M21 rifles until well into the 1980s. (Author's collection)

A US peacekeeper in Haiti during the short campaign of 1994. He is observing through the Unertl scope on his M40A1 rifle, which has been painted to match almost exactly the dull camouflage of his uniform. Note that he has taped extra padding to the stock to raise his cheek and head to a more comfortable shooting position. Current sniping rifles are almost all equipped with adjustable cheek rests. (US Army)

In many modern combat situations, determining who is friend or foe is often impossible. No uniforms are worn, and weapons are seldom openly carried. Here an Iraqi sharpshooter poses with his rifle. It is not an SVD Dragunov but an AK47 variant, probably Iraqi manufactured, fitted with a scope and mount. While not a dedicated sniping weapon, it is a tolerably good sharpshooter's rifle for close to medium ranges. (IPA Photo)

Two Marine snipers in ghillie suits lie in wait. From a matter of a few yards, they would be totally invisible to even an experienced observer. (US Marine Corps)

Master Gunnery Sergeant John Boitnott, I Company, 5th Marines, reloads his M1C Garand. The need for an offset scope because of the clip-loading requirement is obvious in this picture. The rifle has an M82 telescope fitted. (US Marine Corps)

A .50-caliber Browning machine gun, equipped with an 8x Unertl scope, is used as a makeshift sniping weapon somewhere in Korea, September 1951. (US Army)

Captain William S. Brophy at work using his heavy-barreled Winchester Model 70 rifle, with 10x Unertl scope, in Korea, 1952. (US Army)

A Marine sniper fires from cover in the fighting during the Tet offensive. His rifle is a Remington Model 700 with Redfield scope. (US Marine Corps)

A US Army rifleman holds a Raytheon AN/PAS-13 Thermal Imaging Weapon Sight fitted to an M16 rifle. The AN/PAS cannot be detected, as it emits no radiowaves or heat and requires no visible light source to operate. Issued in 1998, some 27,000 are now estimated to be in service, fitted to a wide range of weapons. Unlike many earlier systems, it can be used equally effectively in the daytime. (US Army)

July, 2006. Marine snipers at Fort Hill, Virginia, shoot the new XM110 Semi-Automatic Sniping System rifle (SASS). This example is equipped with a suppressor, and the fired cartridge can be seen ejecting from the port. Its current deployment in Iraq and Afghanistan is expected to bridge the gap between dedicated sniping weapons and infantry rifles, providing both infantry sharpshooters and sniper teams with improved accuracy over the standard M16 rifle. (US Marine Corps)

Sergeant Jeremiah Johnson, a 2nd US Infantry Division sniper, with his M24 rifle in Iraq, May 2005. The long Picatinny-type rail on the rifle can accept a wide range of accessories and a torch is clipped to its side. The rifle's bipod is folded underneath the barrel. (US Army)

With his head raised for the camera, the face of a ghillie-suited sniper can just be discerned, center left. Once in a firing position, with his face covered, he would be invisible. A single shot would be the only clue to his presence. (US Army)

An Army marksman uses an M16 that has been locally fitted with a telescopic sight, which may be either a Redfield ART or a Realist. (US Army)

A Barret Model 82A1A in position at the US Embassy, Monrovia, 1986. (Photo Cpl Jerry Hull, 2/2 Marine Scout Sniper Platoon, via Iron Brigade Armory)

on brackets of a pattern first devised by John Ratcliffe Chapman back in the 1840s. The fact that the Marine Corps was to adopt a sniping rifle in advance of the Army was due not to Marine insistence on providing frontline snipers, but rather to their desire to ensure their competitive rifle teams had the best tools for the job. The Marines were always keen to foster competitive shooting within their ranks and they always fielded one of the best shooting teams in the country. When Winchester produced their new telescopic sight in 1910, Marine armorers mounted a number to match-grade Springfield rifles. The entry of the Marine Corps into the war saw a quantity of these scoped target rifles finding their way to France with them. Although prewar 400 were procured by the Ordnance Department, the exact number supplied to the Marines is unknown. The A5 was mounted above the bore, a great improvement over the side-mounted Warner, but it had a drawback in that it was primarily a sporting scope designed for target use and it had not fared well in military tests, among the reasons being cited:

> The field of view is so small on account of its power … the spacing of brackets is only 6 inches apart, considered a source of weakness … the bolt on the rifle cannot be operated unless the scope is pushed forwards from its firing position … the exit pupil [objective lens] is so small that the sight is of no use in poor light.[13]

In fairness, the scope was never designed to survive hard military service and, despite the criticisms leveled at it, both the British and Canadian armed forces placed contracts for it, some 907 being fitted to British Lee-Enfield rifles. The Marines believed with some justification that the scope was the best then available, as the optical quality was excellent and the body itself robust, and they soon improved on the rather weak Springfield dovetail mounting blocks by utilizing a heavier dovetail block and finer click adjustment drums for elevation and windage. The problem was that the Marines' official order for 500 scopes was not made until comparatively late in the war and few of these contract rifles and scopes ever actually made it to the front in time for combat. In fact, the problems over scopes did not really matter as much as they might have, for there were in the ranks of the AEF many snipers who had learned to shoot excellently just using open sights, and it appears that in combat a large number preferred to do their sniping unencumbered by a delicate telescopic sight. One man, Alvin C. York, used his skills as a champion match-shooter in his native Tennessee to wipe out no fewer than four nests of German machine guns in October 1918, killing 25 crew members with head shots from 300 yards. He eventually forced the surrender of some 132 enemy soldiers. In this ability he was not alone, for as one German soldier recorded in September 1918:

> We had great trouble from the [American] riflemen who were very accurate shots. Three of our troop of machine gunners were shot down one after the other and no one was prepared to take their place. With no fire support from the [machine] guns we were soon overrun and forced to surrender. It was a bitter blow to us who had fought so hard and so well.[14]

There were doubtless dozens of unwitnessed acts of fine shooting by soldiers of the AEF during the hard fighting of 1918. While it is hard to find any accounts of the specific use of snipers, a few glimpses of their use rise to the surface in official reports, such as that to HQ of the US 1st Division, based around Ansauville, which mentions that "effective shooting by the Division's snipers materially assisted the advancing troops. In particular they were able to prevent German snipers from taking too heavy a toll on our men."[15] Such spartan and bland comments belie the quiet heroism of the snipers, many of whom did not survive to tell their tales. Curiously, of those who did see the war to its conclusion, few ever talked openly of their exploits afterwards. No better example exists of this than the almost unknown tale of Herman Davis, a dirt-poor farm boy from Manila, Arkansas.

Drafted after initially being refused for army service (he was 5ft 3in tall and weighed 110lb), Davis arrived in France in late June 1918 as a member of the 24th Division's 113th Infantry Regiment. His slight build and deep knowledge of fieldcraft and backwoods tracking and hunting made him an ideal candidate as a scout and runner. His solitary acts of heroism would have passed unnoticed had not at least one been accidentally witnessed by an officer unconnected with Davis. This event involved dealing with a German machine-gun crew who were pinning down his platoon near Molleville Farm in the Verdun sector in October 1918. Never having actually seen a German, Davis reasoned that as they had a machine gun and were speaking in a language he did not understand, they must be the enemy, so he crawled to within 50 yards of them and shot all four of the crew. The act was witnessed by an artillery observer, who found out Davis' name and reported the quiet act of courage. Blissfully unaware of this, shortly afterwards Davis spotted a dugout from which German reinforcements were pouring. Taking aim with his Springfield he shot 11 Germans one after another, but never thought to mention this event to anyone, until a casual conversation with a hunting friend some years after the war. Later in the month he was observing German troops setting up a machine gun at a distance of about 1,000 yards. When he enquired why no one was doing anything about it, he was curtly told it was too far for rifle shooting. "Why, that's just a good shootin' distance," he said – and then proceeded to shoot five of the enemy before they dispersed in panic. These were the events that were known of; if there were others Davis never thought them worth mentioning. Probably no one was more surprised than Davis himself when in 1919 he was awarded not only the Distinguished Service Cross, but also the French Croix de Guerre with palm and silver star and Medaille Militaire, and was named number four on General John Pershing's list of the 100 Heroes of the World War. Typically of his breed, for the rest of his sadly brief life he refused point-blank to talk publicly about his exploits, refuted any notions of heroism, and never wore his medals (in fact, he kept them in his fishing-tackle box with his beloved lures and flies). He died in poverty on January 25, 1923, aged 35 as a result of tuberculosis brought on by gas poisoning. In 1925 a monument and statue to the State's greatest war hero was raised by public subscription, an event that would doubtless have sent Herman heading into the swamps for a lengthy hunting session.[16]

It is impossible to determine the success or otherwise of the American snipers during their tenure in France, but there is little doubt that once they had adjusted to the rigors of total warfare, they became very adept at their task. With regard to the equipment they were using, there is little doubt that the Springfield rifles were certainly as good as any other combat rifle then in use, but the Warner & Swasey had not proved so reliable. The weight of the scope, at 2³/₄lb, caused the mounting screws attaching the base to the receiver to loose or even shear, requiring the base to be soldered in place, and the catch on the scope body could come loose allowing it to slide on its rails, causing loss of accuracy. In order to ensure a reliable zero, some snipers put a strong elastic band around the mount and scope body to ensure it remained in position, but this was hardly good practice. The fact it was offset to the left was not in its favor either, causing the rifle to be canted over to the left unless the shooter was very careful. The Ordnance Department had, by the end of the war, reversed its original judgment of the scope, damning it by stating it to be unsuitable because of its "offset mounting, the closeness of the ocular lens, too high a magnification and too small an exit lens, excessive weight and bulk, problems with moisture and dirt ingress, too much slack in the windage and elevation adjustment."[17] Nevertheless, it is easy to be critical of the Department for adopting it in the first place when there was so little else available. Perhaps the most pertinent comment on the Warner was made by Herbert McBride, a Canadian sniper with much sniping experience of it, who said, "in my opinion ... when compared to the others we had at the date and time, it was a pretty good sight."[18]

Throughout World War I, there were continual attempts by the School of Musketry at Fort Sill, Oklahoma, to find improved telescopic sights and mounts for the M1903 Springfield. Many were tried and rejected, including a German Goerz scope with a very practical rail mount of a type that was to reappear in World War II, a commercial Zeiss prismatic (curious in view of the fact one would have thought the army had learned its lesson with prismatic scopes) and scopes manufactured by Frankford Arsenal, Stevens, and Winchester. It was the Winchester M1918 that at least initially proved the winner. Further tests revealed a number of deficiencies, including lenses coming loose and brackets fracturing. Despite a number of initial improvements being made and an order being placed with Eastmann-Kodak of New York, the order was never completed as still more modifications held up the manufacturing process. This foolish situation continued for almost seven years until 1925, when development work was stopped by the Department of Ordnance and few of the orders for 32,000 were ever supplied. As a result the Army sniper program was left in limbo and this sorry state of affairs was to continue right up to 1941, when American involvement in a new war suddenly brought home the pressing need not only for sniper training, but also for a rifle to train with.

Chapter 7

WORLD WAR II – UNPREPARED AND UNEQUIPPED

As Europe prepared itself for another war with Germany in 1939, America stood apart, unwilling to embroil itself but watching with concern as the forces of Fascism moved westwards across central Europe. There was little initial worry over any danger of US involvement, although practical help for Britain in the form of Lend-Lease was soon organized to provide equipment and materiel. How long that state of affairs would have continued is open to conjecture, but events forced matters to move quickly when Japan attacked Pearl Harbor on December 7, 1941, and the Army and Marines were thrown into a state of confused readiness. US soldiers were still mainly armed with the weapons that had seen them through World War I, but since 1925 work had been in progress by the brilliant John Garand on a design for a new rifle to replace the aged Springfields. His semi-automatic rifle, the M1 Garand, had been finally adopted for service in January 1936. Ammunition development had also been under some scrutiny, many Ordnance men believing that a smaller, very high-velocity bullet was just as effective and far easier to carry and shoot than a large, heavy bullet. It was really the old "big slow bullet versus smaller faster bullet" argument all over again, and in reality there was no straightforward answer. Simultaneous experiments with a potent new .276in cartridge were halted, however, when the Army Chief of Staff,

Douglas MacArthur, decreed the new service rifle must be chambered for the tried and trusted .30-06 cartridge. In retrospect it was to prove a wise decision. Still, it did little to alter the fact that, when war was declared against Japan, although the US Army had a new battle rifle it still possessed no snipers or modern scoped rifles, other than some stored Springfields dating back to the previous war. In a prescient move, the President of the Board of Equipment had written in April 1941 to the Chief of the Army that insofar as snipers were concerned:

> There was no special training program ... contemplated by the army and no steps are being taken to procure special equipment. Special equipment is costly ... procurement problems at this time and supply problems in case of active operations would be difficult.[1]

In simple language, he suggested that the Army might like to organize something now, before it was too late. Alas, by December it was almost too late and for the rest of the war the snipers were to be issued with a makeshift sniping rifle and scope combination that was never more than adequate.

While the Marines were to be fully engaged with the Japanese in the Pacific theater, the Army had its hands full in Europe. The size of the Army excluded the use of any commercially purchased rifles for sniping, so the recently adopted M1 Garand was the clear choice. There was a significant problem with this, however, for the semi-automatic Garand had to be clip loaded and ejected its spent cases, with some force, from the top of the receiver, precluding the fitment of an over-the-bore scope. As a result, the Ordnance Department went to work to acquire and test a number of telescope and mount combinations. Meanwhile, the combat soldiers were getting increasingly desperate for a sniper rifle. There was one option in the shape of the reliable old Springfield 1903, but the problem as ever was what to use for mounts and sights. Wartime production demands meant that whatever was chosen had to be readily available, reasonably priced, and proven to be reliable. The design of the Springfield had been simplified in late 1942 to speed up production and in January 1943 the "US Rifle, caliber

151

.30 M1903A4" sniper rifle was introduced. It no longer had the fine quality and finish of the earlier Springfields, but was nevertheless a good, serviceable weapon. The scope and bases settled on by the Ordnance Department were commercial items comprising a Redfield "Junior" mount onto which a small Weaver Model 330 telescopic sight was fitted. The scope was a comparatively low-power item, 2.5x, and while it was simple and relatively robust the lack of power was to prove a problem in the field. In addition, the fitting of the Weaver required a modified bolt to be issued to prevent it snagging on the scope. These scopes were eventually renumbered in Army nomenclature as the Model 73B1, but they were to remain essentially the same for the duration of the war, being phased out in late 1944 after some 28,360 had been issued. The combination rifle and scope were reputedly accurate out to 700+ yards, although the lack of magnification was its main shortcoming at extreme ranges. This did have an unexpected benefit, though, for later in the war it meant that urban sniping at relatively close ranges was easier than with a high-power scope such as the Unertl that the Marines were using.

Supplying the equipment was one thing, but the Army also had to find the men to use it. This was also something of a trial, for there was no extant tradition of sniping in the Army. When asked for volunteers for sniping duty, one puzzled veteran asked "Sniper? What the hell does a sniper do?"[2] The Army based in North Africa and Sicily had to hurriedly improvise training courses for the men, but these varied in effectiveness and duration. Training, such as could be provided, was almost identical to that of the previous war. According to the syllabus for the US 36th Division, it comprised a three-week (later four-week) course consisting of: fieldcraft, camouflage, observation and intelligence gathering (now a higher priority than before), construction of hides, shooting, weapon and equipment care, and counter-sniping. There was nothing within its content that any Great War veteran would not have immediately recognized. In practice, volunteering for sniper duty did not always work out as it should. One North African veteran, an excellent shot, was handed a scoped Springfield rifle and told he had just been promoted to Squad Sniper:

I had no idea how to use it and practiced every minute I could on tin cans I set up. My buddies got fed up with the "crack, crack" of the rifle so a few other guys and I in the same situation set up our own unofficial sniper squad and pooled information. It took weeks for us to become proficient and we ended up being pretty good but we never did get any training. I guess not many of the other men liked what we did and they thought we were just a bunch of killers. We had long range shooting there [North Africa] but targets weren't plentiful, whereas Sicily was the opposite and we got the bejeezus shot out of us there. Only two of us came through that unhurt.[3]

The official statistics reinforce his point very well, for 80 percent of the US Fifth Army snipers in Italy became casualties. One of the major problems facing the largely untrained snipers was that they were fighting German snipers who had gained invaluable experience across Europe and in Russia. Many German snipers had built up sizable tallies and the inexperienced Americans were no match for them, despite their enthusiasm. Initially the Germans were unused to being the targets and the Americans thought they were going to have an easy ride:

I volunteered for sniping in Italy in late '43 and was given a nine day training course behind the lines. It wasn't enough but it was all the time the army could spare ... I took my rifle into the field and we holed up in a small olive grove on a steep hillside. We couldn't believe how casual the Germans were about exposing their men and it was like a turkey shoot for a couple of days. But they damn quickly began to retaliate and mostly we didn't know where the hell they were shooting from. One morning my buddy Charlie was spotting for me and he suddenly said "There's ..." Then there was a crack and he went real quiet and I ducked down just as another bullet smashed through the branch where my head had been. I dragged him back but he was dead, shot through the forehead and out the back of his helmet. I had to leave him there, which hurt me bad, we had been through so much together. Things got real hard for us after that. We were fighting Nazis [snipers] who were good and well-equipped, and we had to make do with what we had, which wasn't much. Our rifles had lousy little 2.5 power scopes and we couldn't match the Germans on range, though in the street fighting we were pretty even matched I'd say.[4]

In practical terms the snipers' lives had not been helped because of a simple decision by the Ordnance Department. In order to speed up production it had elected to issue the M1903A4 rifles without any iron sights. As urban fighting became more commonplace during the Italian and French campaigns, it became clear that if the scope was damaged, or dismounted for any reason, the sniper had a rifle that was effectively useless for close-quarter fighting. As a result, many snipers elected to carry carbines or submachine guns (captured German MP40s were popular), but the lack of versatility of the Springfields was a constant complaint that proved to be virtually insoluble while they were in service. Meanwhile, the Ordnance Department was well aware of their limitations and had been hurrying up the development work on the sniping variant of the Garand semi-automatic rifle. There were a number of problems to be overcome, though, for while the Garand was an excellent infantry rifle, arguably the best of World War II, it fell short as a sniping weapon in a number of areas. Semi-automatics did not perform well in terms of accuracy compared to bolt-action rifles. There were many more moving parts for which blueprint-perfect fit was required to ensure reliability. In addition there was the complexity of a gas recoil mechanism that could and did give problems. The automatic ejection of the spent cases was noisy and in bright sunlight the tell-tale glint of the cases as they were flung from the receiver could quite literally be the death of a soldier or sniper. Finding a scope mounting was also proving difficult for it had to allow for the loading and ejection system of the rifle, which required an entire eight-round clip to be inserted through the top of the receiver, preventing an over-the-bore scope mounting. Testing showed that an offset mount, fitted on the left of the receiver, was suitable and while not perfect it did have the benefit of leaving the iron sights in place. Quick-release commercial Griffin & Howe mounts were used, but the main stumbling block was in deciding what scope to use.

As with the Marine Corps, the Army eventually opted for a commercially available sight, the 2.5x Lyman Alaskan. It was available in large numbers and in late September 1944 it was officially adopted as the Model M81, although in short order it became the improved M82. It had a post reticle instead of the usual crosshair, and while Lyman supplied the bulk of them some secondary production was begun in January 1945 at the Wollensak Optical Company of Rochester, New York, to help meet demand.

According to the statistics some 6,896 M1C sniping rifles were supplied to the Army up to August 1945 but the new weapons were to be very rare beasts indeed in the front lines, for even by the very end of the war very few had found their way to Europe. Testing showed the Garand to be accurate to about 600 yards with issue ball ammunition, somewhat less than the performance of the Springfield, but with good-quality ammunition this could be raised to 900 yards or more. As with previous generations of sharpshooters, the snipers were very particular about the quality of ammunition they had, having distinct preferences, some even having supplies of match-grade commercial cartridges shipped from home for field use. Issue ammunition could certainly vary wildly: "The ammo we used was not match grade; it came right out of the green boxes. Sometimes you got misfires with it; sometimes a round simply went *poof!* and you had no idea which way it went."[5] There were compensations with the Garand, though, for the semi-auto mechanism allowed the possibility of a quick follow-up shot and in close fighting the rapidity of fire was invaluable.

For the vast majority of US Army snipers who landed on the French beaches on June 6, 1944, and who fought through the *bocage* country, the reliable old Springfield was to be their only weapon. These saw heavy use, for there was little fighting more onerous and exhausting, both mentally and physically, than pushing yard by yard through the dense and impenetrable tangle of heavily defended ancient trees and bushes that criss-crossed the French countryside in Normandy. Reporter Ernie Pyle wrote of the fighting:

We had had snipers before, in Bizerte and Cassino and lots of other places, but always on a small scale. There in Normandy the Germans went in for sniping on a whole-scale manner. There were snipers everywhere in trees, in buildings, in piles of wreckage in the grass. It was perfect sniping country … and it was like hunting a needle in a haystack. They picked off our soldiers one by one … it wasn't safe to move into a new bivouac area until the snipers had been cleaned out.[6]

For the snipers the fighting seemed endless:

The strain of hedgerows wore on you. It felt like we had fought all the way across France and should be damned near to Germany. We just kept going until the next machine gun ambush or next sniper … If there was a world outside these hedgerows none of us expected to see it again.[7]

A single well-concealed German sniper could cause chaos and initially the inexperienced US soldiers suffered accordingly. One platoon officer ordered his men to keep moving in the face of accurate sniper fire. "I ordered a squad to advance from one hedgerow to another. During the movement one man was shot by a sniper … the entire squad hit the ground and they were all picked off, one by one, by the same sniper."[8] Taking on the Germans was a matter of keen observation, cunning, and above all, patience, for an impatient sniper inevitably became a dead one:

I kept my head low as I started to scan the hedgerows through my scope. The German sniper was no slouch. He had already picked off two of our boys. I detected a large dark knot high in the top of a tree. I studied it a second and was about to slide past when it moved. I watched it intently, finally concluding it must have been a bird … I scoped on down the hedgerow. When nothing else stirred, I returned to the knot for lack of anything more probable. The more I looked the more it resembled a man hugged tight to a tree trunk. Several minutes passed. The sergeant fidgeted.
"I want him to break first" I explained.
The next time the knot moved I knew it wasn't a bird. I drew in a deep breath filled with the smell of the rich soil in which I lay, let half of it escape

then gently stroked the trigger. The rifle recoiled. I saw the tree shaking violently. I squeezed off another round. The German turned loose his perch just like a squirrel does and bounced off the limbs down through the tree until his body hit the ground.

The redheaded sergeant pounded me on the back.

"That murderin' sonovabitch!" he shouted, "You got him."[9]

Fighting was made all the more miserable by the unseasonably wet weather that turned fields to liquid mud and made rifles and equipment rusty overnight. The soldiers learned that the only way to deal with the hedges was to soak them with gunfire and grenades, leaving snipers on the flanks to deal with any Germans flushed out. It was slow and painstaking work. The American snipers, a few of whom were Italian campaign veterans, learned quickly about the rules of engagement in the bocage; basically there were none. In Italy some 36th Division sniper squads contained Sioux Indians who routinely scalped their victims, a practice they continued in France, doubtless providing the Germans with some interesting psychological problems among their troops. While in Italy this habit had not exactly endeared them to their own comrades; by the time the fighting had moved to France there was no longer any tolerance for Nazi snipers and no quarter was asked or given. Captured snipers, of either side, would be routinely shot (as indeed were many ordinary prisoners). Correspondent Ernie Pyle touched on this in one of his wartime dispatches from Normandy:

Sniping, as far as I know, is recognized as a legitimate means of waging warfare. And yet there is something sneaking about it that outrages the American sense of fairness. I had never seen this before we landed in France and began pushing the Germans back. In past campaigns our soldiers would talk about the occasional snipers with contempt and disgust. But in France sniping became more important, and taking precautions against it was something we had to learn, and learn fast. Snipers killed as many Americans as they could and when their food and water ran out, they surrendered. Our men felt that wasn't quite ethical.[10]

Certainly on the Allied side, while there was still a dichotomy in attitude towards the snipers and their craft, the prevalence of German snipers and the toll they took on American soldiers meant that many infantrymen's attitudes changed as the war dragged on:

> Many of our buddies didn't like what we did and called us "ten cent killers" [a reference to the cost of a cartridge] but when they were pinned down by a Kraut sniper in the hedgerows it was always "Get a damn sniper up, quick" and they were happy enough that we dealt with them. Then we were hero's [sic] for ten minutes.[11]

THE MARINES' WAR

The Marines were desperately in need of a better telescopic sight for their rifles and prewar they had begun to look in earnest for a replacement. The Winchester's successor, the Lyman 5A of 1928, was a much improved design with a stronger body and greater field of view, but by the start of the war it was an outmoded design. In a review of optical sights, the Marines' ordnance personnel had recommended that a scope needed to be sourced that was of "about 8x with an object lens of about one to one and a half inches, medium fine crosshair reticle and double micrometer quarter minute click mounts."[12] To meet these criteria was not actually so difficult, as mounts were available off the shelf and there were three scopes to choose from, Lyman, Fecker, and Unertl. All were long-bodied tube designs of 8 to 10x. After tests, the Marines decided to adopt the Unertl, its 8x (in reality 7.8x) body being mounted in micro-adjustable saddle mounts of a design harking back to the previous century. One unusual function of these sights was that after every shot, the body of the scope slid forwards under recoil and had to be pulled back or "returned to battery" to enable the next shot to be made. This configuration prevented a quick follow-up shot and caused some irritation amongst snipers, who often made their own arrangements, frequently involving pieces of rubber inner tube. When supplied, the commercial scopes were actually fitted with recoil springs, but the Marine Corps insisted these were taken off in case they caused jamming due to grit or sand.

At least the rifles were no problem, with almost 1,000 match-grade Springfield weapons available. In keeping with their desire to have the best tools for the job, the Corps had also tested some commercial rifles, including the excellent Winchester Models 54 and 70. The Model 70 was a target and hunting rifle that had been introduced in 1935. It was available in several forms and in three weights of barrel: standard, heavy, and bull, the latter weighing an impressive 13^1/$_2$lb, coincidentally the same as many commercially made Civil War sharpshooters' rifles. Much of the pressure on the Corps to adopt the Winchester came from General George Van Orden, who, along with Captain Calvin Lloyd, was on the Marine Corps Equipment Board. In 1942 they submitted a report titled "Equipment for the American Sniper" strongly recommending the adoption of the Model 70 but to no avail, for the rifle had been officially rejected by the Corps as "insufficiently sturdy" and with "difficult to procure parts."[13] That may have been the official response, but the rifle impressed enough Marines for some 370 to be purchased and adopted into semi-official service. They were mostly fitted with 8x Unertl scopes making them today one of the most collectible of military sniping rifles. Some Marines bought Winchesters privately, Lieutenant John George being a prime example.

A prewar hunter and competition shooter, when George landed at Guadalcanal in November 1943 he carried his own rifle, a lightweight hunting Model 70 fitted with a commercial Lyman Alaskan telescopic sight. Although he had no training whatsoever in military sniping and was forced to find out the hard way, he soon unwittingly discovered many lessons that previous generations of sharpshooters had learned:

It was this first trip that taught me it was not wise … to search with binoculars or scopes for more than thirty minutes at a time, especially if the ranges are long. The eyes should be turned away and rested for a bit every few minutes. There is no substitute for resting the eyes. The only thing to do is find something green and shadowy and look toward it without trying to concentrate vision on any part of it. In searching for sniping targets one needs the last fine edge of normal [or abnormal] vision.[14]

Despite his lack of training, it was not long before targets presented themselves, the Japanese being unused to facing such accurate enemy fire, although it wasn't always at long range:

Another shape moved by the boulder and I shifted the rifle over the parapet so I could look through the scope. "It's a Jap" I almost yelled out loud. I actually refused to believe what I was seeing. Now I dammed [sic] myself for having held fire for so long. The Jap squirmed backwards while I took aim and, in doing, he turned his face my way. He slipped down so that all I could see of him was his face and his helmeted head. But at 80 yards the face was enough target. I must have been pretty steady at the moment of the shot because I remember being able to set his chin precisely on the flat-topped post in the Alaskan reticle. My bullet struck him squarely in the teeth and he pitched on his face, giving a single convulsive jerk.[15]

George had discovered an important factor in sniping that had been taught since 1914, which was to aim at the teeth of the target. The reasons for this were threefold. It ensured instant death for the victim as the spinal cord was severed, while reducing any likelihood of bones deflecting the bullet, as well as allowing for under- or over-estimation of range. If the shot were a little too high or too low, a killing shot would still be made in the head or upper chest. George also learned to operate for most of the time with an observer, who used binoculars or a spotting scope, enabling his shooting partner to rest his eyes and relax tired muscles between shots.

The Marines needed to set up a training school and do it quickly. Like the Army, they had no official sniper program but they did have the backing of senior officers such as Lieutenant-Colonel George Van Orden as well as a hard-core of experienced and enthusiastic shooters in their ranks who were ready to learn. Desperately trying to push the Corps towards adopting a proper training policy in 1942 Van Orden and Gunnery Sergeant Calvin

A. Lloyd had produced a detailed report for Washington on the need to produce trained snipers, detailing not only the practical benefits but also the psychological. "His game ... is to pick off with one rapidly delivered shot, a single enemy. He must harass the foe ... until his rifle 'crack' becomes a menace feared more than the shrieking shells."[16] Amazingly, Washington agreed and in late 1942 training camps were established at Fort Lejuene, Camp Pendleton, and Green's Farm in San Diego, California. A five-week course was planned staffed by gunnery sergeants, universally known as "gunnys," who were all expert riflemen, many also being championship Marine target shooters. One unique part of the course was the Corps' insistence on snipers mastering 1,000-yard shooting, no easy task to learn or teach but later to prove invaluable in combat. This training was, of course, established too late to help during the first stages of the war in the Pacific and no trained snipers were initially available, although there were many expert marksmen like George who exacted a steady toll on the Japanese. Indeed, the first Congressional Medal of Honor awarded in the war went to the commander of the Scout/Sniper platoon, 1st Lieutenant William Deane Hawkins; he and four snipers were the first men ashore on Betio Island, on Tarawa atoll. All five launched a courageous attack on virtually the entire Japanese defense system and were soon joined by the remainder of their platoon. After five days of fighting, the scout/snipers had suffered 50 percent casualties and Lieutenant Hawkins had paid the ultimate price.

In terms of equipment the Marines were rather better served than the Army, for while their mix of Springfield and Winchester rifles and Lyman and Unertl scopes proved a logistical nightmare for the Corps armorers, they did at least give the Marines the capability to engage the enemy on more than equal terms. Their skills were sorely needed too, for the Japanese proved to be masters of camouflage and fieldcraft, as the Americans found to their cost when they began island-hopping in the Pacific. As with their Army counterparts in Europe, the Marines suffered heavily in the face of sniper fire for they had no specialized camouflaged clothing. Whereas Japanese snipers were issued with special rattan capes that blended perfectly with the jungle, and heavily netted helmets in which foliage could be entwined, the Marines wore their issue green herringbone twill (HBT) fatigues which did, after a time, fade to a very practical gray-black color. There was an issue of camouflage fatigues as well, in the shape of the M1942 one-piece suit which was not much liked, in view of the rampant dysentery most men suffered from, but it was improved when modified to be issued as a two-piece uniform. Almost all Marines wore the reversible helmet cover and these became practically an identification badge for the Pacific veterans.

Initially, though, the inexperienced Marines were at the mercy of the Japanese defenders, one company on Guadalcanal losing ten men one after the other to a single Japanese sniper, resulting in the worst possible scenario when an entire advance was abruptly halted because the men lacked the experience to move forwards into the face of aimed fire. The Japanese used both scoped and ordinary sighted rifles and were trained to shoot out to medium ranges of about 400 yards, more than enough in jungle conditions, as George's 80-yard shot evidenced. Generally they were armed with 6.5mm or 7.7mm Arisaka rifles, many of which were fitted with a 2x or 4x scope, an unusual optical sight as it was fixed with no provision at all for adjustment of either windage or elevation. John George, who tested many captured rifles, wrote that "They were extremely accurate out to 400 yards always shooting to the point of aim. I dismounted the scope several times but it seemed not to affect the zero."[17] The Japanese snipers were also masters of camouflage as well as proving incredibly patient, so underestimating them inevitably proved to be a dangerous error.

The Marines' rifles and scopes performed reasonably well in the harsh conditions. The Unertls, although prone to water ingress and requiring careful handling to prevent damage to the mounts, were to provide good service for the Corps for some 30 years, their high power making them ideal as both spotting and long-range shooting scopes. In the right terrain the Marines' Unertls gave them the advantage of being able to engage the enemy at very considerable distances. While jungle was common at sea level, much of the geography of the Pacific islands was hilly with widely scattered vegetation and scrub, and this proved an excellent sniping ground for

Marine snipers such as Private Dan Cass who took the Corps unofficial prize for the longest shots while fighting on Okinawa. Pinned down by a distant machine gun, Cass and Carter, his observer, were summoned. Carter looked intently through his spotting scope:

"I found them."

"Where?"

"There."

"Godammit, where there? There's a lot of *there* out there."

"I estimate twelve or thirteen hundred yards" Carter said, discouraged.

After some quick calculations, spurred on by hopelessness, I slipped a tracer round into the chamber of the Springfield. Carter glued his eyes to the spotting scope. "Pick her up an inch!" he curtly advised. I adjusted the scope elevation knob and dropped the cross hairs onto the Japanese machine gun nest. I fired and worked the bolt, fired and worked the bolt. The machine gun fire ceased. Then "They're running." Several minute figures scurried from the barricades. That was when I took a deep wavering breath. I remembered what the captain had said before we left the ship. "We expect you to do your job." I had done my job, hadn't I?[18]

Cass' experiences were not unusual, but in much Pacific fighting there was no chance to use the potential of the Unertl or any other scope for that matter. Along beachheads and in dense jungle, range counted for nothing and one serious disadvantage for the snipers was that in close combat with the Japanese a scope such as the Unertl had a field of view of about 10ft at 100 yards, impossibly narrow for target acquisition, and it could not be focused down to perform at close ranges. Out of necessity during the jungle fighting, most snipers found it more practical to shoot with the iron sights on their rifles. Marines pinned down by Japanese snipers who were invisible in the treetops or dense foliage soon worked out the best means of dealing with them, either by raking the trees with machine-gun fire, or by using case shot from small field guns. Neither method guaranteed success, though, and the Marines soon evolved the "buddy system," a counter-sniping tactic that proved extremely effective. A Browning gunner equipped with a .30-caliber Browning Automatic Rifle (BAR) would rake the suspected area with fire, while the sniper and a buddy with a Thompson submachine gun watched for movement. When the firing stopped, the Japanese sniper would often move, either to change position to somewhere less dangerous or to see if a shot was possible, at which point either the sniper or Tommy-gunner would take his shot, depending on range. "Sometimes the Nips were so close to us that the Tommy-gunner would open up and literally knock him out of a treetop above us. Often they were behind us, having let our men pass under them. They were hell to locate and kill."[19] It was a good system and could be worked by two men provided they had complete faith in each other's ability and it was to prove its worth in future wars.

TOWARD THE END

There had been some useful innovations filtering their way through to the snipers, and possibly the most interesting for the future history of sniping had been the introduction of the first infrared night-sight. Although only fielded in very small numbers, the Infrared Sniperscope M1 was fitted to an unlikely rifle, the little M1 T3 .30-caliber carbine. The limited range of the scope, of about 300 yards, made its use with anything larger a waste of time and it was also susceptible to damage through shock, so the almost negligible recoil of the M1 made it an ideal choice. Conceived in 1943 it was first used the following year in the Pacific campaign, but from the outset its major drawback, aside from its bulk, was the requirement for a huge battery pack to power it. Even in a relatively static position it was to prove less than practical. The Marines found it better to put their faith in old-fashioned technology, as ex-Marine Frank Booth wrote:

> Contrary to popular belief, the value of the sniperscope … was greatly over-rated. [While] we found they were of greater value in a jungle perimeter use … the ground forces were supported by … an endless stream of flares. These proved to be of greater help in detecting the enemy than any other device.[20]

As with any new technology, the infrared scope was still in its infancy and the Sniperscope was to resurface again in the Korean War.

As they advanced across Europe, the Army snipers had to learn how to deal with a new form of threat, urban sniping. The villages and towns of central Europe provided the perfect backdrop for German snipers, who used tactics perfected at the end of World War I to delay the advancing Allies. Small numbers of snipers, with light machine-gunners in support, occupied roof spaces, ruined buildings, and basements, directing accurate fire at the Americans. Some of the GIs had learned how to deal with the menace in the Italian campaign, but most were new to this form of sniping and working out how to deal with the Germans was difficult. The easiest method was simply by directing a friendly tank to shell, or simply drive over, the suspected sniper's hide, but tanks weren't always available:

> We were held up by a sniper on the main road into the town. No one could spot where he was and we raked the buildings with thirty cal machine gun fire. As we moved forwards there was a "crack" and another of our boys folded up and everyone hit the ground. The Lieutenant gave me the nod and we took his binoculars and my buddy and I got to the top floor of a house with a good view of the square. Some of the boys used the helmet on a stick trick and it worked! It drew a shot from an upstairs window nearly opposite us and we only saw the rifle flash because we were high up, looking into the window. It took ten seconds to finish the Kraut, though even with the scope I couldn't make him out clearly. When we advanced we found him on the floor, lying on top of his rifle, a semi-auto Mauser. My shot had gone right through his chest. He was dressed all in black and was invisible to anyone outside and I still have the scope I took from that rifle.[21]

"Buddy" tactics adopted from the Pacific were also successfully used, with BAR gunners and snipers working together, although the experienced Germans were generally much less likely to be drawn into giving away their locations and most wisely withdrew to new positions after firing one or two shots. It was hard fighting, but it was to prove very useful experience for the future in what was later to become known as Fighting In Built-up Areas (FIBUA). Despite the development work on the new Garand M1C, the Army snipers would continue to use their venerable Springfields to fight their way across France and into Germany. No figures exist for the specific losses of snipers during the European campaign, but from June 1944 to the end of the war in May 1945 Army returns for replacements and rotation of men through sniper schools would indicate something in the region of 85 percent losses, roughly the same as that of British snipers during the same period. It is a moot point whether the lack of specialized clothing for snipers contributed to this figure, for unlike the carefully thought-out uniforms issued to Berdan's Sharpshooters in the previous century, neither the US Army nor the Marines provided any specialized clothing for use by snipers, unlike both the German and Japanese armies. Later in the war camouflage clothing, which had been the subject of much Army experimentation since 1941, did become more widely available, but snipers normally had to beg, borrow, or steal it and often captured German camouflaged smocks would be pressed into service. In Europe, Army snipers wore normal service fatigues of varying patterns, initially the M1941 or "Parsons" field jackets and later the M1943 (possibly the most practical uniform jacket to come out of World War II), although a white parka and trousers were available late in the European campaign for winter use; but the snipers generally created their own camouflage on an "as required" basis.

As the war dragged to an ignominious and weary end in Europe in May 1945, the Marines were still battling across the Pacific, island by island, and fighting on Okinawa was not easing up. Still armed with their eclectic mix of Springfields, Winchesters, and an assortment of scopes, the Marine snipers who had survived were by now a highly skilled and hard-bitten bunch. Not for them were there any happy V-E[22] day celebrations, as Marine Dan Cass recalled. "At exactly noon, every gun on the island and every ship's gun fired one shot to celebrate V-E day. I fired my victory round across a marsh at a battered tree trunk. It was a good thousand yards away. I hit it too. Then we got up and pushed on."[23]

In September 1945 the end of the war with Japan brought to a close the most costly conflict in human history. It was a war that had started with weapons and tactics that would not have been unfamiliar to soldiers at the turn of the century and it ended with a frightening glimpse of total warfare, with civilian populations and economic heartlands thousands of miles from the fighting being targeted by carpet bombing and ultimately nuclear weapons of staggering power. The infantry of most of the warring countries returned to find their economies shattered and no homes, often not even any cities, left and their families dead or scattered.

For the American troops, home was at least something inviolate, untouched by the ravages of war, and they were happy to exchange their uniforms and weapons for civilian clothes. For the snipers who came back there was seldom any reason to talk about their war, for few civilians wanted to listen and fewer still understood the lives they had led:

> I never once told my folks or wife about what I had done. As far as they knew I was just another G.I. and I guess I never talked about what I did until the last few years. As I got older I couldn't shake off the memories of what I had seen and done and I guess ours was a different kind of war, a personal war and when you look into the faces of the men you kill, it will always leave some kind of impression. I don't regret what I did, it had to be done to stop the Nazis but would I do it again? I don't know.[24]

Time, however, is a great healer. The Marine snipers returned their well-used Winchesters to reserve stores and the Army, which throughout World War II had never actually begun an official sniper training program, took its old Springfields back, packed them in grease, and forgot about sniping. For America's politicians and military, other matters were more pressing for a new menace was emerging. The Cold War was about to begin.

Chapter 8

COLD WAR, HOT WAR

America was not alone in ignoring the lessons learned about the deployment of snipers during World War II. It is an unfortunate fact of life that once a perceived danger ceases to exist, the defenses erected, either physical or mental, are invariably quickly dismantled. In the immediate postwar era this was perfectly true of almost all of the Allied combatants. It was only the USSR and China who continued with training programs, Russia uniquely having decided to pursue the development of a semi-automatic rifle both for general infantry issue and also as a sniping weapon. Elsewhere, the situation reverted to normal. Britain put all of its Enfield No.4 [T] sniping rifles into store and ceased development work on a proposed new rifle, and large numbers were subsequently sold off into the commercial trade. The United States stored its aged Springfields, but to its credit the Department of Ordnance sensibly managed to persuade Washington that with nearly 7,000 completed M1C rifles on hand it was worthwhile continuing the development program to perfect the mounting system. In part this was due to fears that the Cold War, which was at its height from 1948 to 1953, would escalate into a major conflict, with the USSR at its epicenter. War did come, but from an entirely unexpected direction, the little known country of Korea.

In June 1950 the communist-backed North Korea invaded the southern provinces, at the time under the protection of the newly formed United

Nations, forcing an armed conflict that the Western powers would have preferred to avoid. From October 1951 North Korean forces were supported by Chinese regular troops, providing huge numbers of both men and weapons. It was to prove a curious war from a tactical point of view, with the Marines landing on the beaches of Inchon in a manner reminiscent of Guadalcanal a decade earlier, then digging in to relive the trench warfare days of 1917–18 in a frontline zone referred to as the MLR or Main Line of Resistance.

Few soldiers or Marines had any idea what to expect, fighting Chinese troops being beyond the experience of anyone in the US military. What they certainly didn't bargain on was to be immediately on the receiving end of accurate, aimed sniper fire.

As had been the case in the early days of World War I, at first this shooting was not recognized as being anything more than infantry rifle fire, or "blind" shots with the resultant casualties being regarded as particularly unlucky casualties. However, as the troops began to settle down in the trenches that had spread across the country, it soon became apparent that the pattern of shooting was quite deliberate, particularly as the ranges involved were long, often in excess of 600 yards. The Korean/Chinese troops (commonly referred to by GIs as "Chicoms") were primarily armed with Soviet-supplied 7.62mm Mosin Nagant rifles with the excellent PE or PU telescopic sight. They were a battle-proven combination, used to great effect during World War II, and the Chinese had many hundreds in their arsenal. Sniper training was also given to selected marksmen and the largely anonymous Chicom snipers initially made life very difficult for the NATO troops. The famous story of the commander of the 3rd Battalion, 1st Marines, having the binoculars shot from his hands as he observed the enemy lines underscored the need for strong retaliatory action. As he nursed a badly cut hand and bruised head, the colonel raged "It's a hell of a situation when the C.O. can't even take a look at the terrain he's defending without getting shot at. Something has got to be done about those goddam snipers."[1] On inquiring where his Marine snipers were, he was even more exasperated to be told there were none. The Marines' response was direct though – find men, train them, and track down enough scoped rifles to equip them. How they managed to do it was soon mirrored by other units along the line, both Marine and Army.

Initial enquiries made at the base armory showed there were supplies of both optically equipped Springfield M1903A4 and M1C rifles. When asked why they hadn't been issued the simple reply was that "no one had asked for them." Scratch-built ranges had to be made and sufficient men selected. While the squads were theoretically formed on a volunteer basis, several good shots were informed by their gunnery sergeant that they were to report for initial training the next day. One Army private who was selected was an expert rifleman who had shot for a Rangers rifle team. He commented that "as I was the only man in the company with any rifle team or shooting experience, the CO called back and requested a sniper rifle for me. 'Hamilton, that makes you the company sniper.'"[2]

The 3rd Marines formed a sniping squad comprising six two-man teams per company, while the 5th decided on eight-man teams operating independently within their companies. They were sent to a range that the engineers had constructed half a mile behind the front lines and then given a two- or three-week course of instruction by the gunnys. This took exactly the same form as had been used in the previous war and most of the instructors were themselves ex-snipers. The scratch-built 600-yard ranges initially used packing crates cut into man-sized shapes for targets until some sharp-eyed Marine noticed that fired 155mm artillery shellcases were almost exactly the same size as the torso of the average Chicom soldier. Before very long the puzzled artillerymen began to wonder why all of their discarded shellcases were disappearing. Lack of suitable range space made 1,000-yard shooting difficult to teach, but the theory was covered, as much of the terrain in Korea was open land separated by high ridges. It was nearly impossible to practice long-range shooting outside of the actual combat zone, though.

Generally, the issue sniping rifle for Marine and Army snipers was to be the Garand M1C, which had only been accepted for Marine service in 1951, and Korea was to prove its first use as a combat sniping rifle. All rifles were shipped to Korea heavily packed in Cosmoline grease and the sniper's first job was to clean it off, not an easy task as the tiny bottle of cleaning fluid supplied for the purpose was wholly inadequate. "The sniper rifle was a brand new M1C with a 4x scope and cheek pad. It was packed in Cosmoline. I had a helluva time scrubbing off all that Cosmoline with the little can of kerosene that came with the weapon."[3] The Garand proved to be a competent but not outstanding sniping rifle. It had several shortcomings, the most serious being its limited range and inadequate scope power. It was generally believed that the barrel was not heavy enough to provide accuracy beyond 600 yards, particularly when using standard-issue ball ammunition. However, the snipers had learned that this could be improved upon if heavier armor-piercing bullets were used and they "liberated" stocks of the ammunition whenever they could find it. It improved the apparently limited capability of the M1C and the low-powered scope did not always prove a stumbling-block, as Master Gunnery Sergeant John Boitnott recalled:

> I was lying along a forward parapet and when [Private First Class] Friday ran through, someone took a shot at him. I thought I saw movement on a hill mass across a valley. That area was about 670 yards away. I called Friday and told him to come to me ... the enemy sniper rose again to fire, and that time I saw him clearly. One shot, one dead North Korean sniper. Friday and I teamed up, with him running the trench and me shooting the enemy for two more kills, which seemed to entertain about everybody on our side. Over a two day span I made 9 confirmed kills in 9 shots at ranges from 670 yards to 1250 yards.[4]

Certainly, the 2.2x M82 (later renumbered the M84) in scope was simply not powerful enough for extreme ranges, and the Marine ordnance armorers knew it, but it was the usual problem of how to obtain sufficient quantities of the right type of scope at short notice. In fact, the whole issue of supply and manufacture of these rifles was to be a catalog of confusion. The first M1C rifles were beautifully made and finished, "the best finished and tightest M1's I ever saw" as one armorer wrote,[5] but the bizarre situation had arisen that in order to provide enough rifles to the infantry between 1,500 and 4,000 M1Cs were requisitioned and stripped of their scopes to be issued as ordinary rifles. However, the sudden demand from the MLR for sniping rifles caused a flurry of activity as armorers searched high and low for scoped rifles to send to the front. In the meantime, the Department of Ordnance was already working on an improved version, the M1D. This was simplified to aid production, but crucially it had a heavier barrel, providing better accuracy. It also did away with the old Griffin & Howe mounts, each of which had to be individually drilled, tapped, and collimated with its rifle, in favor of a single point mounting, soldered to the barrel and using a thumbwheel to permit easy attachment or removal of a scope. In order to achieve sufficient numbers for sniper issue, some 14,325 standard M1 rifles were selected for conversion. The old M84 scopes were also under close scrutiny, and the Marines had tested a number of alternatives, settling on an improved Stith-Kollmorgen "Bear Cub" hunting scope. Originally in 2.5x, the modified scope was a far more practical 4x, but despite the best efforts of the Ordnance Department and Springfield Armory, these improvements were not introduced until early 1954 and were to prove just too late to see service in Korea, although they were to be used in anger elsewhere in the world within a comparatively short time.

As Marines had discovered in the Pacific during close-quarter fighting, the loading system of the Garand could prove a liability as it ejected the used cartridge clip with a loud "ping" when the magazine was empty, alerting the enemy to the fact that the rifle was temporarily unloaded, and wise soldiers kept a .45in pistol close to hand. In Korea the shortage of men required the snipers to be employed as regular infantrymen and this meant that they were often in the middle of mass Korean attacks where the firepower of the semi-auto M1C proved invaluable.

Meanwhile, both Marine and Army snipers were beginning to wage their own quiet war on the Chicom soldiers, using whatever was to hand. This included some Winchester Model 70s with Lyman Targetspot 10x or Unertl 8x scopes, the venerable Springfields with Lyman or M74 scopes, M1C rifles that, while mostly equipped with M82 scopes, sometimes had either Lyman Alaskan or Weaver 330s fitted. Obtaining spares was always a problem and any usable scope would be pressed into service.

Despite the long ranges encountered, for which the Unertl's 8x magnification was in constant demand, much of the trench sniping was to take place at considerably closer ranges, in places the front lines being less than 200 yards apart. The manner of combat engaged in by the Koreans in the MLR, using mass-wave attacks, meant that snipers often found themselves in situations for which sniper training had no ready answers. Sergeant Chet Hamilton recounted what happened when his patrol was caught in a sudden advance by Chicom soldiers and trapped in a thinly defended section of trench. Having rapidly shot four of the enemy who tried to run to safety, Hamilton sat and waited:

> The Chinese settled down to hold their end of the trench and we settled down to hold ours. We weren't more than fifty yards apart. We couldn't get away, but they couldn't get away either, because I or one of the others ... picked them off whenever they tried. It turned into a stalemate ... mostly just fast skirmishes ... until we started running out of ammo. We started using Chinese weapons we picked up off the dead. The stench of rotting dead was overpowering. We fought from what was literally a mass grave. Some of us were wounded. The shelling continued. One part of the trench that was [originally] seven feet deep was only four inches deep. Our lines eventually sent out a rescue attempt and managed to open an escape route.[6]

Bloodied and demoralized, the platoons limped back to the MLR. Hamilton and his men had been trapped for over a week. The Chinese tactics of using huge bodies of troops advancing in seemingly endless lines meant that accurate sniping was often unnecessary. Browning machine guns killed them in their hundreds, but as one veteran said, "no matter how we knocked them down, they just kept coming." Often, the Marine snipers took the war right to the enemy's front door, the 3rd Battalion sending its snipers out to harass entrenched Koreans from a ridge some 400 yards away. Their commander, Lieutenant Gil Holmes, placed his men in a loose skirmish line and ordered them to fire at will. The communist troops had no idea where the fire was coming from and literally ran in circles:

They tried to set up a machine-gun to our direct front and one of my boys knocked out the gunner ... the company commander was running about like a madman ... but his people were crumbling all around him under a steady stream of well-aimed fire from our sharpshooters. They returned fire but it was ineffective, they didn't seem to have a fix on our position.[7]

Some novel tactics were also tried, in particular the use of huge searchlights with pink filters to illuminate the Korean trenches. These filters helped the snipers use their scopes without being blinded and they took full advantage of it, killing large numbers of sentries, while at least one Army sniper with a sense of humor deliberately put a bullet through the spade being wielded by a trench-digging Korean soldier. From their high vantage points on the crags and ridges, the snipers were able to provide vital information about possible Chicom attacks and troop movements and even occasionally help out advancing American forces:

I felt helpless watching [the American attack] from the sandbagged trenches on the Erie until I noticed something. It was only four hundred yards across the valley ... my position put me almost on the same level with the Chink defenders... [In] order for the Chicoms to see our troops and fire at them down through their wire ... they had to lean up and over their trenches, exposing wide patches of their quilted hides. That was all I needed. All I had to do was go down the trench line, settle the ... reticle on one target after the other and squeeze the trigger. The fight for the hill lasted about two hours. Bt the time the GIs withdrew ... my barrel was so hot ... that I could hardly touch it. You could smell the cosmoline being cooked out of the metal. I know I shot at least forty chinks ... bodies had to be stacked up in the Chinese trenches.[8]

A particular problem facing the snipers in Korea was the atrocious winter conditions, with -50°F being commonplace, for which none of the NATO forces were prepared. Chinese soldiers wore eminently practical quilted suits and captured ones that were big enough for the Americans were prized, but mostly they had to improvise, the snipers suffering badly because of their exposed positions and inability to move around. Two hours was the maximum a man could stand without the danger of frostbite setting in, and packing boots with straw or paper, layering up with two or three sets of underclothes and loose outer garments (very heavy greatcoats prohibited free movement and proper positioning of the rifle), and two woolen caps helped. Hands were always a problem, for heavy gloves prevented a man from using the trigger and a good solution was to wear heavy mitts, with woolen gloves inside. The left hand taking the weight of the rifle could remain covered, while the right mitt had a slit cut in it along the length of the forefinger seam, allowing the vital trigger finger to be slid into the firing position for long enough to take a shot. One small but vital item issued from late 1949 was an observation telescope of the type typically found on competition shooting ranges. Hitherto, the military had issued binoculars for observing, but, as the British had discovered in World War I, they were nowhere near as efficient or powerful as a telescope. The M49 scope, mounted on a tiny but sturdy tripod, soon became an invaluable item of equipment for snipers, its 20x magnification capable of spotting enemy movement up to 10 miles away in clear weather conditions. It didn't take very long for the Americans to gain the upper hand in the fight for sniping superiority, the Chinese troops learning very quickly that careless exposure usually meant death. As the commander of the Marines' 3rd Battalion commented with satisfaction, "In nothing flat there was no more sniping on our positions. Nothing moved out there but what we hit it."[9]

While in most respects Korea was to prove just another small, costly, and militarily inconclusive war, it did raise a number of practical issues in terms of the deployment of specialist troops and their weapons. As usual, no thought had been given to the deployment of snipers until it became clear that an immediate response was needed to meet the enemy's threat, and even that was done purely at local level. No official training was given for snipers and, with the cessation of hostilities, rifles were once again returned to store and men reverted to normal infantry roles, to be mustered out of service in due course.

Yet there were some who had fought in Korea who did not believe that the military needed to reinvent the wheel with regard to sniping every time a conflict broke out. Some were serving officers who had considerable World War II sniping experience, others had brought their own hunting rifles to the war, much the same as many British officers had done in World War I. There were even a few senior officers in the Marines and Army who felt strongly enough to bombard their seniors with requests that sniper training and weapons be permanently established as an accredited military specialism. One of these men was an Army ordnance captain named William S. Brophy. He made it his mission in Korea to convince the Army, at every level, that they should be teaching, training, and supplying their own snipers with the best instructions and weapons available; in his opinion the best weapon system was the heavy-barreled Winchester Model 70 rifle, with a Unertl scope. He believed that, if suitably equipped, Army snipers could match the Marines in ability and results, as well as create their own invaluable sniping and intelligence units. It was an uphill struggle, he said. "The first reaction was not encouraging due to the feeling that the equipment I was demonstrating would be easily damaged and not be handled by the average soldier."[10] His approach was direct, lecturing commanding officers on the benefits of sniper deployment then following up by simply demonstrating his ability to hit targets at 1,000+ yards, a demonstration that invariably resulted in a Chicom soldier requiring urgent medical attention. Officers were certainly impressed, one commenting he had never seen shooting like it in all his career, but the Army was utterly rooted in the belief that any sniping rifle adopted must be a variant of the service weapon, and as they did not even have a sniper program for the Garands in service, there was little hope that they would approve use of commercial weapons. In fact, the US Army did not instigate a sniper training program until 1984 when, ironically, they adopted what was effectively a commercial Remington rifle.

If Brophy was banging his head against a metaphorical brick wall, he was certainly not the only one experimenting with non-standard sniping rifles, albeit of a slightly larger size. World War II had turned out some interesting weapons, some more effective than others, but the US Army had been particularly interested in the development by both the USSR and Germany of large-caliber antitank rifles. Although the thickness of tank armor had made the weapons largely useless by 1942, the Soviets in particular had adopted a considerable number of 14.5mm PTRD and PTRS rifles as sniping weapons, their armor-piercing bullets being capable of penetrating sniper shields, light armor, concrete, and several courses of brickwork. A few had scopes fitted locally, but most were used over open sights, with great effect. Indeed, some British .55in Boys rifles had been drafted into service in the Pacific for dealing with Japanese snipers, the trunk of a palm tree being no hindrance whatsoever to a Boys' bullet. The initial development work on these large-caliber sniping rifles appears to have been due primarily to Major F. Conway, who was then based at Aberdeen Proving Ground in Maryland, who appreciated from very early on the great potential of such weapons. Accordingly, at some point in 1946 his armorers had fitted a Browning .50-caliber barrel to a captured German PzB39 rifle and he tested it, commenting dryly that "ear protection was highly recommended."[11] It was accurate, though, with targets of 12in x 12in being regularly hit at 1,000 yards.

This unofficial development work was not regarded with any seriousness by the Army and unsurprisingly it was left to the Marines in Korea to make the earliest practical use of big-bore weapons for sniping. The 1st Battalion may have been the first unit to mount a scope on a .50-caliber Browning machine gun, a Unertl robbed from an unserviceable Winchester or Springfield. The Browning fired in single-shot mode proved unexpectedly effective, with a hit capability well in excess of 2,000 yards, and enthusiastic unit armorers continued to experiment. Ordnance artificer R. T. Walker was seconded to work with allied Nationalist Chinese troops in Korea and managed to acquire half a dozen Boys rifles from Canadian armorers who had little use for them, which he re-barreled in .50 caliber and then test-fired using double charges. Happy that the guns were safe to use, "We concentrated on smoothing out the action … we installed a block of steel in the magazine well, which served to strengthen the action and function as a loading block."[12] These guns were used at ranges in excess of 1,100 yards with some success, but only on an ad hoc basis, the military not yet taking seriously the pioneering work undertaken by Conway or Walker. Few could have foreseen what their work would eventually lead to.

HOT WAR – VIETNAM 1961–73

After the Korean War ended, the inevitable running-down of sniper deployment began. For the Army this was an almost immediate process, as no real program had begun anyway and the Army simply recalled its rifles and limited itself to ensuring each infantry squad had a designated marksman to act as sharpshooter if required. For the Marines it was less drastic, with competition shooting still greatly encouraged. (Immediately after the war, Staff Sergeant D. L. Smith, using a Marine Model 70, had won the National Match championship at Camp Perry.) There was still some limited sniper training available at Quantico, but it was not regarded as a priority requirement. While it may appear that everyone in the military had 30-second memories with regard to the value of sniping it should be remembered that there were a significant number of factors that acted against the idea of forming sniping units, particularly in times of peace:

1. In the world of military politics, there were very few high-ranking officers to support the case for snipers.
2. Commanding sniping units was not "career" soldiering and only a very few enthusiastic officers were prepared to limit their chances of promotion by doing so.
3. Sniping was by its very nature a clandestine occupation. Few snipers liked the limelight or were prepared to discuss what they did or what they accomplished. For example, eliminating enemy artillery to allow an infantry attack was seldom recognized as attributable to snipers.
4. Sniper training and equipment was regarded as expensive, although in practice it was not as long as scoped rifles existed in service.

5. There existed a distinct antipathy towards snipers as combat soldiers, with the lingering attitude that it was somehow an unfair way to wage war.

In another hitherto unknown country, the threat of war had also been simmering. French influence in Vietnam had kept a lid on a tense situation for years, but their authority had been severely eroded following the debacle of Dien Bien Phu in 1954, which eventually resulted in the French pulling out of Southeast Asia. The communist North was fighting a bitter war against the republican South at a time when anti-communist feeling was running high within both the US government and military, so when America finally entered into the conflict in Vietnam in 1961 it was already facing a well-organized, highly motivated enemy.

The first troops sent to Vietnam were marginally better equipped than their Korean War forebears, but not by much. The uniforms had changed a little, with lightweight tropical combat fatigues being issued, but almost everything else was the same as seen in World War II. In terms of weapons, there had been some advances, however, for in 1957 the infantry were issued with a new rifle to replace the Garand. The M14, although it strongly resembled a Garand in form and function, had been designed to incorporate a number of improvements. Crucially it was chambered for the new 7.62mm NATO cartridge. There had been much debate over the adoption of this new cartridge, it being less powerful than the tried and trusted .30-06, and many believed it incapable of making 1,000-yard shots. The M14 also had a 20-round detachable box magazine eliminating the twin bugbears of trying to top-up a partially used magazine, and having a noisily ejecting ammunition clip. It was 1lb lighter than the M1 and from a sniper's point of view it usefully had been manufactured with a groove and screw recess on the left side of the receiver similar to that of the M1D, to allow for a night sight or telescopic sight to be fitted. Unsurprisingly, though, no scope had actually been selected or mounting system designed. Despite the M14's introduction, the Garand soldiered on in a sniping role, the M1C having been finally replaced by the improved M1D with its integral scope mount, although both models were to serve side by side for some time to come.

THE RAW MATERIAL

By the end of 1965 there were over 38,000 Marines in Vietnam and the war was darkly reminiscent of the Pacific campaign. Many of their officers and gunnys were Pacific veterans and a fair percentage were also top-ranking competitive shooters, which was to provide the Corps with a sound foundation for the formation of a sniper training establishment. Captains D. W. Adams and J. R. Foster had won half a dozen times between them at Camp Perry, while captains Bob Russell and Jim Land had for years been pushing the Marines to establish a formal training program. Land had run the sniping school in Hawaii in the early 1960s, the only such school in existence in the whole US armed forces, and it provided the only recognized qualification that allowed snipers to become accredited military specialists. Then there were sergeants such as George Hurt, Marvin Lange, Don Reinke, Don Barker, V. D. Mitchell, and E. R. England, who between them had won almost every shooting prize going at Camp Perry and in national matches around America.

Some idea of the level of experience within the Corps can be gleaned from the story of Gunny Mitchell, who had been a sniper instructor at Camp Matthews, California, and was the only man to have won all three major shooting trophies: the Pershing, Boone, and DuPont. Aside from technical ability, he also had a wealth of practical sniping experience, having served in that capacity on Saipan, Tinian, and Iwo Jima, as well as in Korea. If ever there was a man born to instruct the neophyte snipers it was Gunny Mitchell, and despite having retired in 1964 he was unique in being re-enlisted into service in 1967 at the specific request of the commandant of the Corps.

While there was undoubtedly a solid core of experience within the Corps, the greater difficulty was in obtaining the authority to gather the men together to form a cadre of instructors. The situation was helped dramatically when late in 1965 the commanding officer of the Marines' 3rd Division gave Russell his blessing to form an in-country training school. Some potential instructors proved difficult to extract from their units; many were serving in rear-echelon supply or transport units, but man by man Russell pleaded, cajoled, or bullied their commanders into releasing them. Some idea of the difficulties facing him can be gathered from the fact that aside from having no instructors seconded to him, he had nowhere designated as a range, no training equipment and little idea how to set up an effective training program. Moreover, as a competitive shooter he had no practical sniping experience, so Russell did what any self-respecting commander would do; he decided to go sniping and find out exactly what the pitfalls were. Armed with Winchester Model 70s and Unertl scopes, he and his gunnys took to the field, Sergeant D. Barker becoming the first US sniper to make a recorded kill in combat in Vietnam. The instructors learned quickly, and within two months they had the basics of a course mapped out. All sniper recruits had to be volunteers, expert riflemen (having qualified by shooting at least a score of 225 out of 250 possible) and be recommended as suitable by their commanding officers. At Hill 327 in Da Nang, a temporary 1,000-yard range was bulldozed and once again artillery units nearby were puzzled by disappearing shellcases.

Shortly afterwards, in September 1966 the commander of the 1st Marine Division ordered Captain Jim Land to train up its own Corps snipers:

> I want you to organize a sniper unit within the First Division. Captain Russell in the third division started training snipers last year. I want mine to be the best in the Marine Corps. I want them killing VC [Vietcong] and I don't care how they do it, even if you have to go out there and do it yourself.[13]

Land took him at his word and with other some experienced gunnys he followed Russell's example, going on sniper missions to learn of the problems the hard way. He had "acquired" a number of excellent instructors/snipers, including Sergeant Reinke and also Sergeant Hathcock, who had at one stage been badly misplaced as a provost sergeant but had still managed to amass a considerable amount of in-country sniping experience. With the help of a skeleton staff, Land was able to set up a school also based near Da Nang.

The urgent need for snipers made three-week courses impractical at first, so initial courses at both schools lasted three days, though this was later extended to a week. Rifles for the 3rd Division school were a hodgepodge of available weapons initially comprising 53 Model 70s, 20 M1Ds, and 58 Unertl scopes, but as Carlos Hathcock commented, they were mostly junk: "We needed something more modern that could and would survive the heat and moisture ... the Winchesters were good sticks in their time but they weren't built for Vietnam. They were built for target ranges and competition back home."[14] Despite the brevity of training, there was little doubt that the program quickly proved effective, for in three months the 1st Brigade's 17 snipers accounted for more enemy than any combat battalion in the Corps and 3rd Brigade had racked up over 60 kills. What the instructors needed now was more of the raw material to turn into trained snipers. Land was interested not only in the mechanics of shooting, but in the psychology of it. At a time when soldiers were expected to kill without compunction and the understanding of mental problems such as Post Traumatic Stress Disorder (PTSD) was in its infancy, he mused over what sort of men made the best snipers and why. It was a question that had bothered British instructors in World War I, and they had found, by trial and error, that "game hunters, trappers, prospectors, surveyors, lumberjacks and poachers"[15] made the best snipers, not Bisley or Camp Perry champions. Why this should be so was questioned by Land, who was particularly interested in what motivated his young volunteers. Mostly, they were men who were confident, self-reliant, and often economical with words (Hathcock records spotting for an entire day with his partner Burke, whose sole words in that time were "There's one" as he spotted a Vietcong). They also had to possess great patience, as well as above-average shooting ability. Neither should they hold any personal animosity towards the enemy, as Land recorded:

There is no hate of the enemy. Psychologically, the only motive that will sustain the sniper is knowing he is doing a necessary job and having the confidence that he is the best person to be doing it. When you look through a scope the first thing you see is the eyes. There is a lot of difference between shooting at an outline ... and shooting at a pair of eyes. Many men can't do it at that point.[16]

The climate precluded the wearing of specialized clothing such as ghillie suits and sweat turned any clothing green or camouflaged black in color, so snipers simply wore their issue green M62 jungle utilities or the four-color leaf pattern camouflage utilities issued from 1968. The heavy M55 or M69 body armor jackets were avoided if at all possible, but sometimes were necessary. They were, as one 9th Division Marine officer said, "hard to live with, and sometimes impossible to live without."

Once on a mission, like all combat soldiers, snipers had to carry everything they required on their backs although most tried to move as lightly burdened as possible:

> The two of us traveled light. I carried a canvas bandoleer containing eighty-four rounds of match grade … ammo, two canteens, a Kabar combat knife, a .45 pistol, compass and map, and a few of the smaller cans of C-rations … Burke carried the same. In addition … we had the Winchester Model 70 … an M14 rifle, binoculars, a radio and a high-powered spotting scope. As soon as we returned from a mission we prepared our gear for the next so that we were always ready to go at a moment's notice.[17]

Longer patrols, of several days' duration, required more: additional rifle ammunition (usually two 84-round bandoliers), haversack (captured Vietcong haversacks were much favored), with cold rations such as tinned meat, crackers, jelly, and peanut butter, which meant avoiding having to light a fire that could give away their positions. They also carried a minimum of spare clothing, a waist belt with two or three water canteens, a pistol and holster with ammunition, and a first-aid pack. Radios were vital for calling in artillery or air strikes, but understandably few wore the flak-jacket unless ordered to, reasoning that their load was heavy enough in tropical heat without adding to it. Conditions were often appalling, with swamps, impenetrable jungle full of razor sharp leaves (these inflicted deep cuts that instantly became infected), leeches, jungle sores, and "bugs so big that they looked like they were right out of a Hollywood movie. Except these bit or stung, or both. I hated the centipedes most, some were a foot long and their bite was like a knife stab."[18]

Lying in their hides, watching and waiting and unable to move other than to stretch stiff limbs, often soaked through or broiled by the sun – the sniper's life was hard on the nerves and body so the sniper teams had to trust and understand each other implicitly. Sniping was a type of fighting that particularly played games with the men's nerves, for the means of waging war practiced by the North Vietnamese and Vietcong were utterly alien to the Americans. Here were no heroic pitched battles, just constant ambushes, hit-and-run raids, clandestine booby-traps, and behind-the-line sabotage.

The situation for infantry and snipers alike was highly problematic, for simply determining who was their enemy was difficult enough, as one officer commented:

When everybody is wearing black pajamas, who do you shoot? Even the North Vietnamese regulars who wear uniforms are not identified by rank. So all we can do is shoot the one who looks different in any way. Our snipers watch the enemy and if we can see one who is giving the orders, we shoot that one. If we see four VC who look identical, but three are wearing black sneakers and one is wearing white sneakers, we shoot the one wearing white sneakers.[19]

This selection policy was unfortunate if you were an innocent Vietnamese farmer with only one pair of sneakers, and it was hardly a scientific way to wage war. If there was one thing the US troops were certain about, though, it was the fact that from the beginning, they were under constant, accurate sniper fire from soldiers they had been told were amateurs incapable of making aimed shots.

The North Vietnamese were actually well ahead of the Americans in terms of training and equipping their snipers. With a plentiful supply of the same scoped ex-Soviet Mosin bolt-action rifles used in Korea, equipped with 4x PE or 3.5x PU scopes as well as some Tokarev SVT40 semi-automatic sniping rifles, they trained volunteers for three months. The course involved every aspect of infantry and guerrilla warfare, as well as normal sniper training. Captured manuals indicate that these courses covered shooting up to 1,000 yards, about the limit for a Mosin, but concentrated on short- to medium-range (200–500-yard) shooting. As no sniper in the field had access to an armorer or workshop, he was instructed in basic gun repair. Spares kits were supplied for each rifle containing springs, screws, firing pins, and scope cleaning kits.

As with their American counterparts, these men considered themselves an elite and competition for places was correspondingly high. The snipers worked in infantry platoons with three squads of ten men each, the purpose of the platoon being in part to protect the sniper. Many snipers were seconded to Vietcong units, to whom they gave basic sniping instruction. This low-level training was one reason that many Vietcong snipers were not as effective as the regular North Vietnamese Army (NVA) men, much to the relief of the US soldiers. One sniper who was hidden near a Marine strongpoint at Hill 811 proved singularly inept:

> This guy had fired as many rounds as his predecessor but he hadn't hit a damn thing. If we blew him away the Vietnamese might replace him with someone who shot straight. My men even started waving "Maggies drawers" at him, a red cloth that we used to signal a miss on the range. He stayed there the whole of the battle – about two months – fired regularly, and never hit a man.[20]

THE REMINGTON RIFLE

The volunteer snipers had to be trained with what was to hand, which were mostly Winchester Model 70s and some old Springfields. The Marines did not accept the M1C or M1D as adequate for serious sniping use, one report even condemning the M14: "M14 rifles with conventional sights were found inadequate for precise long range shooting."[21] In view of the age and wear of their original Winchesters, a number of weapons were rebuilt between 1956 and 1963, at the Marine facility in Albany, Georgia, and all were re-barreled in their original .30-06-caliber chambering. With more snipers taking to the field, the demand for weapons meant that a number of new rifles were also acquired, fitted with 24in medium-heavy barrels mounted on special-order sporting stocks. These were supplied by the now retired Brigadier-General Van Orden via his company, Evaluators Ltd. They were fitted with Redfield match iron sights and often, though not exclusively, Unertl or Lyman scopes. The number that found their way to Vietnam is not proven but over 1,000 Model 70s were purchased and certainly very many of them found their way to Vietnam to serve as quasi-official sniping rifles. The problem of rifle supply was exacerbated when in 1964 Winchester ceased production of the Model 70.

Fortunately in the interim the Marine Weapons Training Battalion at Quantico had been looking hard for a replacement issue sniping weapon. What they needed was:

> … a sniper rifle, not a target rifle. A target rifle is expected to put all its shots into a very small group after some adjustment of the sights. The sniper's rifle must put the first shot of any day into the same spot as the last shot of any day. A sniper gets no sighting in shots and he doesn't intend to put ten shots into the same target.[22]

Certain parameters needed to be met, the Marines stipulating that any sniping rifle must be chambered for the now universal 7.62mm cartridge, have a free-floating barrel with rust-free coating, a stock with integral cheek rest and mounting for a telescopic sight. The best-suited off-the-shelf rifle to meet these criteria appeared to be the Remington Model 700. It had a 24in medium-heavy target barrel, and the action used a tested and reliable Mauser-type locking system. Rifles were slightly modified, being selected only if their barrels met with blueprint dimensions. All barrels were glass-bedded into the stocks and were free-floating, in other words no part of the barrel touched the stock other than where it bolted in at the receiver. The free-floating design was derived from a lesson in accuracy learned many decades before at Camp Perry and the 1,000-yard ranges of Creedmoor. The science of harmonics aimed to prevent any interference with the vibration of the barrel that was generated with each shot, thus ensuring that, theoretically at least, every bullet would be placed identically to the last. Feed ramps were polished to ensure smooth loading of the cartridge into the chamber. The receiver was drilled to enable a strong but simple Redfield mounting base to be fitted for the scope. The close-grained stock was heat and vacuum treated to prevent warping or shrinkage and all parts except the bolt were parkerized. A checkered butt-plate was fitted to prevent slipping and in deference to the rifle's intended role, no iron sights were fitted. A steel magazine and trigger-guard from the Winchester Model 70 was fitted, with triggers adjusted to 4–4^1/$_4$lb, but this could be altered by unit armorers to suit an individual shooter's preference. As usual, finding the correct scope was proving difficult, but a Redfield 3 x 9 Accu-Range variable power unit was eventually selected, finished in matt black. The variable power would, it was hoped, help solve the problems of switching between long- and short-range shooting and the scopes had an internal range scale that helped with judgment of distance. At 9^1/$_2$lb with scope, the new rifle was not overly heavy and it was capable of very accurate shooting indeed with sub-MoA (under 1in grouping) accuracy at 100 yards. As the issue of quality ammunition was always such an important factor, the rifles and scopes were to be used only with 173-grain 7.62mm M118 Lake City National Match ammunition, which had been introduced in the mid-1960s in response to pleas for high-quality ammunition to be supplied to snipers. It was of the quality expected for competitive shooting, where 1,000+ yard accuracy was expected. The new weapon was adopted for service on April 6, 1966, and designated the Model 700, although it was soon given the nomenclature M40. It was to prove a success from day one, and snipers' fears about the rifles being less powerful or accurate than the old Winchesters soon proved groundless. Sergeant Chuck Mawhinney, who was eventually to become the top scoring Marine sniper in Vietnam, discovered the properties of the Remington quite early on:

The armorer issued me a brand-new M40 Remington 700. My part of the Arizona territory [Combat zones were given US friendly code names] was perfect for a sniper, tree lines, rolling hills and rice paddies. One morning I spotted movement at about 1200 meters, it was four VC watching us in a little group. I worked the bolt, setting the scope at a thousand and touched off the first shot, and missed. My spotter called out corrections and my second shot hit the target in a puff of dust and blood. I fired a second round and the other two broke for it and ran to the trees. Later the colonel told me the range was closer to 1500 yards and wrote me a commendation. Really, I was surprised I hit them at that distance.[23]

The very necessary requirement for first-round hit capability meant that, like all snipers, the Marines kept a very close eye on their rifles, rarely letting other soldiers handle them, except possibly other snipers, and all hated having to return them for checking by the unit armorers. No matter how carefully the work was done on a rifle, the smallest alterations to the scope mounting, reticle, or trigger pull meant a stint of re-zeroing. Mawhinney had his checked over and warned the armorer not to alter anything. When it was returned he had to head straight out on patrol without being able to check its zero. Suddenly an enemy soldier appeared 300 yards away:

It was an easy shot, and I centered on his belt buckle and fired. He started and looked up with a sort of "What the fuck ...?" look on his face. I cranked off another round, aiming at the right of the target, but that didn't work. He just stood there. I aimed high, I aimed low and shot dead center, but meanwhile he decided someone must have been shooting at him, so it was in his interest to quit Tombstone. I was really pissed, he should never have got away, but when I checked the zero the rifle was shooting five feet high and off to the right.[24]

If the North Vietnamese were well supplied and trained, for the new Marine snipers life was somewhat more complex. The Corps in the south of the country faced a geographical problem that was quite different from that in the north, which was Army territory. The heavy jungle often made the use of 1,000-yard rifles impossible as dense vegetation and head-high elephant grass blocked out any view except for an immediate few yards. As sniper Ed Kugler said, "It was pretty fruitless to carry a weapon that could shoot for over a thousand yards in jungle where I couldn't see twenty feet."[25] In a firefight the Marines usually needed firepower, not accuracy, and many sniper patrols carried Army M14s, while a few had even managed to beg or borrow suitable scopes. This weaponry gave the teams an impressive level of firepower, with the sniper's partner being able to provide accurate fast-firing backup. On some operations, Marine snipers even elected to carry scoped M14s instead of their Winchesters. Private Gary Reiter, detailed for Hill 51, a renowned hot-spot, stored his bolt rifle: "I went back to the scoped M14 with as much ammo as I could carry. You definitely wanted ammo if you were going to do this kind of work."[26] What they really needed was a light semi-automatic weapon that could be carried in addition to their sniping rifles. Fortuitously, in February 1967 the Department of Ordnance hoped it had solved the problem with the issue of the M16 as the new frontline combat rifle for all armed forces. It was never designed to be used for sniping, for its tiny .223in bullet was too light (53 grains as compared to 150 grains for the US 7.62mm M59 ball) and it had a limited range and poor stopping power at anything over 300 yards. For months, many Marines clung to their M14s, as faith in the new rifle was limited, but eventually most of the old rifles were returned to store. The sniper units were exceptions, for their requirements were different from those of the infantry and most Marine units managed to squirrel away sufficient M14s to satisfy their occasional needs.

THE ARMY GOES SNIPING

While the Marines were organizing themselves to meet the problems of enemy sniping, the Army was still proving obdurate in establishing specialist schools outside of normal military requirements. Nevertheless, from the arrival of the first infantry units in Vietnam, it was patently clear that there was a serious need for trained snipers. Fortunately the Army was not bereft of its own sniping supporters. Lieutenant-Colonel F. Conway had equipped four M14 rifles with M84 scopes in 1958 and one had been used by Captain R. Wentworth with great success to win a world championship in the same year. From the Army's arrival in Vietnam up to 1967, no sniper training at all was provided, but at least some tests had been undertaken by the Ordnance Department at Springfield to determine if it was feasible for the M14 to be successfully adapted to sniping requirements. Conway's mounting system was copied from the M1D and worked well enough, but no further development work was undertaken until the Army was in Vietnam and suffering losses from North Vietnamese snipers:

> We had two men on guard by the bridge when one dropped suddenly, followed by the sound of the rifle. Everyone dived for cover but we didn't know where the hell the shot came from. Charlie had snipers! We didn't and there wasn't a damn thing we could do except pour fire into the treeline opposite.[27]

Although the Army had some platoon sharpshooters, they used issue rifles and without optical sights were no match for the better-equipped Vietnamese. Moreover, they worked as ordinary infantry grunts without the freedom to run the "search and kill" missions that the Marines enjoyed, and this severely limited their operational use while doing nothing to force Vietnamese snipers onto the defensive.

A report commissioned in 1969 into the use and employment of snipers was seriously critical of the Army's lack of trust and understanding in the capability of snipers:

> The role of snipers is not that of other specialists such as mortar teams or machine gunners ... and they are often wrongly employed when used in ambush. The unique capability of the sniper to instill terror through swift, silent, mysterious death is not fully appreciated or capitalized on.[28]

Some senior commanders, in particular Brigadier-General J. S. Timothy and Lieutenant-General Julian Ewell, commanding the 9th Infantry Division in the Mekong Delta, were also becoming increasingly frustrated at the Army's lack of direction, and they began to take matters into their own hands. They were disturbed at the apparent inability of their troops to return accurate fire and Timothy conferred with the Army Marksmanship Unit at Fort Benning. The US Army Marksmanship Training Unit (USAMTU) was also concerned that the shooting training program they had devised was not achieving what was expected. They had adopted a policy called "Trainfire" using the rapid-fire capability of the new M16s, and recruits were taught to shoot at pop-up targets at known ranges, using volume rather than accuracy of fire to achieve a result. Invariably, this meant missing the target if it was moving or was at an unknown range, a normal enough scenario in combat conditions.

After some heated exchanges of correspondence, in July 1968 the USAMTU sent out Major Willis Powell and seven senior NCOs to begin a sniper training program. Powell wanted to do things thoroughly and the team's first priority was for proper ranges to be constructed. While the range work was in progress, an 18-day course was prepared, based partly on the Marines' tutelage. It took four months of hard preparation before students began arriving at the school, although initially the Army's selection process was somewhat convoluted. As a result many potential students failed to make the grade, some 50 percent being washed out. It was November by the time the first course of snipers graduated, 76 men in total, and the Army High Command watched expectantly for results. They were to be sadly disappointed, for by the New Year a mere 19 kills had been registered. The reason was simple, as Private Crosse explained:

Although I trained as a sniper, I was just another dog-faced grunt in the squad, pulling patrols and guard. I didn't even get issued a sniper rifle, only the M16. When we got hit by a VC sniper the lieutenant started yelling for me, but with the M16 I couldn't do anything. I went to the captain and told him sending me on a sniper course then using me as a grunt was stupid. He agreed and I got an immediate issue of an XM-21 which really pissed the lieutenant. He kept putting me on point and it was some weeks before they started pairing us up and really using us for what we'd been trained for.[29]

A report on the failure of the snipers to achieve anything notable was written by Ewell and backed up exactly the comments made by Crosse: "most company commanders could not care less [about snipers]. They just used snipers as any other riflemen. Consequently we directed assignment of snipers to the battalion HQ and held battalion commanders responsible."[30] Faced with the requirement to produce results, line commanders at last began to use their snipers properly, particularly in the counter-sniping role and to remarkable effect; up to April of 1969, 346 enemy were killed by Army snipers, the true number being probably near double that. It was not only the Marines who produced excellent snipers. Sergeant Adelbert Waldron of the 9th Division won two Distinguished Service Crosses for his outstanding shooting, leaving Vietnam with 113 confirmed kills.

The US Army had never been comfortable with the idea of using commercial weapons in any role and having adopted the M16 they looked at trying to utilize it for sniping. The few rifles that were locally modified with the attachment of scopes proved to be only of limited use, one of the problems being the inability of the light bullet to punch through vegetation. Indeed, tests with both the .223in and 7.62mm ammunition proved that while both could be deflected by striking objects such as leaves or twigs at extreme range, the little M16 bullet would actually become ballistically unstable even at close ranges (under 220 yards) by hitting something as fragile as a blade of grass, whereas the bigger M14 bullet was not unduly influenced by anything in its path until it began to lose stability at 550 yards or beyond. Nevertheless, the shortage of suitable sniping rifles did ensure that a few M16s were locally converted by unit armorers into makeshift sniping rifles. If used with a heavier target bullet hits could be registered out to 700 yards, and some snipers used them to good effect in a limited role, but the M16 was never designed for such use and scoped examples remained in the minority.

The answer therefore seemed to lie in adopting a sniper rifle already chambered for the 7.62mm NATO ammunition and the Army had but a choice of one, the M14. In 1966 the Army Weapons Command (AWC) had looked more closely at the work undertaken by Frank Conway and decided it had some merit. Experiments were undertaken to develop a hinged scope mount that was by then quite unnecessary for the M14, for its box magazine had rendered clip-loading redundant. Considerable effort was wasted on the project, and while the AWC did eventually produce a solid, fixed mount using the M1C's Griffin & Howe base and M84 scope (of which there were large numbers in store), it proved an acceptable sniping rifle when used with match-grade M14s. It was only really an interim solution, though, and the AWC continued in its quest to find a more suitable rifle/scope combination.

The USAMTU had faced the same problems in choosing the M14 as the USSR had done in selecting the semi-automatic SVD Dragunov. Choosing any semi-automatic rifle to provide extreme accuracy was fraught with problems, for they had to be hand-built from selected parts to the closest possible mechanical tolerances if they were to prove to be both reliable and accurate. The manufacturing process necessary for the M14 sniper rifles is instructive, showing not only how labor intensive and expensive it was, but to what lengths the USAMTU went in order to ensure the rifles were suitable for issue. It required:

1. Total disassembly.
2. Barrels triple checked for trueness and uniformity of dimension.
3. Barrels installed with perfect headspacing.
4. Internal parts modified to prevent loosening. (Gas pistons were polished as were gas cylinders, which were also welded and internally polished, with all mating surfaces stress-relieved and polished.)
5. Flash suppressors machined and polished to ensure perfect barrel alignment.
6. Removal of all moisture from the stock by means of heat/vacuum then injection of epoxy under pressure to seal the stock, preventing warpage and swelling.

7. Stocks bedded internally to provide a solid mount for the barrel.
8. Triggers polished and adjusted to between $4^1/_2$ and $4^3/_4$lb pull.[31]

At the end of the process the Army had a rifle that was good for 1,000-yard shooting. As proof Sergeant Waldron notched up a spectacular kill with his M14 from a moving boat patrol boat at a range of 1,000 yards, when he shot a Vietcong sniper from a treetop. But the main problem still lay in finding a reliable optical sight, and in this quest the Army was extremely fortunate to have a quiet genius in their ranks. Lieutenant James M. Leatherwood was stationed at the Weapons Department, Fort Benning, and he combined his twin interests in mathematics and shooting to try to solve the eternally vexing problem for snipers of ensuring that their range estimation was exact. Over- or under-estimation at long ranges was sure to result in a missed shot, as snipers had to grapple with not only allowing for bullet drop but also compensating for windage. His solution was simple but effective; he placed a ring with an internal cam in front of the ocular lens on a commercial Redfield 3 x 9 scope, so that the act of turning the power ring automatically adjusted for bullet drop at any range up to 1,000 yards – providing the scope was used in conjunction with M118 match ammunition. In trials in 1967 ten scopes provided to the 9th Division proved successful, snipers reporting first round hits at 650 yards and USAMTU marksmen had achieved 10in groups at 1,000 yards. "All you had to do was turn your scope until your target's picture was dead center, you couldn't miss; the weapon was so easy to shoot it built up our confidence, thinking no target was too far away."[32] With the introduction of a simple but effective quick-release screw mount that used the threaded hole in the left side of the receiver, the combination of M14 and Auto-Ranging Telescope (ART) was adopted and in service by the end of 1968, when the first 50 were built and shipped to Vietnam by the USAMTU. The rifle soon became known officially as the M21. Unlike the Marines, the Army was sold on the benefit of the M21's rapidity of fire and ability to be used with specialist equipment such as silencers or night-scopes, Major Willis Powell even demonstrating his new rifles to the

Marines sniper school. "They have a moving target at 300 meters … and they fire one shot on each pass. I put seven out of seven in the heart area of the target on one pass … [but] they are sold on the bolt-action with the Accu-Range scope.[33]

THE NIGHT WAR

The Army also made considerable use of night-sights, silencers, and suppressors, all of which they found invaluable in Vietnam. Suppressors (as opposed to silencers) muffle the sound of a shot and hide the tell-tale flash of the discharge, but could be used with any service ammunition without affecting performance. Silencers were generally used for clandestine operations or for very short-range sniping, typically at under 200 yards. While they almost totally masked the sound of a shot, they only functioned with special sub-sonic ammunition that drastically limited the range for the shooter, although at night this was not a real issue. "Charlie may have ruled the days, but we ruled the nights. I got most of my kills with my M21 at night and they had no way of fighting us."[34] The development of night optical devices that had begun with the bulky infrared Sniperscope in 1944 had continued through the Korean War when some units were supplied with them for sniping use. By 1961 the Army had developed the T-1 Infrared Weapons Sight, which could fit on both the Garand and M14. No longer powered by a truck battery, but by a small Nicad cell that could be belt mounted, it vastly improved the practicality of such devices. Calls for a more portable unit capable of medium-range combat began to come thick and fast from Vietnam, as the Vietcong used the cover of night to make hit-and-run attacks and generally made the Americans' lives a misery. The system that was developed was the AN/PAS-4 active infrared which actually worked best in total darkness. One early problem was that it magnified any glare from external light sources back into the observer's eyes, temporarily blinding him, so in late 1965 a new device, the AN/PVS-1 Starlight scope was produced by a subsidiary of Xerox, Electro-Ordnance Systems Inc. Development was transferred to the Army Engineer Research Laboratories and an improved version, the AN/PVS-2, was issued, which was to see the most use in Southeast Asia. It was a compact unit by the standards of the time, $17^1/_2$in long, $3^1/_2$in in diameter, and weighing 6lb. It worked in much the same manner as the production of a TV picture, light being trapped by fiber-optic lines, focusing it into a tube with a photo-emissive surface, which magnified the available light by some 40,000 times, making warnings about not looking at bright lights through the Starlight seem rather superfluous. While it did not provide an image of daylight clarity to the sniper, it did give a solid green image that was particularly sensitive at picking out movement.

When allied to the use of a suppressor the M21 became a potent night weapon. The Army snipers were taught to use the scopes at 164, 328, and 656 yards (more officially, 150, 300, and 600m) and unlike the Marines they included night shooting in their syllabus. Private James Gibbore shot 14 Vietnamese sentries one after the other using a Starlight scope, and the Army was able to take on the night infiltrations of the Vietcong on their own terms. Private Crosse recalled his first kill at night:

> I was in the tower [observation tower] when Brunt said "There's something moving, by the gates." I took a look through the starlight and sure enough, there was Charlie, crawling under the wire, dragging a bag. I said "I see him" and steadied the rifle on the sandbags. I took a deep breath which I half exhaled, then lined him up and squeezed the trigger. The rifle went "thud" and recoiled into my shoulder and I got the scope back on target. The VC was lying motionless so we radioed down to the watch office and they decided to leave him there until morning, in case it was a booby trap. When the patrol collected him he had a bullet through the top of the head and was carrying a primed satchel charge. I think that shot was about 425 meters, which was pretty good at night.[35]

THE BEGINNING OF THE END

It was clear from the results of both Marine and Army snipers in Vietnam that having a proper training program more than paid dividends. Intelligence was gathered that would have been impossible to obtain by any other means, often resulting in damaging air or artillery strikes. The enemy were demoralized by the use of snipers and became less confident about showing themselves in day or at night, and rewards were offered to Vietcong or NVA troops for the killing or capture of American snipers. Perhaps most importantly, the morale of the US soldiers was greatly improved by knowing they had their own snipers. At first there had been a palpable animosity towards the newly trained snipers when they returned to their units after training. Because of their novelty, unusual hours of work, and the fact they occupied billets or "hootches" together and not with other infantry or Marines, they were regarded with suspicion, a not uncommon occurrence and similar to the experience of snipers in World War II. Nicknames for them ranged from the hostile, "Murder Incorporated" or "The Assassins," to the more genial, such as "The Hunting Party," "The Headhunters," or, in the case of a squad commanded by a lieutenant from the Midwest, "Craig"s Cowboys." It was noticeable, though, that over time, as the work of the snipers became better understood, the animosity began to disappear:

> Our Lieutenant had been hit by a VC sniper and the boys were real mad. "Get the sonofabitch" "Waste the motherfucker" they hissed as I worked my way forwards … he [the Vietcong] wasn't too bright because he took a second shot just after we had got set up and we both saw the flash from his rifle against the dark foliage. He was across a clearing in a spider-hole so Brunt opened up with the M14 while I worked round. I got to fifty yards of his hide and waited, the scope to my eye. Eventually the lid of the hole lifted, just an inch or two but that was enough, it was the closest shot I ever made. When we got back that night the boys gave us all the beer they had. Jeez, we felt like shit the next morning …[36]

Having established its program, the Army began to turn out snipers at a high rate, and as they filtered back to their units it became apparent that finally they were taking the war to the enemy, rather than waiting to become targets themselves. From January to July of 1969 alone, Army snipers accounted for 1,139 enemy personnel and the Army recognized the value of its rifles by officially adopting the XM21 as its standard sniping weapon, in 1972. Throughout the rest of the war, Army and Marine snipers were widely employed right across the Southeast Asian combat zone, accounting for somewhere in the region of 6–7,000 Vietnamese combatants.[37] Crucially, they embarked on a very fast learning curve, and by the end of the war they were arguably the most experienced military snipers in any military command. In view of future events, this was perhaps just as well.

Chapter 9

A CHANGING WORLD

The military have always been very good at coming up with new terminology to cover any given situation: "friendly fire" to describe the accidental targeting of their own men, "collateral damage" to explain civilian casualties or destruction of non-military targets, and "low intensity conflicts" (LICs) referring to what had previously been known as minor conflicts. The actual number of LICs that have occurred around the world since the end of World War II is shocking, for it has been calculated that there has never been a single day in which a conflict is not in progress somewhere in the world. America has been involved in no fewer than 28 since 1945 and in most of them, at some or other time, snipers have been called upon to utilize their skills.

Increasingly, the form taken by these "small wars" is very specific, involving scenarios that require special tactics to be developed. Aerial bombing of suspected areas or the use of heavy artillery to neutralize resistance are invariably inappropriate, as quite often the "enemy" are local civilian inhabitants, indistinguishable from any others, and their attacks can be unpredictable, very rapid, and often over before any response can be coordinated. In some cases, locally raised forces may be trained and guided by "advisors" from other countries and a very complicated situation may result, as in Angola in the 1970s and 80s or Grenada in 1983. There have been Russian advisors in Cuba, Cuban advisors in Angola, Chinese in Korea and Vietnam, and Syrians in Iraq – the list is almost endless. Exactly how the US military, or any other NATO power for that matter, is to differentiate between friendly and insurgent forces is a conundrum, particularly in the increasingly sensitive 21st century, where the media are constantly poised to point accusatory fingers at what they regard as ineptitude or callousness on the part of intervening forces.

The political situation after the Cold War was novel, with the Western powers initially being perplexed as to the best methods of dealing with the new threat of terrorism. Following the terrorist atrocity of September 11, 2001, it was obvious that the type of threat that America and the rest of the NATO forces were facing had changed dramatically. There was also an increasing necessity for the covert use of their forces outside of localized war zones as foreign powers secretly aided and abetted warring factions. To prevent media intrusion, much of what happened was surrounded by a heavy veil of secrecy as to exactly who was doing what, with whom, and where.

It was during the Vietnam War between 1963 and 1975 that it began to become clear to both the ground forces and the media that there were things occurring in places where they should not, in particular the clandestine use of US Special Forces in supposedly neutral places such as Cambodia and Laos. Snipers also played their part, although they seldom knew exactly where they were being detailed to accompany the Special Forces teams. One Marine sniper was ordered to assist a reconnaissance team that would be inserted into an unspecified location by helicopter, and he was told to take on any suitable targets that presented themselves. When he enquired how they would get out of trouble if they were discovered he was told "There will be no help for you. You are not officially there, get out as best you can."[1] While on the surface there may appear to be something romantic about the notion of the lone sniper on a dangerous mission, the reality was very different. Snipers were particularly detested by the NVA and being caught was a nightmare that haunted all of them. Many simply vanished on missions and their names are recorded along with the many other Missing in Action (MIA) statistics of the war.

After their military service, some ex-snipers found settling into the humdrum routine of civilian life too tame for them and became mercenaries, hiring themselves out to any governments who would pay for their skills. Who they were and where they served is a closely guarded secret but they appeared in the Congo, Angola, Rhodesia, various Arab–Israeli wars, and the Falklands conflict in the 1970s and 1980s, and in Croatia and Bosnia in the 1990s. Most held loyalty only to whoever paid them and many of their employers could see little difference between their acting as military snipers and as paid assassins. One ex-Vietnam veteran, working in West Africa in the late 1970s, was offered a very large sum of money to kill a senior "friendly" general whose loyalty was suspect. He refused on the grounds that he was a paid soldier not a contract killer. For the snipers it was a fine line but an important one, for they needed to believe that the work they did was both professional and also necessary to help save the lives of the comrades they worked with, regardless of their cause. It can be argued that this line existed only in their minds, but belief is nothing if not subjective and most managed to retain their professional integrity. However, when a man becomes an inadvertent sniper, perhaps by being "volunteered" for the job by a senior officer or even falling into the profession by accident, he is often unable to cope with the stress of his chosen profession (although it must be emphasized that the fall-out rate is tiny). This can cause serious long-term problems as snipers struggle to deal with their consciences.

Finding any ex-snipers who were prepared to talk about post-service problems was difficult, but one, called William, did discuss candidly his unusual career as an irregular sniper in a very brutal LIC during the early 1970s.[2] As a young American college graduate he was taking a shoestring holiday on a cruise ship prior to beginning the hunt for a job back in the United States. The ship called into the port of Dakar, Senegal, when he was approached by two English-speaking Frenchmen who suggested they might have some worthwhile employment for him. They asked if he had any particular skills, and were very interested to learn that he had a good knowledge of explosives, gleaned from working with dynamite on the family farm. Their offer was straightforward: in return for an extremely high salary, paid into a Swiss bank account, he would nominally become an employee of the regular Angolan Army. It seemed a crazy arrangement to William, but then the two men started talking about payment in terms of sufficient money to set up the young man very comfortably indeed. Against his better judgment, the lure of adventure allied to a pressing need for hard cash found him agreeing to the terms. Short of money and with college debts to pay, to William it seemed a golden opportunity and he was bundled into a jeep, about to become the least trained irregular sniper in history.

At an army base he was asked to provide proof of his expertise with explosives on an old tree stump. Having blown an unnecessarily large crater ("I used waaay too much dynamite") his future suddenly looked very uncertain. "I was on my own in a strange country and no one knew where the hell I was. If I was shot and buried I would simply have disappeared forever." The worrying situation was resolved when he pointed out to a Portuguese mercenary that he happened to be a very talented long-range competitive shooter. Once they realized he knew far more about rifles than explosives, they offered him employment to shoot. The snag was that his battlefield was Angola, at the height of the bloody and complicated civil war of 1973:

> The men told me I would be supplied with everything I needed, weapon, clothing, maps, food and dropped behind the Angolan lines by helicopter. I'd then target "anyone white" as these were invariably Cuban or Soviet advisors helping the Angolan rebels. After a two-week mission wreaking as much havoc as I could, I would return on foot to one of the friendly Angolan camps to be resupplied and have some rest. In the meantime I would have to evade rebel search parties, fend for myself and live pretty much a totally nomadic life.

For most snipers, there is a period of instruction that mentally settles them into the profession they have chosen. They are trained to kill and accept what they do as an inevitable part of their chosen profession. For William, this process never happened:

I was taken to a military camp and then kitted out with everything. Military fatigues with no insignia, haversack, maps, binoculars, food packs, everything. My first rifle was a commercial Winchester Model 70 with a long Unertl scope on it. It was at least a scope I was familiar with.

Within a week he was in the bush, totally unprepared and about to make his mark in his own small private war. "It was a very hard learning curve, I had to master bush camouflage, work out escape routes, learn to lie still and just observe for hours at a time. I got crawled over and bitten by things science has no name for." His savior took the form of the grizzled Portuguese mercenary he had first met, who passed on all of his hard-learned experience. "Without him I would have died really fast in the bush. He took me under his wing and it was due to him that I survived my first few weeks." Working in the bush was grueling, physically and mentally:

I didn't wash at all for the two weeks I was working, soap smells a mile off and the locals didn't use it. It was hotter then Hades all the time and the best I could do was wash my fatigues in a river by bashing them with a rock occasionally. It was easy to lose all track of time, so every day I knotted a piece of twine until it had fourteen on it.

William began to take a steady toll of "foreign advisors" and he soon learned the wisdom of doing nothing even when a good target had appeared. "It often was not worth compromising myself for the sake of an easy shot, although there were times when I over-rode my own judgment." After deciding two Cubans were too tempting a target to let go, he killed both in three seconds then was taken by complete surprise as a hidden mortar team began to pound the hillside he was on. Another time he was heading back to his base when a Soviet Hind gunship appeared from behind a hill and roared over him, fortunately failing to spot him in the bush. It was a lonely existence fraught with troubles:

... supply was my major problem. I was always short of water and on more than one occasion someone else's canteen saved me. If possible I would go through the effects of someone I had killed to see if they carried anything worthwhile such as medicine, purification tablets or just food.

His weapons were suspect too, the Winchester scope having been poorly mounted – he had to use up precious ammunition to re-zero it. "The ammunition supply was never guaranteed, what I got was sometimes years old and had been stored God-knows-where or for how long." He always tried to get as close as possible to guarantee a shot, but this was tempered by the need to ensure he could get away and also avoid the skilled trackers who accompanied the rebels. "Ranges were an absolute minimum of two hundred yards up to a max of around eight hundred."

What was most difficult for William to come to terms with, though, was the rationale for his employment:

I didn't really know who my employers were; though I was paid by the Angolans I had no idea who was backing them and I was never sure who I was targeting. Normally it was pretty clear they were rebels, but they would often fraternize with regular army troops and camp together. The French were helping the regular army and so were the Americans. I shot Cubans and Russians but never anyone in Portuguese uniform or kids, even if they were armed.

When his Portuguese mentor left the unit, he was given a young American as a partner. "He knew nothing about anything and he was a liability who was going to get us killed. I eventually stopped working with him and went out alone most for the rest of my time." His return to a rest camp meant a debriefing:

Who had I seen, where were they, who had I shot? The rest camps were mainly in Rwanda and were small outfits run by warlords. These guys were not rebels, they were using Angola for its wealth, diamonds were plentiful and oil was being discovered. The warlords would trade sides for money and run drugs, diamonds, anything. Politically, they didn't give a shit.

The uncertainty of his existence began to play on his mind:

> Always in the back of my mind was the knowledge that if I was caught, they
> would make sure I had a long, lingering death and I always had a loaded
> pistol on me to make sure I wasn't captured alive. I kept a single round with
> a notched bullet in my shirt pocket, so I could even find it in the dark.

When William's aged Renault car, which was looked after by a local family
in Dakar, was the target of a bomb which destroyed it and the driver, he
decided enough was enough. "I had done a year in-country and I decided to
go before someone terminated my contract with another bomb, or simply
shot me in the back one day." He left everything he owned in his hotel and
slipped away by local bus and boat, eventually making his way to Europe,
where he went into hiding for two years. As an irregular he had become a very
skilled sniper, but he had been killing with no ideology to back up his work
and few friends or comrades to help justify what he did. The psychological
impact on him was devastating. "I spent the next ten years paranoid and totally
screwed-up and I guess it took twenty years or so for me to come to terms
with that."

His comments about his likely fate in the event of capture had long
antecedents, harking back to the Revolutionary War days when American
riflemen were likely to be bayoneted by British troops if caught. Throughout
the years, the attitude toward the captured sniper had changed very little.
During the Falklands War of 1982, British paratroopers were pinned down
by very accurate shooting from a rock outcrop at Goose Green. They took
casualties but were unable to dislodge the snipers. Their own snipers managed
to retaliate and ensure that the Argentinean troops kept their heads down,
while the Paras advanced. After a brief close-quarter fight with entrenched
infantry, the two snipers were captured:

> … they had proper commercial scoped rifles and they had caused some heavy
> losses but neither spoke Spanish – they spoke English with American accents
> but didn't say much. They knew we were pissed off with them. Some of the

lads took them away and we never saw them again. We all knew they were killed, but no one spoke about it.[3]

Certainly, some ex-Vietnam snipers found it impossible to settle down to a life of dull routine, and they craved the excitement of combat. One, an Army sniper of Mexican extraction, said that:

After bustin' my guts for a year in Nam, the army kicked me out, like: "You done what we want, we don't need you no more, get lost." Well, I was pretty screwed up – most of us were, so I thought "Well fuck you, I'm gonna keep fighting for who the hell I want," so I did.[4]

He went to South America and fought in El Salvador and Nicaragua between 1979 and 1982, where his knowledge of jungle fighting was invaluable:

We got given all kinds of shit to do, take out some paymaster or general or spook, mostly we didn't know who the hell we were shooting, but as long as I got paid, I didn't much care. I guess some were "advisors" and could have been American, Russian, anything. It was tough, as tough as Nam, and we didn't have the backup that the US military provided. If you got sick or wounded, your squad were your only way out. If they hated your guts, they left you and you were a dead SoB. Mostly it was run and hide warfare, like we'd get dropped near our target, do what we did then get out as best we could. There were a few of us contractors [mercenaries] and we kept pretty tight. The other guys, mostly young dudes, didn't understand us and said we were crazy to do this for money. I guess we were, but I guess I was suffering with PTS [Post Traumatic Stress] so nothing made much sense. Mostly it was OK till we were on R&R then it got harder and harder to cope. Drugs were easy, they cost like nothing and I had a bad habit. Eventually I just stopped to function, combat left me unmoved, I would kill without compunction. I just didn't give a fuck. One day my buddy Carlos told me it was time to get out. So we both just walked into the jungle and headed for the border. In the US we did time for drugs and all sorts of shit and man, it took years to get my head straight. I don't even drink beer now. I look at what I did and it's another world, another person, it wasn't me. I was lucky, so, so lucky, I got a life back.

In the wake of the Vietnam War, the US military was at last taking a more professional approach to the use of snipers and their equipment, and the adoption by the Army of the accurized M14 as their official sniping rifle was certainly a step in the right direction. Yet there was still some disquiet about the use of a semi-automatic weapon, with its consequent cost and complexity. Keeping them functioning properly in Vietnam had eventually required National Match armorers being drafted in to ensure the rifles were repaired to the specifications needed to ensure accuracy and reliability. Nevertheless, the USAMTU had finally learned that there was no substitute for training soldiers to shoot their rifles accurately, and marksmanship courses were reinstated to ensure a better standard of general shooting. Meanwhile, regular army snipers were also doing what they were paid for in a number of remote places around the world, with the Army taking an active role in LICs in places such as Beirut (1980s), Grenada (1983), Somalia (1992–94), Bosnia (late 1990s), Afghanistan (2001–), and Iraq (1990–91, 2003–). Every location was different and each held its own surprises, with the snipers needing to learn quickly and absorb new lessons, particularly as many of these actions were now no longer considered straight military intervention, but were termed "policing" or "peacekeeping." As a political consequence, rules of engagement for all troops, and snipers in particular, had become far more complex since the days of white sneakers in Vietnam, where the orders were simply, "If the enemy is holding a rifle, shoot him."

In the face of increasingly unrealistic demands for political correctness, and with no little influence from the media, the requirements to ensure that no one ever became the victim of "collateral damage" meant that restrictions were placed on the rules of engagement that bordered on the ludicrous. Many snipers witnessed appalling atrocities, without being able to respond. One Marine sniper in Lebanon in the 1980s was forced to watch a whole company of unarmed Lebanese soldiers being massacred in cold blood. Another team coming under fire in Beirut in 1983 was denied permission to return fire, as no one could find an officer senior enough to give his authority. Fortunately other NATO peacekeeping troops serving alongside the Americans did not require such a convoluted system and simply shot back, usually to great effect. In Beirut one frustrated Marine sniper commented that "We aren't keeping the peace, the Israelis are – they got loaded weapons. The ragheads know they'll get their asses shot off if they pull anything with them."[5] In practice the rules of engagement became so restrictive that it was all but impossible to retaliate and this had the unconsidered effect of making the Americans favorite targets. Troops in "safe" compounds were the target of suicide bombs, as happened at the US Embassy during the Marines' tenure in Beirut (1982–84). They were continually subjected to random fire directed at them from distant buildings, the high-angle bullets plunging into the area, injuring men and causing chaos. After one compound in Beirut was particularly heavily targeted the snipers were finally given the go-ahead to discourage the shoot-and-run gunmen and a pair of Marine snipers took to their hide on the rooftop. Eventually a Lebanese gunman appeared on a rooftop and emptied his AK magazine in the direction of the compound. Not only was he not expecting retaliation, but at 900 yards' distance he believed he was safe. A single shot from the sniper dropped him in his tracks. A companion, puzzled by the sudden silence from the roof, then appeared and also dropped as a bullet found its target. The sniper relaxed behind his M40A1, but not for long. His observer said, "Oh, oh, there's number three." The third man looked at his two comrades then raised a clenched fist at the Americans and a third shot dropped him. The two snipers exchanged wordless glances, then the observer stiffened, as a fourth man appeared, examined the bodies and looked around him in puzzlement. He too dropped as the sniper fired. At dusk a US patrol entered the building and recovered their weapons.[6]

Elsewhere, fellow Marines simultaneously engaged in an LIC a long way from the desert were facing different problems. The island of Grenada had become a political hot-spot in the early 1980s as Cuban "advisors" had occupied the island. This situation was being seen not only as an acute political embarrassment, but also as a potentially destabilizing influence in the Caribbean, so in October 1983 Army and Marine troops landed on the remote island, the Marines thundering ashore in a textbook beach landing. Few thought they would meet much in the way of resistance, but they were wrong. They were also surprised by the number of Cuban snipers who were very professional and well armed. They soon began to make life very difficult for the advancing US troops. A Marine platoon had been pinned down by one such sniper who had forced them to take cover on the outskirts of a town. The sniper's fire was preventing them crossing the open stretch of land in front and the inexperienced soldiers instinctively to͟   ͞ m the hidden menace. This began to have a ripple effect as the advancing troops on their flanks also began to falter and the entire action was in danger of grinding to a halt. The call "sniper up" quickly came:

"The Lieutenant's got to get on, he can't let one shooter hold up everything."

"Well this is no ordinary guy over there, Hell, he's getting off round like he has a machine-gun."

"He's accurate too, nobody's up staring but us."

The sniper was concentrating on his telescopic sight. "Now if I was over there I might just slip into that shadow ... then I'd put a round right up this way."

The sniper waited with outward patience. The observer said "He's down near there, I got a glimpse of him moving."

CRACK. The Remington bucked a little in recoil. The sniper was already working the bolt ... just as a long rifle barrel poked onto sight ... a fatigue-sleeved arm flopped into the sunlight and lay motionless.

"Signal the Lieutenant that we got the guy."

"He's already moving."

"You just want to police up that sniper's rifle. It's got a scope on it."

"It's a Dragunov, we've studied them."

"I didn't know Cuba had them."

"Well they don't have this one anymore."[7]

At the short ranges they were often firing at, the American Marine snipers suffered from a recurring problem of being unable to use their scopes, although the variable power did prove useful when their magnification was reduced to its minimum 3x, sufficiently low to deal with most relatively close-range targets. Even so, sharpshooting at very close ranges was left to the infantry, the snipers being unable to obtain rapid enough target definition through their scopes.

At entirely the opposite end of the spectrum, Army Rangers of the 75th Infantry Regiment not far away from the Marines on the island were using their M21s to silence enemy mortar teams at ranges in excess of 900 yards at Point Salinas:

> The Rangers experienced heavy and accurate mortar fire from the Cuban positions and a sniper team were ordered up. They managed by accurate fire to silence the Cubans and drive off the mortar teams, killing eighteen enemy in the process. As a result resistance collapsed enabling the Regiment to advance and secure the position.[8]

THE ARMY REEVALUATES

Having officially adopted the XM21 as its service sniper rifle in 1972, the Army had been reasonably happy with its performance, although many rifles were now beginning to show their age. At the start of 1976, as a result of requests from the Airborne Divisions, the USAMTU began a program of refurbishment for the 342 M21 rifles stored at Fort Benning. Whether refurbishment of these weapons was the best long-term route to take was a problem for the Department of Ordnance, so a series of comparative tests were undertaken with some of the best contemporary rifles to see if there were any worthwhile gains to be made from selecting a new rifle. The rifles tested were:

1. Issue M21.
2. Accurized M14 with M84 scope.

3. M14 National Match rifle with Redfield 3 x 9 scope.
4. M16 with 3 x 9 Leatherwood/Realist scope.
5. French FRF-1 with Model 53 4x scope.
6. AR10 with a Dutch 3x Artillerie Inrichtengen scope.
7. Winchester Model 70 with Weaver 3x scope.

The results were not too surprising, with even accurized M14s being capable of good shooting, commonly achieving sub-two minute (2in) ten-shot groups at 100 yards with an effective range of 700 yards. The test board's conclusion at the time was that there were "no significant differences between the test items and the standard M21 from an accuracy standpoint."[9] Moreover, a second crucial point was also raised, namely that "The test soldiers unanimously reported that they preferred a semiautomatic sniper rifle with externally loaded magazine."[10] These results effectively ensured that the M14-derived semi-auto sniping rifles would remain as the Army's primary sniping weapon for the foreseeable future.

However, the Army was well aware that there were always going to be limitations placed on the long-range capabilities of the M21, as well as consequential problems with maintenance. There had also been some complaints from the Airborne Division over the damage the rifles sustained when used in airborne operations. The question posed was in what direction were they to go when the M21 eventually reached the end of its service life? Did they replace it with an uprated model, a new semi-automatic rifle, or even a bolt-action weapon? There were other considerations, too, such as the inevitable costs and delays involved in the sourcing of a new weapon and the selection of a suitable scope. The M21 continued in service for over a decade, but in March 1985 a survey was sent out to Army units to compile information on their requirements for a sniping rifle, with the aim of understanding exactly what was demanded of a new weapon. It was soon clear that for producing the level of accuracy that snipers now demanded, a bolt-action rifle would be the primary choice for the Army. The major contender to provide this was the Remington Arms Corporation, which had so much experience in supplying the Marines with their M40s.

Remington duly set up an evaluation team to try to work out the major parameters for production of a new weapon. "The team defined seven major items for considering the rifle action: the rifle action, the stock, the scope, a carrying case for the system, iron sights, ammunition."[11] The new rifle was a long-action Model 700 rifle capable of chambering rounds such as the .300in Winchester Magnum or more potent .338in Lapua. A Kevlar-based stock was selected with adjustable butt-plate, and it was designed to be ambidextrous, thus eliminating the need for left-handers to perform prone gymnastics when shooting. It was also non-slip, non-reflective, and had built-in aluminum bedding blocks to ensure perfect barrel fit. The stainless-steel barrels were originally sourced from a private contractor, Rock Barrel Company of Wisconsin, although Remington eventually took over production, interestingly adopting the same rifling as used in the prolific AK-47 rifles. The trigger block was the same as used in the M40 and the magazine held five rounds. The magnification of the old scopes was deemed insufficient, particularly if .300 or .338in ammunition was to be used. Besides, experience showed that virtually all snipers set their 3 x 9 power scopes up to the maximum magnification for shooting, so a fixed Ultra M-3A 10x scope made by Leupold-Stevens was selected. This was a whole new generation of optical sight, filled with nitrogen to eliminate fogging. It had separate focusing and it utilized a radical new reticle pattern, termed Mil-dot, which enabled the shooter to calculate with considerable accuracy the range to his target. In addition range and elevation drums were fast-action so that adjustments could be carried out from 100 to 1,000 yards with one turn of the dial. As if this were not impressive enough, the mounting rail on the rifle was designed to enable the scope to be mounted and dismounted with, as Remington quoted, "less than one-half MOA change in zero."

Remington managed to produce the first prototype, called the Sniper Weapons System or SWS, for testing on October 13, 1987, followed by 100 others, and after exhaustive trials the government approved the rifle in July 1988, to be called the M24. Considering how long it had taken the Army in the past to decide upon and then produce a new rifle this was extraordinarily rapid. The Army report on the weapons was factual, but positive. "The SWS will exceed in test the Government specification of achieving 1.3 inches Average Mean Radius [AMR] at 200 yards and 1.9 inches at 300 yards based on five targets of ten shots each."[12] In tests several snipers achieved sub-12in groups at 1,100 yards.

The rifles, complete with all accessories, were initially $3,980 each although by 2002 this had risen to almost $6,000. It was a far cry from the days of supplying a modified service rifle, and it gave the Army snipers a new edge. Their sniper deployment was also following a different pattern, for the Army had decided to use not only dedicated snipers, but also selected marksmen within each infantry platoon, who usually carried an M21 sniping rifle and could provide accurate medium-range shooting in support of their infantry. Although not technically classified as snipers, many achieved very good kill rates with their weapons. If it were needed, proof of the benefit of the Army's insistence on the use of a semi-automatic sniping weapon came about during a peacekeeping action in Somalia.

In 1993 confused and brutal warfare had broken out in Somalia and a US intervention force was sent in. Two 1st Special Forces Delta Force snipers, sergeants Gary Gordon and Randall Shughart, used their skills to lay down covering fire to protect the crew of a downed helicopter, Shughart's M21 accounting for up to 30 attackers as he fired from the floor of a hovering helicopter. Their request to be landed to protect the surviving aircrew was a suicide mission, but the commanding officer Colonel Harrell took the difficult decision to drop them in. The two snipers fired steadily and competently, downing Somali insurgents with every shot. It was like trying to stem a river, however, as word spread about the downed helicopter. The badly injured surviving pilot, Mike Durant, recalled afterwards: "I heard Gordon cry out as if he'd been stung by a bee, 'Damn, I'm hit.'"[13] He died where he lay next to the wreck. Meanwhile, running perilously low on ammunition, Shughart was no longer being helped by the guns of the hovering chopper, which had been struck by a rocket-propelled grenade (RPG) and was forced to crash land. He walked over to the disabled Durant and handed him Gordon's CAR15 assault rifle, wishing him "good luck."

After two minutes of furious shooting, which echoed around the buildings like a drum, Shughart cried out once and silence fell. Against all the odds, Durant survived 11 days of captivity, the only member of the crew to live. A report on the fight concluded that in the region of 500 Somalis had been killed during the fight, a large percentage falling to the very fast and accurate shooting of the two sergeants. For their part in protecting Durant at the cost of their own lives, sergeants Gordon and Shughart were both awarded the Congressional Medal of Honor.

There was little doubt that the Army's rifles and their snipers were more than fulfilling their role. However, the old M21 was at the end of its life expectancy, but the requirement still existed for a semi-automatic that was capable of assisting the sniper teams to provide fast and accurate back-up, particularly in urban environments:

> The army had the M24 ... then we came along with the .50 caliber, the M-107 ... then units came along with a new requirement. They were looking for [the ability to engage] light-skinned materiel targets as well as personnel with 7.62 mm. They were also looking for a weapon that would be good in a close urban fight as well.[14]

As a result, the Armament Research and Development Center (ARDEC) staff at Picatinny Arsenal were tasked at the start of the 1990s with finding a suitable replacement. The specifications issued to prospective suppliers were detailed. The new rifle had to be: "Accurate to a range of 1000 meters, be man portable, utilizing military M118LR and M993 7.62 x 51mm ammunition ... with a detachable bipod, flash/sound suppressor, high capacity box magazine ... rails mounting surface for fire control [optical scope, aiming light, variable power optics/electro-optics] and night vision capability." Furthermore, it had to have accuracy that was "equal to or greater than the M24 SWS ... and be less than or equal to 1 MOA."[15] In addition, a complete set of cleaning kit, tools, and a carry case had to be supplied with each weapon.

The competition came down to three finalists, Remington, Armalite, and Knight Armament based in Florida. An interesting requirement was that the new rifle had to be specifically tailored for use with the new M118 Long Range ammunition as well as the M993 armor-piercing round. This requirement has been a particular response to lessons learned in Afghanistan, where fighting the Taliban has become progressively harder, and also by the combat requirements of fighting in Iraq and other parts of the Middle East. As Lieutenant-Colonel K. Stoddard of the US Army Test and Command board pointed out:

> The enemy gets smarter. Targets don't stand up and stay there. They get behind things and learn to expose themselves for a few seconds and then they drop down and move again. And when the insurgents come, it may be one, two, three or four guys, they come as multiple targets. [The sniper] may have to shoot through glass or to stop a vehicle by putting rounds into its engine block. It may be that he needs to take a first and second shot before the target can react.[16]

In view of these prerequisites the XM110 Semi-Automatic Sniper System (SASS) was eventually chosen, based on a successful MKII design already in use by Navy Seals, and at the time of writing 15 weapons are undergoing testing at the ATEC base at Fort Drum, New York. The XM is chambered for the 7.62mm NATO cartridge, and is loosely based on the design of the AR10, the predecessor of the AR15/M16 family. It has a free-floating 20in barrel and a specially cast receiver to keep the weight as low as possible. Variable length butt-stock, quickly detachable scope and mounts, with a Leupold Vari-X Mil-dot scope and back-up iron sights, are also fitted. As standard, a bipod, sound suppressor and 5-,10-, and 20-round magazines are supplied. The XM will shoot sub-MoA groups at 100 yards, a far cry from the M1C. As of early 2007, the first of these rifles is now in limited operational use. The price reflects the technology and development, however, for each weapon costs in the region of $7,000. Although it was thought initially that these rifles would replace the M24 it appears that they will be issued in parallel, thus providing the Army with the best of both worlds.

THE MARINES' ROUTE

As far as the Marines were concerned, there was no immediate question of changing their M40s. Some 995 had been issued between 1966 and 1971[17] at a unit cost of $1,114.64. Bearing in mind they were primarily designed as target and hunting rifles they had proved surprisingly durable. By the mid- 1970s, however, they were becoming tired. In 1977 an improved model, the M40A1, was devised that did away with the wooden stock and used instead a McMillan fiberglass, epoxy-bedded stock that was self-colored in a camouflage pattern that would not rub off. The trigger-guard and magazine floor plate of the Remington, which had proved troublesome in the field, were replaced by a Winchester Model 70 pattern, which strengthened the receiver and provided a more user-friendly magazine. The barrel was a 24in commercial stainless-steel Atkinson, free-floating as was the norm, and the work of assembly and testing was done by USAMTU in Quantico, Virginia.

Possibly the most significant change was in the optical system. The old Redfield Accu-Range was conceived as a hunting scope, and it was to its credit that it stood up to the harsh conditions inflicted on it in Southeast Asia. The biggest problems were internal misting, caused by humidity (though this was by no means unique to the Redfield), reticle breakage, and lens separation due to heat, recoil, hard handling, or simply a combination of all three. After considerable testing, including a new variant of the ART scope, the Marines went back to a name that was very familiar to many of them, Unertl. The new-generation MST-100 scope chosen was very different from the elegant long tube of World War II. It was a fixed 10x power with a steel body, powerful enough to deal with the ranges the rifles were capable of shooting out to, with adjustment turrets for windage and elevation marked in click adjustments of $1/2$ MoA, equating to $1/2$in adjustments at 100 yards. Small improvements were made, such as brazing the lower ring mounts onto the mounting base, thus eliminating any possibility of the mounts twisting. The new rifles, designated the M40A1, were capable of one MoA accuracy, which translated to 1in grouping at 110 yards (100m). Sure of their weapon's capability, the Marine Corps Rifle team took their new rifles to Romania to take part in the Cap Match, and won.

The M40A1 began to replace the old rifles from early 1978. As weapons rotated through the MTU at Quantico they were uprated, and by late 1983 all M40s had been converted to M40A1 specification. The use of the Remington was not all plain sailing, though, for there had been inevitable troubles, including some rifles produced with off-center bores, breaking bolt handles, scope mounting problems, and lack of adjustment on the stock to allow for shooters of different physical characteristics:

> I liked the M40A1, it was a good rifle but the scope was always wrong for me and I used to wrap a bandage pad round the stock to raise my cheek. It was supposed to be a 1000 meter rifle but mine was never capable of reliable shooting at that range and I used to get problems with case ejection. Sometimes it just didn't pull the old case out at all and I had to use a blade to extract it. It went back to the shop [armorer] for adjustment and they gave me another, which was way better. I think quality control varied a lot with them.[18]

It was almost inevitable that the M40 would be uprated before long and in early 1996 the M40A3 began to materialize. It still used the same basic 7.62mm short action but was equipped with a Schneider 610 stainless heavy match-grade barrel, and fiberglass stock, with a newly designed Schmidt & Bender 3-12 x 50 scope, and custom designed trigger, trigger-guard, and scope mounts by the D. D. Ross Company. All of which gave a new lease of life to the Remington, improving its accuracy and function albeit with the penalty of a weight increase, up 2.2lb on the old M40A1 to a substantial 16^1/$_2$lb. Testing showed it capable of 4in grouping at 870 yards and even with a silencer fitted it is able to group 5in at 330 yards.

It became operational in early 2001 and has seen considerable service since. Desert conditions in Operation *Iraqi Freedom* have been a tough test of the Remington, but it has acquitted itself well:

> In the Humvee I carried an M16 for suppressive fire and for precision fire the latest scoped rifle ... the M40A3. When we came to road blocks ... word

went back for "snipers up!" The sniper's task was to engage Iraqis manning the roadblocks at long range – 600 to 700 yards, out of range of enemy AK's – with "precision fire."[19]

Unlike the fighting in Lebanon, in Iraq the Marines are no longer encumbered by restrictions on how they operate, and current rules of engagement state that as long as their targets are armed, or if they are attacked first, then they are permitted to return fire. Physical conditions for the snipers, in fact for all troops, are hard, with little sleep, less water, the most basic of food, and a punishing requirement to wear the heavy Kevlar flak jackets in oppressive heat. For much of the early campaign the troops appeared to do little but chase fleeing Iraqis. Eventually the running stopped and some Marines found themselves on the receiving end of enemy fire, but the US soldiers were fighting troops who had little concept of the role of snipers, something that Marine Sergeant Joshua Hamblin had firsthand experience of:

A lone Iraqi soldier, an officer, turned the corner and began walking towards the base. He wore a full uniform ... he probably thought his people still occupied the base, for he strode along as if he were going to work. I set my scope on him and followed him ... an old man dashed from one of the houses ... the old man tagged after him, waving his arms and jumping up and down with frustration. I imagined the old man yammering "Get out of here! They'll kill you." The soldier shrugged a last time, still not understanding ... I squeezed the trigger. It was a perfect shot. I watched the vapor trail of the bullet through the scope as it flew straight into the center of his chest. It impacted with a little puff of dust. His face contorted in pure shock. He looked down at the bullet hole in his chest before he slumped to the ground, still surprised.[20]

Hamblin and his partner Mulder accounted for 32 enemy soldiers in one day. "Mulder and I just watched the show, awed. We – just the two of us – were responsible for all this?"[21] The improvements to the Remington have ensured it will continue as the Marines' front-line sniping rifle for the foreseeable future, but such modifications have proven to be merely the tip of the iceberg in terms of technological advancement, for sniping was about to get much, much bigger.

SIZE MATTERS

While it had become clear that the rifles and scopes in service were a perfectly adequate combination for jungle or urban actions, the emerging threat from within the Middle East and Afghanistan posed a new set of challenges for the sniper, for ranges were almost unlimited and rifles capable of over 1,000-yard shooting were required. As a consequence, ARDEC at Picatinny was tasked with finding a suitable weapon to cope with the long-range requirements. Developing one from scratch was clearly unfeasible in terms of cost and time, so it took its lead from the Marines and looked at weapons that were already commercially available and had known properties in terms of reliability, accuracy etc. ARDEC was sure that before long, larger calibers would be the way forwards for this specialized form of sniping, so they looked to history to help provide an answer. The early experiments in Korea and Vietnam with big-bore rifles such as the .50-caliber Browning and .55in Boys converted for sniping had greatly impressed the people involved, who appreciated that the potential of such weapons was truly colossal.

The problem was in transferring this enthusiasm to the military high command. Post-Korea, between December 1953 and June 1954 the Army Ordnance Corps under the aegis of Major Brophy had also conducted some exhaustive trials on all of the available heavy sniping weapons, including a modified PTRD antitank rifle fitted with both light and heavy .50-caliber M3 BMG barrels and a 20x Unertl scope. Its performance was a surprise to all who participated, for at 600 yards it achieved a mean average 50-round group of 8.63in, as compared to an M1D's 11.4in and the Winchester Model 70's 5.26in. At 1,000 yards it averaged ten-shot groups of between 13.7in and 22.2in while at 1,400 yards it hit a 12ft x 12ft panel with 49 out of 50 shots.[22] The subsequent report concluded that:

It is apparent that the utilization of the heavy-barrel with the caliber .50 sniper rifle improves its inherent accuracy, giving it dispersion characteristics comparable with the Winchester M70 rifle. In addition the flat trajectory, long range and small wind deflection of the caliber .50 M2 ball make the comparisons between .30 caliber and caliber .50 weapons more favorable to the latter as range increases.[23]

There were logistical problems, however, which at the time were difficult to overcome. With a heavy barrel fitted, the rifle weighed an arm-wrenching 43lb, was 69in long and possessed, as the test recorded, an "objectionable" recoil. These shortcomings needed addressing before the rifle could be considered for service, but solutions were not long in coming. There was certainly no problem with the ammunition – the original M2 .50in bullet weighed in at a hefty 759 grains (compared to 174 grains for a .30-06 M1 bullet) and it generated a massive 12,570ft/lb of energy, with a maximum range of about 7,000 yards. In practical terms, there was little that could stop it apart from heavy armor, and it was devastating against soft-skinned targets such as vehicles, aircraft, and command positions. Experience in Vietnam had taught the military that killing the enemy, while good psychologically, was not always the most efficient policy. Wounding was calculated to require eight other personnel (field medics, ambulance drivers, doctors, nurses) with the associated cost, but even more damaging was targeting materiel. This simple tactic had been discovered by German snipers in World War I; shoot a machine-gunner and another would replace him, but destroy the gun and all the gunners in the world are of no practical use. Vietnam saw the beginnings of an extension of this policy of inflicting materiel damage by targeting the North Vietnamese and Vietcong's fragile technology, which was sparse and valuable. Everything that was lost to them required a great deal of effort and energy to replace, and while at the time it was only occasionally possible to put this theory into practice, after the war it was quickly appreciated that the application of a specific policy of targeting war materiel could be greatly assisted by the use of special long-range weapons.

The logic behind this shift was inescapable, for a $1.50, .50-caliber round, fired through the jet engine of a parked-up fighter rendered over $10 million worth of aircraft instantly redundant. Thus in the late 1970s much development work was undertaken to try to produce a weapon that was not overwhelmingly heavy for infantry or snipers to carry, did not generate the terrifying recoil that was associated with such calibers, yet had all the ballistic capability required to ensure it was as accurate, powerful, and practical as possible. While the big .50in Browning machine gun was used on many occasions as a pro tem sniping weapon it was neither man-portable nor particularly accurate unless very carefully set up and heavily sandbagged in place, effectively making it a permanent and thus vulnerable fixture. While Carlos Hathcock uniquely achieved a kill in Vietnam with a Browning at 2,500 yards, such feats were very rare indeed, mainly due to the weapon having being specifically designed for rapid fire in a static or vehicle-mounted role.

If ultra-long-range shooting (in excess of 1,000 yards) was needed, then a dedicated rifle had to be developed, so in the early 1980s it fell to Colonel D. Willis, the commander of the Weapons Training Battalion (WPNSTB) to find a rifle that met Marine requirements. Fortuitously enough, the very weapon they needed was then being developed in the small town of Murfreesboro in Tennessee for long-range target use. An American company named Barrett Firearms Manufacturing had made a short-recoil operated semi-automatic .50-caliber rifle that was compact enough at 57in and light enough at $28^1/_2$lb to be man-portable. More importantly, perhaps, it would fire any extant type of .50-caliber ammunition (ball, armor-piercing, tracer) as far as, if not further than, the shooter could see. In fact, it was capable of out-shooting any optical device then available, with the possible exception of the powerful but impractically fragile 20x or 40x benchrest scopes. There was a downside to this power, of course, for the laws of physics cannot be sidestepped and for every action there is an equal and opposite reaction. In the case of the .50-caliber cartridge, the recoil forces generated were punishing, so the new rifle had both an internal spring and buffer assembly (in miniature similar to the type employed on artillery pieces), as well as a highly absorbent foam butt-pad and new-generation muzzle brake that reduced felt recoil by 70 percent. The new Barrett M82 Light-Fifty proved to be an immediate hit in every sense with civilian long-range shooters when it was released in 1983 and the Marine armorers at Quantico soon arranged a test. They liked what they saw, but for military applications there had to be changes.

For a start it had to be Marine-proof. A substantial mounting rail needed to be fitted for a scope that was tough enough to survive the recoil and powerful enough to provide long-range vision. The Unertl Company was asked to provide a 10x Mil-dot scope that was rugged enough to do the job and things progressed well, so well in fact that by 1990 the new M82A1 was ready for service. The looming prospect of Operation *Desert Storm* suddenly made the Marines' requirement for the Barrett very pressing indeed, and they placed an order subject to the delivery being met within 90 days, which was was almost unheard of in delivery terms. Amazingly it was accomplished, and by January 1991 the United States had its first large-caliber sniping rifle in service. *Desert Storm* was the first real test of the Barrett and it performed remarkably well. Marine snipers used them with particular effectiveness to knock out missile launchers, command bunkers, radar sites, and light armored vehicles. One corporal recalled the work as:

> Real easy, the rifle was so steady and accurate that taking out static targets was quite literally like being in a shooting gallery. We disabled a radar site with two shots from 900 meters. The Iraqis came out [of the bunker] with their AK's but they didn't have a clue where the shots had come from. We were under orders not to waste ammo on them so we packed up and lit out, leaving them running round in little circles.[24]

Taking out enemy snipers was also made easier by the ability of the bullet to punch through almost any construction material. This proved particularly useful in war zones such as Bosnia, where opposing sides fought in ruined buildings in predominantly urban areas. In July 1993 the UN peacekeepers had moved in to be faced with a complex set of problems. The buildings provided perfect cover for enemy snipers, and urban sniping by both sides had become a real problem, targets often being innocent men and women heading to work or queuing for food. The situation was made worse by the widespread availability to the Bosnians of high-quality Russian Dragunov sniping rifles. (Over 350 were estimated to have been supplied by the Russians.) Many of the victims were murdered on sectarian grounds and seldom were the snipers positively identifiable as being from one faction or another. UN snipers – British, French, and American – were told that counter-sniping was their primary task and the rules of engagement were clear: they had to locate the snipers, then warn the relevant regular armed forces that if they persisted in shooting they themselves would be shot. Sometimes the warnings were heeded, other times they were not. Many of the riflemen were not even trained snipers, but young members of local paramilitary units, working alone and wearing no uniforms. As a Marine sniper explained, the task was not easy:

> There were empty and ruined apartments everywhere, each one a haven for a sniper and the jumbled location made it impossible to determine where a shot came from, it just echoed around. We would observe for days to try to pinpoint activity, gradually narrowing it down to a specific building, then a floor and a room. If the guy was good, he'd simply move on and we'd have to start over. Sometimes we were sure we had spotted the guy but if he was not in uniform or carrying a weapon we could take no action.

One Bosnian sniper who had shot several civilians worked around a neighborhood in Grbavica and was finally pinpointed to the rear of an empty apartment. Normal 7.62mm NATO ammunition was deemed impractical, so the Barrett was used. Two shots resulted in silence from the building:

> We never knew for sure if we actually hit him, but the fifty [caliber] acted like a grenade blowing big chunks of brick and concrete into a room, so even if we missed him, he would sure have been hurting.[25]

In Somalia, too, the Marines had begun to earn a healthy respect from the rebels for their abilities, few of the armed street gangs ever having experienced such long-range shooting before. Mogadishu in January 1993 was lawless, violent, and the center of a brutal struggle for supremacy by a number of highly aggressive and well-armed warlords. Equipped with a motley collection of weapons, mostly Russian-manufactured AKs, the Somalis also possessed trucks with the formidable "Zeus" quad-mounted ZSU-23/24 cannon, massive 23mm antiaircraft weapons capable of delivering a building-shredding 4,000 rounds per minute. Demands by the United States for the surrender of the Somalis brought no response and their presence endangered the waiting American Cobra helicopters. Marine sniper Sergeant J. Coughlin was tasked with immobilizing the Zeus with his .50in rifle:

> The Cobras had come to a halt and were hovering just behind our building, their rotors thudding like a mad drummer. The Zeus gunner heard them too and began cranking his weapon up to aim … "Take the shot" said the general, and I fired, taking the big kick of the recoil as my rifle thundered. The heavy round punched through the metal feed tray, then slammed into the gunner like a bowling ball going a hundred miles an hour. The last I saw of him he was flipping upside down over the back of the seat, thin legs splayed in the air, and barefoot because he was blown right out of his sandals.[26]

It very quickly became evident that these large-bore sniping rifles were here to stay, for their firepower was immense and the speed with which second- or third-round shots could be made could not be matched by a bolt-action rifle. As an anti-materiel weapon they excelled, and they were capable of knocking out even armored vehicles at long range, as Marine Sergeant Kenneth Terry showed when he fired two armor-piercing (AP) rounds at an Iraqi armored personnel carrier at a range of 1,650 yards, knocking it out and encouraging the following two vehicles immediately to surrender. The rifles were also found invaluable for target marking:

We used the Barretts to mark targets for LAV [Light Attack Vehicles, mounting 25mm chain-guns] gunners who had trouble picking them up ... the Thermal Sights of the LAV could detect targets a long way away but the image they show often has poor resolution. I could help them better identify enemy troops because of the clarity of my scope.[27]

The Marines believed that the Barrett was a vital addition to their armory and they ordered another 300. The Army had not adopted any large-caliber sniping weapons and it was clear it could not ignore the Barrett's potential on the battlefield for much longer. Curiously, after testing several rifles in 2001, it specified not a semi-auto but a bolt-action version of the Barrett, which flew in the face of its original insistence on the use of semi-automatic sniping rifles. Although the Remington M21 had proven to be a very good combat sniping weapon, the Army was apparently dubious about the advantages in accuracy and maintenance that a semi-auto possessed in a caliber as big as .50in. Further testing actually showed there to be little difference in accuracy between the bolt-action and semi-auto Barretts, and the semi-auto M82A1 was capable of exceeding the requirement of 2.5 MoA accuracy at 300 yards, some actually achieving 1.5 MoA. The Barrett's capability provided the theoretical potential for a 10in grouping at 2,000 yards, and it further became clear that the Army marksmen preferred the rate of fire of the semi-automatic. The Army acquiesced and in fall of 2001 they adopted the Barrett M82 as the XM107.

Combat experience with the Barrett resulted in some improvements being requested. A close-range iron sight was provided for the times when a 10x scope was simply too powerful – ironically the Unertl had also been criticized for not being powerful enough, the effective operational range of the .50in bullet being in excess of 2,000 yards. Marine snipers had found that 1,600 yards was about the limit that target engagement could be positively made and as a result a new range of scopes with magnification of 14x are becoming standard. There were other problems, for the magazines were neither interchangeable, nor numbered to their rifles, resulting in considerable confusion when rifles were being checked after transit:

The five-round magazines we'd been issued are cheap and thin … maybe sufficient for the civilian shooting … but they're not well built enough for extended use during combat. The rounds catch in the magazine, interrupting the feed. We're forced to use a metal file to customize each magazine to each weapon.[28]

Another problem that snipers found when shooting at such ranges was by no means unique to the .50 caliber, though, for the potential of the rifle raised questions about the quality of the ammunition supplied. The M33 Ball proved to be insufficiently accurate at extreme range, understandable in view of its original specification being for a machine gun not a sniping weapon. Barrett themselves began manufacture of match-grade ammunition, and in addition the use of the rifle was greatly expanded by the introduction of Norwegian-developed Raufoss MK211 High-Explosive Incendiary Ammunition, which greatly increased the rifle's destructive power in the anti-materiel role.

As a result there is an improved M83A3 now in service in Iraq, but the story does not end there. Requests for even larger-caliber anti-materiel rifles have been taken seriously and ten prototype 25mm rifles have been produced by the Barrett company for evaluation. The XM109 is a shade under 4ft long and is 11in shorter than the .50 caliber, but the downside is its weight, which is 14lb heavier. The caliber has been "borrowed" from that used on the cannon fitted to AH-64 Apache helicopters. Unlike a helicopter, the human body is not capable of withstanding the recoil of such a caliber (frequent shooting of the .50in has resulted in detached retinas for some snipers). Without the benefit of some very advanced technology to tame the recoil, such a weapon would be impossible to shoot. One tester familiar with the .50 caliber reportedly referred to the 25mm rifle as "terrifying," but Barrett are apparently working hard at reducing the recoil to manageable proportions. The question as to why it is necessary to utilize such a massive caliber has been raised in some quarters. The answer is simply power. The 25mm can penetrate 2in of armor at 200 yards, and it can be loaded with variations of explosive, AP, incendiary, and airburst antipersonnel payloads not practical with a smaller caliber. As to whether it will become a practical frontline sniper's weapon is open to conjecture at the moment.

OPTICAL IMPROVEMENTS

While much time and effort was being directed to weapons improvements, optical technology was also advancing at a quantum rate. One of the most important improvements had come about in late 1944 when German scientists (although Russia also claims to have been responsible) working on camera lenses for aerial photography found that if a coating of magnesium fluoride one five millionth of an inch thick was put onto a lens, it improved the light-gathering properties by 15 percent as well as having the useful byproduct of reducing reflected light. By the 1950s this process was being adopted for all optical lenses, and further experimentation with modern telescopic sights using much larger objective lenses means that manufacturers such as Leupold and Unertl can produce scopes that permit up to 90 percent of available light to pass through them, greatly enhancing their light-gathering properties. The size of objective lenses has also increased dramatically, the early scopes commonly being $7/8$ in whereas modern scopes are now being produced with lenses of almost 2in diameter.

In practice, the extra light gathered through these large lenses allows the modern sniper to shoot well beyond the traditional "sniper's light" of dawn and dusk. Modern scopes are capable of being used in very, very low light conditions where it would be impossible for the human eye to make out any detail at all. This means today's optics are of practical use far longer into failing light than was ever previously believed possible. Neither was the manufacture of the scopes themselves lagging behind, for scope designers are able to produce even stronger bodies out of steel or ultra-light alloys, which can be externally coated to prevent corrosion and provide camouflage. They are commonly filled with inert gas to prevent the eternal problem of fogging, and the advent of modern adhesives and sealants has contributed materially to the reliability of modern scopes, particularly in the harsh conditions of the battlefield. Lenses are no longer glued together with cement that degrades with age or heat, and the incredibly thin wires traditionally providing the reticle are also being phased out in preference for reticles that are etched onto the glass. A focusing difficulty known as parallax, commonplace on earlier-generation scopes, has also been eliminated by the adoption of separate focal adjustment, and scope mounts that allow the body of the scope to be moved forwards or backwards to suit the shooter's eye.

In addition, manufacturers have increasingly turned to computer design to create optical systems and design lenses to perform exactly the function required. In the past, lenses had to be handmade to a set formula known to provide certain magnification and optical characteristics. Since the 1980s, computer design technology, allied to lens manufacture through computer-automated cutting and polishing machines, has enabled high-quality lenses to be manufactured more cheaply and faster than ever before. The cheap imported hunting scopes now available, made using optical plastic lenses, will provide a clearer, brighter image and possess stronger physical characteristics than all but the very best scopes of the 1940s, although there is still no doubt that the finest scopes are manufactured with hand-ground lenses and are accordingly expensive. While the power of military scopes has hovered at around the 10x–14x mark, the performance of new large-caliber rifles such as the Barrett means that demands for scopes of 20x are increasingly vociferous and already examples have been undergoing tests. As General Thomas Holcomb, US Marine Corps, remarked: "There will be time aplenty when the practical limits for small arms marksmanship will be measured not by how far the rifleman can see his target, but by how far he is able to hit any target that he can see."[29] It is also interesting to note that the development of more powerful rifles acts as a spur to the improvement of optics, as the 25mm XM109 goes to prove. In producing such a monster, Barrett were faced with having to design from scratch a new-generation optical system capable of 2,000+ yard performance, while also having to deal with the complex math that would be required on the part of the shooter. The different performance of such large projectiles, particularly when using different payloads such as AP or HE, means complex sets of calculations are needed, dealing with wind, trajectory, air pressure, and temperature, and at present guaranteeing a first-round hit is almost impossible. As a result a computerized optical ranging system (BORS) has been developed by Barrett with the range and ammunition type being dialed in and an on-board computer doing the rest of the calculations. It is also planned to add laser range-finding to the sight. Perhaps the days of the point-and-shoot sniper may not be all that far away after all.

It is not solely the optics themselves that have undergone a radical improvement, for fitting them to a rifle, long regarded as a minor but necessary task, has also been the subject of much revision. In the late 1930s the Marines started a trend by using a more substantial Mann-type tapered base on their target rifles in place of the standard commercial mounting blocks, and this was the beginning of a small but important revolution. No optical sight is of any use if it is not secured rigidly to its weapon and yet from pre-World War II to post-Vietnam the use of ordinary commercial mounting bases was prevalent on military sniping rifles. However, in the early 1980s, a new mount, the Picatinny Mil-Std-1913, was devised by the armorers at the Picatinny Arsenal and was to set a new military standard for US sniper rifles. It comprises a long flat machined top plate with beveled edges to enable a scope with dovetailed mounting rings to be quickly attached to it. The result is a strong and stable platform that enables many different lengths or patterns of scope to be used, as well as allowing for heavier add-ons in the shape of night-vision devices. This capability has become more important than ever over the last decade because of work undertaken on improving the monstrous and unwieldy infrared Sniperscope that was first introduced in 1944.

The electronics industry was in its infancy post-World War II, but leaped ahead with indecent haste in the years after the Cold War. In the late 1950s the industry was led by demands for more sophisticated and smaller rocket guidance systems, and it was assisted by the advent of the transistor and the microchip. Each in their way contributed tiny pieces to the huge puzzle of how to improve a sniper's performance, and the solutions presented themselves in a myriad of forms, many quite unconnected. Night vision was initially developed through the AN/PVS systems by using early television technology. The AN/PVS family of night-scopes have continued to be developed, the PVS-14 now being the latest in an expanding generation of military night-vision devices, and there are also other similar modules available from the SIMRAD Optronics Corp and Military Infrared Company's family of Night Vision Weapons Sights (NVWS). These early units were heavy and had limited range; additionally, they replaced the daytime optical sight of the rifle and each time they were refitted they required zeroing, as did the normal scope, tasks no sniper wanted to do more often than was necessary. It became clear in analyzing night combat experience in Vietnam that a better solution was to have an infrared or thermal device that could couple with the extant scope, thus eliminating the requirement for scope removal and consequent re-zeroing.

The SIMRAD image-intensifier unit overcomes this problem by mounting directly onto the objective lens of the scope, thus converting it to a night-vision device. These intensifiers are not magnifying units – they merely provide an enhanced image – but they work from 25 yards to infinity, require no focusing, and can be quickly removed in bright light conditions. The drawback of the additional weight of about 2.2lb meant that very solid scope mount and rings were required, and the new Picatinny fulfilled this role neatly. It was naturally only a matter of time before telescopic sights began to emerge that had built-in night-vision capability. In fact the Soviet Union was the first to provide some limited night-use capability on its PSO-1 scopes fitted to the Dragunov sniping rifle, with a power cell providing an illuminated reticle that was basic but effective enough for low-light level sniping. For the US snipers, the new generation of night-scopes like the NVWS-4/6 provides them with self-contained night-vision telescopic sights equipped with all of the features expected of a modern military scope: Mil-dot reticle, nitrogen-filled housing, complete weatherproofing, as well as the added ability of a total night-vision capability that can be switched on or off as required. Equipped with a pair of standard elevation and windage turrets, they also have illuminated reticles that can be adjusted for brightness and a focusing drum to allow for adjustment to individual shooters' requirements. Unlike the early Sniperscope, and much to the relief of the modern sniper, all of this is accomplished with miniscule powercells. These new-generation night optical devices are the size and weight of an average day-scope and they provide the latest development in multi-functional optics. Some indication of their flexibility is that the Army Sniper Team recently used both NVWS models to win the International Sniper Competition.

Electronics have also been responsible for an extraordinary improvement in assisting the sniper in achieving those most difficult of things – accurate distance and wind-speed estimations. Laser rangefinders, initially developed for use on golf courses or for hunting, were to prove a godsend for snipers. Provided the weather conditions are suitable (fog, blurred backdrops such as forest, or strong heat haze can result in poor results), then a laser will provide an accurate reading to plus or minus a yard at 1,000 yards or more. Air-speed monitors the size of a packet of cigarettes are able to determine the strength of the wind, from a barely discernable 1–2mph up to a no-point-in-shooting 40 or 50mph gale. Sniper instructors rightly insist, of course, that such aids are to be used as backup only, for first and foremost the sniper must master the art of estimating such things for himself. Relying on technology is fine right up to the point when it ceases working, and if there is no solid core of skill and experience to fall back on then one is rendered helpless. However, when used carefully, such devices can make the sniper's life much easier and are able to provide unparalleled accuracy.

For example, on duty in Iraq, sniper Sergeant J. C. Coughlin's observer spotted an RPK machine gun being brought into action. Having previously prepared a range card detailing all possible locations in front of him, he asked his observer to check the distance:

"Panda, make a laser check for the range of our position to the building."
"Nine hundred and eleven yards boss." That distance was almost perfect, because my M40-A1 … was zeroed at a thousand yards – the length of ten football fields. I adjusted the elevation fine-tuning ring on the scope to nine plus one, which would make the bullet strike exactly 915 yards away … then I scanned back down to ground level. I found possibly the stupidest man in the Iraqi army. The soldier had made an elemental mistake by confusing

concealment with cover, assuming that being hidden in the shadows protected him from a bullet. I took a breath, partially exhaled, and gently squeezed the trigger. Almost instantly, my 173 grain round of Lake City match ammunition exploded in his chest and he spun around … he was dead, my first kill of Operation Iraqi Freedom.[30]

Where the advances in electronics will go in the future is difficult to predict with any certainty, but scopes with built-in rangefinders are in existence. It is quite feasible that scopes fitted with micro-chips and sensors will permit not only range and wind speed but also target speed calculations to be done, providing the sniper with a head-up readout that simply leaves him to dial in the required changes and shoot.

The introduction of new technology can be likened to a game of chess and it reaches back into antiquity. In the same way that the advent of the longbow and crossbow brought about better designs of medieval armor, which in turn worked until the introduction of the firearm, which required still more changes and so forth, our modern reliance on science to come up with solutions is a double-edged sword. Sophistication and miniaturization are the name of the game today. While suggestions that snipers will soon do little more than lock onto targets in the manner of fighter pilots are a tad far fetched, there is little doubt that before the end of the decade their lives will become materially easier, at least where the application of technology is concerned. Though all snipers now wear the universally issued camouflaged combat fatigues, donning their ghillie suits only when required, the clothing is of little consequence because of the latest thermal detection technology. But the chess game continues, for there are now clothes available that are lined with by-products of the coal industry, which effectively neutralize the thermal image that the human body gives off. While this is a clever solution, it is doubtless only a temporary one. For even if he cannot be seen, the modern sniper can still be heard – the use of sophisticated sound location equipment means that the best ghillie suit in the world is rendered useless as the location of a sniper who has fired a shot can be pinpointed by sensors connected by a computer to artillery or missile sites. The location information can be transferred instantaneously to a rangefinder and a retaliatory shot fired before the sniper has reloaded his rifle. To survive in an increasingly hostile environment cunning and intelligence will still be requirements for snipers for some considerable time to come.

A QUESTION OF MORALITY

By the mid-1980s it had become quite clear that the global role of the US military and the West generally was altering. The threat of another world war had receded in the wake of Russia's move away from communism to a more open form of government. This new freedom for the world's other superpower brought with it its own myriad problems, most of which had hitherto been kept firmly bottled up by the state. Not the least for Russia were the ongoing problems in Chechnya, where a bitter civil war (or terrorist campaign, depending on your viewpoint) was being waged. Elsewhere in Europe new hotspots were opening up, and while these were frequently the result of long-standing enmity between localized factions, such as in Bosnia, they were nevertheless the cause for a considerable amount of American and NATO intervention. The Middle East, too, was an ever-expanding source of conflict, with Western Europe becoming actively albeit somewhat reluctantly involved in Middle Eastern politics post 9/11. In addition, there was progressively more NATO military intervention against the aggressive Taliban regime in Afghanistan. If this were not enough, once more warring factions were creating almost insoluble problems in Lebanon, and active Israeli intervention became more frequent as a new threat – suicide bombers – materialized.

Attempting to stop these conflicts was the job of the politicians, not the military, and the morality of these situations was not the soldiers' concern. They were there to protect life and property, and to maintain the balance of power, at least as far as NATO determined. During the many LICs that the United States was involved in few of the ground troops had any real political overview of exactly what was being achieved. Neither was their job made any easier by increasing opposition to military involvement from left-wing and peace groups at home, who had been handed a *cause celèbre* during Operation

233

Desert Storm in the shape of the Barrett rifle. The much publicized power of the big rifle caused considerable controversy after its initial use, for it was deemed by many as unnecessarily powerful and immoral if used against human targets. This in turn raised questions among liberals about the morality of using it as a sniping weapon. This was not new ground, of course, for the legality of sniping had been brought into question before. In 1992 the Department of the Army had been specifically requested to state its legal position with regards to sniping and the unsurprising conclusion was that "A sniper is a lawful weapon system" and his use was entirely in accordance within NATO, Geneva Convention, and Department of Defense guidelines.[31]

While the sniper himself may have been legitimized, his weapon, in the eyes of many, was not. This attitude mirrored the strange dichotomy of previous wars, where certain weapons such as blunt-nosed (dum-dum) bullets, poison gas, or flamethrowers were deemed to be "inhuman" for use against enemy troops, yet wiping out civilian populations by carpet bombing or shredding the crew of an armored vehicle by using depleted uranium shells was quite acceptable. The sniper question was taken seriously by the Department of Defense, however, for a ban on the use of .50-caliber ammunition against anything but materiel targets not only would be near-impossible to enforce, but would encompass all large-caliber weapons including cannon and the Browning machine gun. Such was the publicity given to the question of this morality that even the Marine and Army instructors were confused over the questionable legality of its use, but in true military style, they circumvented it. One instructor informed his sniper students that "The .50 caliber machine-gun can be used against enemy military equipment, but not personnel. So be sure to aim your .50 caliber machine-gun at the enemy's belt buckle."[32] However, the unresolved question caused some disquiet among newly qualified snipers, as Marine Private Anthony Swofford recalled, in an exchange during pre-*Desert Storm* briefings:

> The instructor breaks in. "By the way, you know you can't hit a human target with a fifty caliber weapon, right? It's in the Geneva Convention. So you hit the gas tank on the vehicle, and they get blown the hell up, but you can't

target a couple of towlies [enemy] in an OP calling in bombs. You'll have to get closer with the forty [M40 rifle] or call in your own bombs."

"We can't shoot people with that thing? Fuck the Geneva Convention," a sniper from the Fifth Marines says.[33]

The questions continued to be asked, however, and the cause for the Barrett was not helped by certain extreme right-wing and survivalist groups using it as an icon of American power and freedom. In 1995 the Department of the Army once again had to process a lengthy legal document outlining the legality of the use of such heavy weapons for sniping and the Barrett specifically:

The Barrett and other .50 caliber rifles have been employed by US peacekeeping forces in Beirut, Somalia and Haiti, French forces in Rwanda, and by British, French, Swedish and Norwegian forces in Bosnia. These examples of the practice of the United States and other nations are provided as confirmation of the previously-stated view that anti-personnel use of the .50 caliber is entirely consistent with the law of war obligations of the United States.[34]

Thus consoled, the sniper instructors continue to teach shooting with the M40, M24, and Barrett rifles, but as discussed earlier the question of using even larger-caliber rifles in an anti-materiel role has not been ignored. Tests have been undertaken with a 20mm rifle, hitherto a caliber suitable only in a ground role for antiaircraft use. Perhaps unsurprisingly the results are showing that perhaps bigger is not always better. The benefits of such weapons – range and ability to deliver a number of different types of warhead – are balanced by their excessive weight, muzzle flash, and recoil, and the simple fact that only a hole of a relatively small diameter needs to be made in an object, be it human or mechanical, to stop it functioning. Humans, of course, will cease caring about pretty much any problem except their immediate survival when even a small wound has been inflicted on them, and the delicate electronics of radios, aircraft engines, or controls of missiles tend to be remarkably sensitive about any holes that appear unexpectedly. Testing by both Marines and Army weapons commands are beginning to show that adopting an intermediate caliber, possibly the .300in Winchester Magnum, the .338in Lapua, or the .458in Winchester, might provide them with everything they require in terms of range and power without all of the associated problems of cost, special ammunition, and limited portability. Experiments are continuing, but already some other sniper units, such as those in the British Royal Marines, have adopted the .338in Lapua cartridge as their sniper standard.

Regarding recruitment of the men to use these increasingly powerful and sophisticated weapons, there does not seem to be any shortage of volunteers, although the attrition rate in completing the training in scout/sniping schools is still very high. The courses themselves have come a long way from the impromptu three or four days of World War II. A typical Marine course now lasts six weeks and covers every conceivable topic that a sniper requires including some that he didn't believe he needed to know. Course training at the 3rd Marines Division base in Kaneohe, Hawaii, is now ten weeks' duration and uniquely is also available to Army snipers of the 25th Infantry Division as well as special forces such as Navy Seals. It is broken into three training phases; the first covers navigation (both the old and the new, with map reading as well as GPS use) and basic marksmanship, including range and wind estimation. The second phase teaches field skills such as stalking, camouflage, and target surveillance, and the final phase covers radio communications, advanced surveillance, and reconnaissance techniques. Each phase must be passed. At the end trainees are required to pass their final, tough graduation test and about 40 percent of volunteers fail to make the grade.

Sniper training is the second hardest specialism to pass next to special forces training. Yet much of the sniper's life in combat is neither exciting nor interesting, as Gunnery Sergeant Tisdale, the NCO in command of sniper training at Kaneohe Base, said: 'A sniper selects his target and fires upon it, but … marksmanship makes up only ten percent of being a sniper.'[35] The fact is that despite the faintly heroic image given to snipers, the bulk of their time in a combat zone is dull, uncomfortable, and apparently unrewarding, as Private Swofford found in his time as a sniper in Iraq:

> We arrive back at First Marine Division Headquarters where the other snipers have spent the week bored to death on the roof. Accidental discharges are always a concern when two-thirds of the Marine Corps have live ammunition hanging from their bodies. There are also accidental *on purpose* discharges, when the Marine decides it's about time he fires his rifle or blows something to hell because he sits there with all this firepower ... The AOPDs usually occur when two Marines have been sitting together on observation post for days or weeks, looking for what they're not sure, and they've talked themselves nearly to death.[36]

The Army and Marines have at last appreciated the fact that no amount of technology or training can turn a man into a sniper, for the basic elements required for this job are hard-wired into the brain of the individual. Some men are born hunters, others are not, and despite the attempted use of psychological profiling there is no infallible test as to whether a man can look at his enemy and pull the trigger. Most can, a very few cannot, and the majority of snipers have no qualms about their past or current employment and are content with their chosen profession. I have spoken to many snipers, past and present, and they tell the same story. "I did it because every enemy soldier I killed meant some of our boys lived" is a nearly universal *raison d'être* and it is also a sound and honest one. The enemy soldier a sniper shoots may just be the one who would, the following day, have killed his officer, NCO, or a fellow sniper.

One method of dealing with the business of killing is the de-humanization of the enemy. This is not unique to snipers of course, for it is a trait shared by frontline soldiers across the ages who adopt nicknames for their enemy. Redskins, Redcoats, Yankees, Rebs, Heinies, Huns, Krauts, Commies, Chinks, Gooks, Charlie, Slopes, Skinnies, Ragheads, Towlies – the list is almost endless. Unlike other soldiers, though, regardless of what he calls his enemy it is more difficult for a sniper to disassociate himself totally from his actions, for there exists none of the remoteness in killing that protects other specialists such as an artilleryman or machine-gunner. As Captain Robert Russell succinctly commented in Vietnam, "Sniping is a very personal war, for a sniper must kill calmly and deliberately, shooting carefully selected targets, and must not be susceptible to emotions … they will see the look on the faces of the people they kill."[37] It was axiomatic that few enjoyed seeing the results of their shooting at close hand and some snipers I met exhibited post-conflict qualms about what they did, with certain incidents remaining embedded forever in their minds. One Vietnam veteran was distraught at the time for having had to shoot a heavily armed and pregnant Vietcong woman. Another recalled shooting a sniper in Bosnia who turned out to be 15 years old. James Gibbore, a Vietnam sniper who shot 14 Vietcong in one night, found that it raised uncomfortable questions he could not easily answer:

Could I, would I, have taken a man's life just because he was the enemy? Could you do that? Think about it? Now think about how it would feel to carry that picture in your mind all the days of your life. Fourteen men lay dead … this is only one of the pictures I carry around all the days of my life.[38]

Every sniper had his own method of dealing with his job – Jack Coughlin wrote that after any action he would retire somewhere quiet to allow himself a "private two-minute nervous breakdown" after which he returned to duty as normal but he added, however:

I remembered each target vividly, seeing them again just as I had with my scope when I blew away the last moment of their life. These regular little sessions with myself are as close as I come to thinking of the enemy as individual human beings who might have families and dreams and identities of their own. Today they were trying to kill Americans, so I had no choice but to do my job before they could do theirs.[39]

Others put their past behind them and successfully returned to civilian life. Chuck Mawhinney, the highest-scoring Marine sniper of the Vietnam War, said of his return home, "I just got on with work and raising a family and trying to earn enough to get by. I did what I had been trained to do to the best of my ability and I always slept well." His words were echoed by most other ex-snipers, who filed away their experiences in a secure mental compartment and got on with the difficult business of just living. Snipers regarded their profession as necessary and their war as private, and while they would occasionally talk among themselves about their shared experiences few cared to discuss them with outsiders. Yet, interestingly, many still hunt for relaxation, although some said they had never subsequently picked up another rifle. "I killed enough" was one Korean War veteran's comment. None I met exhibited any pleasure in killing, although there was clear satisfaction at good shooting resulting in immediate kills. In some cases maturity and retrospection had clearly replaced youthful callousness but this is nothing new – one Civil War sharpshooter recalling that he once shot a Yankee officer solely to steal his fine boots.[40] As one Vietnam veteran told the author:

> We were eighteen, nineteen, we had the guns, the training and a mandate to use them. I liked being able to hit at Charlie … when you've got a bolt-rifle with a thousand yards of range you are a battlefield god. You're the one to decide who lives or dies.[41]

Most of the snipers were very young men during their military service and young men are not known for their humility, patience, or desire to avoid a course of action that may be dangerous. As with their forbears, the Minutemen of the Revolutionary War and the sharpshooters of the Civil War, killing was a matter of doing their job and they did it as dispassionately as they could. They did not normally see the end result of their handiwork at close range, although post 9/11 there has emerged among some snipers a desire to publicize their actions by means of mobile-phone camera technology. Many images appear now on the internet that military censors would have had a fit over only a few years ago. The psychology behind this phenomenon is complex, but there is doubtless an element of revenge for the actions of the World Trade Center bombers. However, while they are not to anyone's credit, such acts are not unique and certainly have antecedents in World War I, when photos of dead Allied soldiers were often found on German soldiers to the puzzlement and disgust of Allied troops. Yet even in the callousness of war, there is humanity, a point at which a target ceases to be an object and becomes a human being; and crossing this line can be almost an epiphany for some. One World War II veteran told of helping staunch the blood from a young German machine-gunner he had just shot. "I knocked out the gun and our boys took the position with no casualties so I saw no reason not to help the kid. I chose to shoot him, and I chose to try and help him." During Operation *Iraqi Freedom* sniper Jack Coughlin had twice shot a running Iraqi soldier, eventually losing sight of him in the chaos of events. He was soon called to see a wounded prisoner who had two gunshot wounds:

I looked at the wounds and they looked about the right size. Was this the guy I had shot? The Iraqi refused to talk and his dark eyes flashed in anger, but there was some fright. He said the first bullet hit his left arm … then another shot went through his shoulder. I asked why if he wanted to give up, he didn't throw down his rifle and take his boots off. He said if he tried to do that his own side would have killed him. Weird conflicting emotions swept over me. I was glad that I had not missed a target, but I was also strangely delighted that this guy had survived. Never had I felt a personal responsibility for the safety of an enemy combatant, so this sudden kinship was unexpected, and it was kind of cool. I felt he had earned a new lease on life. I called him "Achmed" because I didn't know his real name. By doing so I crossed the invisible line of humanizing my enemy.[42]

APPENDIX

PERCUSSION RIFLES

AMERICAN TARGET RIFLES

Although not adopted as an official pattern by either the Federal or Confederate armies, so many of this type saw service during the Civil War that it seems reasonable to include a generic description.

Percussion muzzle-loading rifle, single shot, cal. between .45 and .55in

Overall length:	42–48in
Barrel length:	24–30in
Weight:	17–45lb
Sights:	Many types fitted – globe, peep, ladder as well as early telescopic of Malcolm or similar pattern. Scopes were commonly slightly longer than the barrel length and were usually brass bodied.
Bullet velocity:	between 800 and 1,400fps, ball or conical bullet

Berdan Model 1859 Sharps rifle

Percussion breech-loader, single shot, cal. 52in

Overall length:	49.2in
Barrel length:	30in
Weight:	8lb 8oz

Sights: iron ladder, graduated to 800 yards
Bullet velocity: approx 1,500fps, 370-grain conical bullet

London Armoury Company Enfield Pattern 1853 rifle musket
Percussion muzzle-loading rifle, cal. 58in (.577in British)
Overall length: 55in
Barrel length: 39in
Weight: 9lb 8oz
Sights: iron ladder graduated to 900–1,250 yards, depending
                on model
Bullet velocity: approx 900fps, 530-grain minié bullet

Whitworth rifle
Percussion muzzle-loading rifle, single shot, cal. 451in
Overall length: 49–52.5in
Barrel length: 33, 36, or 39in
Weight: varying, but average of 8lb 12oz
Sights: iron ladder, graduated to 1,200 yards
Bullet velocity: approx 1,500fps, 530-grain Whitworth hexagonal bullet

BOLT-ACTION RIFLES

Model 1903A1/A4 Springfield rifle
Bolt action, cal. 30-06in, 5-round box magazine
Overall length: 43.2in
Barrel length: 24in
Weight: 8lb 10oz
Sights: Telescopic Unertl or Fecker 8x and Weaver 330, Lyman
                Alaskan, M72/M74/M82/M84 2.5x
Bullet velocity: 2,715fps, 165-grain M2 ball

Winchester Model 70 rifle
Bolt action, cal. 30-06in (later 7.62 x 51mm), 5-round box magazine

Overall length:	44in
Barrel length:	varies depending on model, but heavy barrel normally 24in
Weight:	7lb 2oz
Sights:	Telescopic, Unertl, Fecker or Lyman Targetspot 8x
Bullet velocity:	30-06 – 2,640fps, 173-grain M72 match; 7.62mm – 2,550fps, 173-grain M118 match

Remington Model 700 (M40) rifle

Bolt action, cal. 7.62mm, 5-round box magazine

Overall length:	41.6in
Barrel length:	24in
Weight:	9lb 8oz
Sights:	Telescopic, 3 x 9 Redfield/Leatherwood ARTI
Bullet velocity:	2,550fps, 173-grain M118 match

Remington Model M40A1 rifle

Bolt action, cal. 7.62mm, 5-round box magazine

Overall length:	43.9in
Barrel length:	24in
Weight:	14lb 7oz
Sights:	Telescopic, Leatherwood ARTII then MST-100 Unertl 10x
Bullet velocity:	2,550fps, 173-grain M118 match

Remington Model M40A3 rifle

Bolt action, cal. 7.62mm, 5-round box magazine

Overall length:	44.25in
Barrel length:	25in
Weight:	16lb 5oz
Sights:	Telescopic, MST-100 Unertl 10x and Schmidt & Bender 3-12 x 50
Bullet velocity:	2,670fps, 168-grain M118LR/AA11 ammunition

Remington M24 SWS

Bolt action, cal. 7.62mm, 5-round box magazine

Overall length:	43in
Barrel length:	24in
Weight:	15lb 2oz
Sights:	Telescopic, Leupold Mk4.M3 10x
Bullet velocity:	2,720fps, M118LR/AA11 ammunition

SEMI-AUTOMATIC RIFLES

Garand models M1C & M1D

Semi-automatic gas-operated action, cal. 30-06in, clip-fed, 8-round box magazine

Overall length:	43.6in
Barrel length:	24in
Weight:	9lb 7oz
Sights:	Telescopic, various but normally M82/M84 2.5x or Stith Kollmorgen Model 4XD 4x
Bullet velocity:	2,715fps, 150-grain M2 ball

M21 & XM21 Sniper rifles

Semi-automatic gas-operated action, cal. 7.62mm, 5- or 20-round box magazine

Overall length:	44.1in
Barrel length:	22in
Weight:	11lb 4oz
Sights:	Telescopic, 3 x 9 Redfield/Leatherwood ART
Bullet velocity:	2,750fps, M118LR/AA11 ammunition

M25 & XM25 Sniper rifles

Semi-automatic gas-operated action, cal. 7.62mm, 5- or 20-round box magazine

Overall length: 44.3in
Barrel length: 22in
Weight: 10lb 10oz
Sights: Telescopic, Bausch & Lomb 10x Tactical, also Leupold Ultra Mk4 10x
Bullet velocity: 2,750fps, M118LR/AA11 ammunition

XM110 Semi-Automatic Sniper System

Semi-automatic gas-operated action, cal. 7.62mm, 5-,10-,15-, or 20-round box magazine

Overall length: 39in
Barrel length: 20in
Weight: 10lb 8oz
Sights: Telescopic, Leupold Ultra Mk4 10x
Bullet velocity: 3,300fps, M118LR/AA11 ammunition

Barrett Model 82A1/XM107

Short recoil-operated semi-automatic, cal. 50in BMG, 10-round box magazine

Overall length: 57in
Barrel length: 30in fluted
Weight: 28lb 8oz
Sights: Telescopic, Unertl 10x, Leupold Vari-X IV 4.5-14x and Swarovski 4.5-14 x 40 fitted
Bullet velocity: 2,925fps, IMI M33 633-grain ball

NOTES

CHAPTER 1 NEW WORLD, NEW WEAPONS

1. Petersen, H. L., *Pageant of the Gun*, New York, 1967.
2. Lavin, J. D., *A History of Spanish Firearms*, New York, 1965.
3. Two examples exist in the Royal Armory in Madrid and date from the mid- to late 15th century. One is in .50 caliber, while the other has a 1.6in bore.
4. Hackluyt, R., *Virginia Richly Undervalued*, London, 1609. Translated in *Tracts and Other Papers by Peter Force*, Washington, 1846.
5. Brandon, W., *The American Heritage Book of the Indians*, New York, 1961.
6. Cipolla, C. M., *Guns, Sails and Empires. Technological Innovation and the Early Phases of European Expansion 1400–1700*, New York, 1965.
7. Pegler, M., *Powder and Ball Small Arms*, Wiltshire, 1998.
8. Lavin, op. cit.
9. H. P. Biggar (ed.), *The Works of Samuel de Champlain*, Toronto, 1922–36.
10. Pegler, op. cit.
11. Strachey, W., *Historie of Travaile into Virginia. Early English and French Voyages 1534–1608*, New York, 1906.
12. Its origin is disputed, but it is believed to have been in common use in Europe by the early 16th century.
13. Priestly, H. I., *The Luna Papers*, 2 vols, De Land, 1928.
14. Ibid.
15. Ibid.
16. An excavated example exists at Jamestown.
17. *Journal of New Netherlands*, British Museum Library, London.
18. Petersen, H. L., *Arms And Armor in Colonial America*, Pennsylvania, 1956. Manifest by the governor of Mexico, Don Juan de Õnate, May 1597.

19. Hof, Dr Arne, *Encylopedia of Firearms*, New York, 1964.
20. Smith, J. A., *True Relation of Such Occurrences and Accidents of Noate as Hath Happened in Virginia*, reprint New York, 1907.
21. Strachey, op. cit.
22. Bourne, W., *Inventions and Devices Very Necessary for all Generalls and Captaines*, London, 1587.
23. Petersen, H. L., *Arms And Armor in Colonial America*, Pennsylvania, 1956.
24. Shurtleff, N. B. (ed.), *Records of the Governor and Company of Massachusetts Bay in New England*, Boston, 1853–54.
25. Chatelain, V. E., *The Defenses of Spanish Florida 1565–1763*, Washington, 1946.
26. Stetson Collection, J. P. Yonge Library of Florida. Governor Cabrera's letters, October 8, 1683.
27. Ibid.

CHAPTER 2 WINDS OF CHANGE

1. Government Proceedings, 1640–42, National Records Office, Kew, London.
2. US Bureau of Census, *Historical Statistics of the United States*, Washington DC, 1961.
3. Bartlett, *Records of Rhode Island*, Rhode Island, 1936.
4. *Acts Orders and Resolutions of the State of Virginia*, 1638, Virginia State Records Office.
5. Act of Parliament, March 4, 1628, National Records Office, Kew, London.
6. Brown, M. L., *Firearms in Colonial America 1492–1792*, Washington DC, 1980.
7. R. Woddey of Boston and W. Everenden of Massachusetts.
8. Woodward, W. E., *The Way our People Lived*, New York, 1966.
9. Brown, op. cit.
10. Hanger, G., *To All Sportsmen and Particularly Farmers and Gamekeepers*, London, 1814.
11. The Royal Fusiliers and Royal Welch Fusiliers.
12. *A Generall State of the Ordinance 1685–1691*, report of the Board of Ordnance, Royal Armouries Library, HM Tower of London.
13. Blackmore, H., *British Military Firearms*, London, 1961.
14. Ibid.
15. Brown, op. cit.
16. Pargellis, S. (ed.), *Military Affairs in North America 1748–1765*, New York, 1936. Letter from Braddock's campaign, July 25, 1755.

17. Zaboly, G., *American Colonial Rangers*, Oxford, 2005.
18. Pegler, M., *Powder and Ball Small Arms*, Wiltshire, 1998.
19. Muir, B. W., *American Rifleman*, January 1971.
20. Kindley, R. L., *Guns Magazine*, January 1956.
21. Letters Patents Nos 44, 162 and 711, 635. The Patent Office.
22. Grant, W. L., *The Voyages of Samuel Champlain 1604–1618*, New York, 1907.
23. Merwyn Carey, A., *American Frontier Firearms Makers*, New York, 1935.
24. Massachusetts State Library.
25. Weld, I. Jr., *Travels Through the States of North America and Canada 1795–7*, reprint New York, 1928.
26. Church, T. and B., *The History of Philip's War, Commonly Called The Great Indian War*, New Hampshire, 1829.
27. Minute Books of the Board of Ordnance, HM Tower of London.

CHAPTER 3 REVOLUTION

1. US Bureau of Census, *Historical Statistics of the United States*, Washington DC, 1961.
2. Wilson, J. G. and Fiske, J. (eds), *Appletons Encylopedia of American Biography*, 6 vols, New York, 1889.
3. Wilkinson, N. B., *Explosives in History. The Story of Black Powder*, Chicago, 1967.
4. Declaration of Rights, October 14, 1774; Trade Suspension December 1, 1774.
5. Massachusetts Historical Society, Boston.
6. Pegler, M., *Firearms in the American West*, Wiltshire, 2002.
7. Brown, M. L., *Firearms in Colonial America 1492–1792*, Washington DC, 1980.
8. Barker, J., *The British in Boston*, Cambridge, Massachusetts, 1924.
9. Ibid.
10. Neumann, G. C., *American Rifleman*, July 1967.
11. Brown, op. cit.
12. Huddlestone, J. D., *Colonial Rifleman in the American Revolution*, Pennsylvania, 1978.
13. Bright, J. R., "The Rifle in Washington's Army," *American Rifleman*, August 1947.
14. Scheer, G. F. and Rankin, F., *Rebels and Redcoats: The Living Story of the American Revolution*, New York, 1957.

15. Barrett, A., *An Account of the Battle of Concord by Capt. Amos Barrett*, ed. by True, H., New York, 1904.

16. Adams, C. F. (ed.), *Familiar Letters of John Adams and his wife Abigail Adams During the Revolution*, New York, 1892.

17. Hanger, G., *To All Sportsmen and Particularly Farmers and Gamekeepers*, London, 1814.

18. Yee, G., "The Longest Shot Ever," *Muzzle Blasts Magazine*, date unknown.

19. Hanger, op. cit.

20. Walcott, W., *The Republic Magazine*, Boston, 1832, University of Chicago, Durett collection.

21. Hanger, op. cit.

22. Hanger, op. cit.

23. Peters, R., *Report to the Council of Safety*, October 26, 1776, Maryland Archives, Morristown National Historical Park.

24. Dann, J. C., *The Revolution Remembered. Eyewitness Accounts of the War for Independence*, Chicago, 1980.

25. *The Middlesex Journal*, December 31, 1776.

26. Gilchrist, M. M., *Patrick Ferguson*, Edinburgh, 2003.

27. One of Ferguson's personal rifles is in the Smithsonian Museum, Washington DC; the other is in The Royal Armouries Museum, Leeds, England. Three more service rifles exist: one in the National Army Museum, Chelsea, London, another in the Army School of Infantry Museum, Warminster, England, and one in Morristown National Park, New Jersey. One of some later militia pattern rifles is also held in the Smithsonian Museum.

CHAPTER 4 HEADING WEST

1. Purchased by President Jefferson from Napoleon in 1800 for the sum of $23 million.

2. Irving, W., *The Adventures of Captain Bonneville*, Oklahoma, 1967.

3. Audubon, M. R., *Audubon and His Journals*, New York, 1899.

4. *American Rifleman*, July 1956.

5. Ross, A., *Adventures of the First Settlers on the Oregon or Columbia Rivers*, Michigan, 1967.

6. Garvaglia, L. A. and Worman, C. G., *Firearms of the American West*, vol. 1, Colorado, 1984.

7. Pike, Z., *An Account of the Expeditions to the Sources of the Mississippi River*, reprint Michigan, 1966.

8. Lewis, M., *The Lewis and Clark Expedition*, reprint New York, 1976.
9. American State Papers, *Military Affairs*, vol. 1, Washington DC, 1818.
10. Chamberlain, S., *My Confession*, New York, 1967.
11. Gale, J., *The Missouri Expedition, 1818–1820*, ed. by Nichols, R. L., Oklahoma,1969.
12. "Civil War Smallarms," *American Rifleman Supplement*, Washington DC, undated.
13. Pepys, S., *The Diaries of Samuel Pepys*, November 11, 1663, reprint London, 1986.
14. *The Journal of Natural Philosophy*, July 1799. Courtesy of the Royal Society, London.
15. One such exists in the Royal Armouries Museum, Leeds, England.
16. US Patent, June 19, 1824.
17. *The London Directory of Business and Trades*, January 1828, Guildhall Library, London.
18. Garavaglia and Worman, op. cit.
19. Ibid.
20. Ibid.
21. Bosworth, N. A., *Treatise on Rifle, Musket, Pistol and Fowling Piece*, New Hampshire, 1846.
22. Cooke, P. St George, *The Conquest of New Mexico and California*, New York, 1882.
23. Davidson, D., *The Army and Navy Journal*, August 1864.
24. Chapman, J. R., *The Improved American Rifle*, 1844, reprint New York, 1926.
25. Senate Document ex. 6.0, 36th Congress. Report of the US Military Commission to Europe, 1855–56.
26. Ibid.
27. Garavaglia and Worman, op. cit.
28. Annual Report of the Chief of Ordnance, 1856, National Archives, Washington DC.
29. Garavaglia and Worman, op. cit.
30. Maury, D. H., *Recollections of a Virginian in the Mexican, Indian and Civil Wars*, reprint New York, undated.

CHAPTER 5 THE SHARPSHOOTER'S WAR

1. Gorbunov, N., unattributed, translation provided by Alexi Vassilipov.
2. *The Army and Navy Journal*, August 1864.

3. Record of the Chief of Ordnance, 1863. National Archives, Washington DC.

4. Meyers, A., *Ten Years in the Ranks of The US Army*, New York, 1922.

5. Aschmann, R., *Three Years in the Army of the Potomac, or A Swiss Company of Sharpshooters in the American Wars*, Bern, 1972.

6. Sword, W., *Sharpshooter; Hiram Berdan, His Famous Sharpshooters and Their Rifles*, Lincoln, Rhode Island, 1988.

7. *Detroit Daily Advisor*, August 22, 1861.

8. *New York Times*, August 7, 1861.

9. Katcher, P., *Sharpshooters of the American Civil War*, Oxford, 2002.

10. Aschmann, op. cit.

11. Katcher, op. cit.

12. Hastings, W. H., *Letters from a Sharpshooter. The Civil War Letters of Private William B. Greene. Co G, 2 U.S.S.S. Army of the Potomac 1861–1865*, Wisconsin, 1993.

13. Stevens, C. A., *Berdan's United States Sharpshooters in the Army of the Potomac*, 1892.

14. Stevens, C. A., *Berdan's United States Sharpshooters in the Army of Minnesota*, 1882.

15. Young, J. D., *A Campaign with the Sharpshooters. The Organization of the Riflemen in the Confederate Service, Philadelphia Weekly Times*, January 26, 1878.

16. Ibid.

17. Ibid.

18. Sword, op. cit.

19. McAfee, M. J. and Langellier, J. P., *Billy Yank: The Uniform of the Union Army 1861–1865*, Philadelphia, 1999.

20. Katcher, op. cit.

21. Stevens, op.cit.

22. Aschmann, op. cit.

23. Inspection report of the 1st USSS, November 1, 1862, December 19, 1862, National Archives, Washington DC.

24. Trepp, C., *Papers. Letters from Captain Isler September 24, 1862*, New York Historical Society.

25. Sword, op. cit.

26. *Detroit Free Press*, January 24, 1862.

27. Ibid.

28. Preston, T., *Letters March 10, 1862*, University of Michigan Collection.

29. Sword, op. cit.

30. Marcot, R. M., *Hiram Berdan, Military Commander and Firearms Inventor*, California, 1989.
31. Ray, F. L., *Shock Troops of the Confederacy*, North Carolina, 2006.
32. Confederate State Papers, April 2, 1862, National Archives, Washington DC.
33. Katcher, op. cit.
34. Ripley, W. Y. W., *A History of Company F. 1st United States Sharpshooters*, Rutland, Vermont, 1883.
35. Benson, B., *The Memoirs of a Confederate Scout-Sniper. The Civil War Memoirs of Barry Benson*, ed. by Benson, Susan, Athens, Georgia, 1992.
36. Katcher, op. cit.
37. Blackford, S. L., *Letters From Lee's Army, or, Memoirs of Life in and out of the Army of Virginia During the War Between the States*, 1896, reprint. Lynchburg, 1996.
38. Blackford, op. cit.
39. Dunlop, W. S., *Lee's Sharpshooters, or The Forefront of Battle: A Story of Southern Valor That Has Never Been Told*, 1899, reprint Dayton, Ohio, 1988.
40. An earlier prototype had actually been invented by Isambard Kingdom Brunel and made by Westley Richards based on an 1843 idea proposed by Robert Moore.
41. Sword, op. cit.
42. Watkins, S., *Company Aytch. A Side Show of the Big Show*, Nashville, 1882.
43. Kent, W. C., "Sharpshooting with Berdan," *Civil War Times Illustrated*, May 1976.
44. Marcott, R., *Civil War Chief of Sharpshooters, Hiram Berdan*, Tuscon, 1989.
45. Ripley, op. cit.
46. Ibid.
47. Katcher, op. cit.
48. *The Illustrated London News*, December 5, 1863.
49. McMahon, M., *The Death of General John Sedgewick*. Quoted in C. Buel and R. Johnson, *Battles and Leaders of the Civil War*, New York, 1887–88, reprint, New York, 1956.
50. Minnich, J. W., "Confederate Rifles," *Confederate Veteran Magazine*, No. 30, 1922.
51. Stevens, op. cit.
52. Morrow, J. A., *The Confederate Whitworth Sharpshooters*, private publication, 2002.
53. Ripley, op. cit.
54. Ripley, op. cit.

CHAPTER 6 GLOBAL WAR

1. Report of the Chief of Ordnance, 1900, National Archives, Washington DC.
2. Ibid.
3. Report of the Chief of Ordnance, 1908, National Archives, Washington DC.
4. McBride, H. W., *A Rifleman Went to War*, Arkansas, 2002.
5. Senich, P., *The Pictorial History of US Sniping*, Colorado, 1980.
6. Report of the Chief of Ordnance, 1916, National Archives, Washington DC.
7. The term "sniper" had by now become commonplace, superseding other established words like marksman or sharpshooter. It seems to have been born out of the trench warfare of 1914–15 when British regular army troops who had served in India brought the word with them. Its original use, which dated back to the late 18th century, had hitherto referred only to bird hunting, of which the snipe was one of the fastest and most elusive of game birds. By 1915 it was firmly established in the soldier's vocabulary to refer to the deliberate targeting of one man by another and had been widely adopted by the media, although in Germany snipers were still referred to as *Scharfschutzen*, literally "sharpshooters."
8. *600 Days in Service. A History of the 361st Infantry Regiment*, AEF, no publisher, 1919.
9. Penberthy, E., *The British Review*, London, 1920.
10. First Army, *Hints and Tips for Snipers*, printed First Army School of Sniping, 1916.
11. Lecture Notes by Captain F. I. Ford, 1st Leicestershire, National Firearms Collection Library, Royal Armouries, Leeds.
12. Instruction O.B. 1158, First Army, dated June 10, 1917. NFCL ibid.
13. Report to the Chief of Ordnance by the Army School of Musketry, December 18, 1915, National Archives, Washington DC.
14. *A History of the War Record of the 174th Infantry Regiment, 1914–1918.* Berlin, 1922.
15. Winstone, J. C. (ed.), *History of the 1st (AEF) Division 1917–1919*, Society of the 1st Division, Philadelphia, 1922.
16. Ross, Margaret Smith, "Herman Davis, Forgotten Hero," *Arkansas Historical Quarterly*, vol. 17, Spring 1955.
17. Report to the Chief of Ordnance, ibid.
18. McBride, op. cit.

CHAPTER 7 WORLD WAR II – UNPREPARED AND UNEQUIPPED

1. Report to the Director, Plans and Policies USMC, dated April 8, 1941. National Archives, Washington DC.
2. Sasser, C. W. and Roberts, C., *One Shot, One Kill*, New York, 1990.
3. Penney, J. D., Corporal, 82nd Airborne, personal correspondence with the author.
4. Ibid.
5. Sasser and Roberts, op. cit.
6. Pyle, E. T., *Brave Men*, New York, 1944.
7. Sasser and Roberts, op. cit.
8. *Battle Experiences of the First US Army*, quoted in American Combined Operations in France, 6 June–21 July 1944. ed. by M. D. Doubler, US Army Command, Washington DC, 1988.
9. Sasser and Roberts, op. cit.
10. Pyle, op. cit.
11. Penney, op. cit.
12. Senich, *The Complete Book of US Sniping*, op. cit.
13. Report dated July 29, 1942, to HQ Quartermaster, Marine Corps, National Archives, Washington DC.
14. George, J., *Shots Fired in Anger*, Washington DC, 1981.
15. Ibid.
16. "Equipment for the American Sniper," A report to the US Board of Ordnance by Col. G. Van Orden and M/Sgt C. A. Lloyd, Washington DC, 1942.
17. George, op. cit.
18. Sasser and Roberts, op. cit.
19. "Pacific Fighting," *Leatherneck Magazine*, October 1944.
20. Booth, F. H., *American Rifleman*, Letter in Reader's Comments, August 1946.
21. Daley, T. N., letter to the author.
22. Victory in Europe Day, May 7, 1945.
23. Sasser and Roberts, op. cit.
24. Daley, op. cit.

CHAPTER 8 COLD WAR, HOT WAR

1. Senich, P. R., *US Marine Corps Scout Sniper WWII and Korea*, Colorado, 1993.
2. Sasser, C. W. and Roberts, C., *One Shot, One Kill*, New York, 1990.

3. Ibid.
4. Boitnott, J. E., in Chandler, N. and R., *Death From Afar*, vol. 2, Maryland, 1993.
5. Dunlap, R., *Ordnance Went Up Front*, Plantersville, 1948.
6. Sasser and Roberts, op. cit.
7. *Marine Corps Gazette*, May 1953.
8. Sasser and Roberts, op. cit.
9. *Marines Corps Gazette*, August 1954.
10. Senich, P., *The Pictorial History of US Sniping*, Colorado, 1980.
11. Senich, P., *Limited War Sniping*, Colorado, 1977.
12. Walker, R. T., "Team Shots Can Kill," *Marine Corps Gazette*, December 1963.
13. Sasser and Roberts, op. cit.
14. Chandler N. and R., *Death From Afar*, vol. 2, op. cit.
15. Armstrong, N., *Lectures on Sniping*, private publication, 1916.
16. Sasser and Roberts, op. cit.
17. Chandler, N. and R., *White Feather: Carlos Hathcock, USMC Scout Sniper*, North Carolina, 2005.
18. Crosse, E., correspondence with the author.
19. McGuire, F., "Snipers – Specialists in Warfare," *American Rifleman*, August 1967.
20. Page, T. and Pimlott J., *Nam. The Vietnam Experience. 1965–1975*, London, 1988.
21. Senich, P., *The Pictorial History of US Sniping*, op. cit.
22. Report of the Marine Corps Equipment Board, op. cit.
23. Vide C. Mawhinney.
24. Ibid.
25. Kugler, E., *Dead Center*, New York, 1999.
26. Sasser and Roberts, *Crosshairs on the Killzone*, New York, 2004.
27. Ibid.
28. US Army Combat Development Command, Trip Report, Sniper Program, April 28, 1969. US Army Military History Institute, Carlisle Barracks, Pennsylvania.
29. Crosse, op. cit.
30. Ewell J. J., and Hunt, I. A., *Sharpening the Cutting Edge. The Use of Analysis to Reinforce Military Judgement*, Dept of the Army, Vietnam Studies 1974. US Army Military History Institute, Carlisle Barracks, Pennsylvania.
31. US Army Concept Team, *Sniper Operations and Equipment*, report February 23, 1968, Lieutenant-Colonel F. B. Conway, US Army Military History Institute, Carlisle Barracks, Pennsylvania.

32. Gibbore, J., *Soldier*, New York, 2002.

33. Correspondence Major Powell to Colonel Bayard, quoted in Senich, P., *The Long Range War*, Colorado, 1994.

34. Crosse, op. cit.

35. Ibid.

36. Ibid.

37. Figures provided by differing US Departments disagree on this matter. Some authorities put the official figure at 4–5,000, others maintain the figure was as high as 10,000.

CHAPTER 9 A CHANGING WORLD

1. Ward, J. T., *Dear Mom, A Sniper's Vietnam*, New York, 1991.

2. All William quotations taken from personal interview.

3. Personal interview.

4. Personal interview.

5. Sasser and Roberts, *One Shot, One Kill*, New York, 1990.

6. Vide Lieutenant-Colonel R. D. Bean, USMC.

7. Chandler R. and N., *Death From Afar*, vol. 1, Maryland, 1992.

8. Army Command Report on Operations in Grenada, undated.

9. *The Marksman*, March 1976, USAMTU monthly newsletter.

10. Ibid.

11. Poyer, J. and Marcot, R., "Remington Sniper Rifles," *Remington Society of America*, Journal 1st Quarter 2000.

12. US Army Training Circular No. 23-14, "Sniper Training and Employment," June 14, 1989.

13. Durant, M., *New York Times*, November 6, 1993.

14. Association of the United States Army, *The Army Review*, July 1, 2006.

15. US ARDEC, Request for Proposal, W15QKN-05-R-0433, November 30, 2004.

16. Association of the United States Army, op. cit.

17. Numbers issued: 1966: 700, 1967: 62, 1968: 87, 1969: 137, 1970: 8, 1971: 1. Courtesy of the Remington Army Company.

18. William H., correspondence with the author.

19. Coughlin, J., and Kuhlman, C., *Shooter*, ed. by Davis, D. A., New York, 2005.

20. Sasser and Roberts, op. cit.

21. Ibid.

22. Report of sniping rifle tests, Army Development and Proof Services, Aberdeen Proving Ground, Maryland. Reprinted in full in Senich, P., *The Complete Book of US Sniping*, Colorado, 1988.
23. Ibid.
24. Correspondence with the author.
25. Ibid.
26. Coughlin, op. cit.
27. Poole, E., quoted in "Practical to Tactical," *American Rifleman*, April 2004.
28. Swofford, A., *Jarhead*, London, 2003.
29. Chandler N. and R., *Death From Afar*, vol. 3, North Carolina, 1994.
30. Coughlin, op. cit.
31. Report by the Department of the Army, Office of the Judge Advocate General, September 29, 1992.
32. *Marine Corps Gazette*, January 1988.
33. Swofford, op. cit.
34. Report by the Department of the Army, Office of the Judge Advocate General, April 21, 1995.
35. *Marine Corps Service News*, September 3, 2003.
36. Swofford, op. cit.
37. Pegler, M., *The Military Sniper Since 1914*, Oxford, 2001.
38. Gibbore, J., *Soldier*, New York, 2002.
39. Coughlin, op. cit.
40. Ray, F. L., *Shock Troops of the Confederacy*, North Carolina, 2006.
41. Correspondence with the author.
42. Coughlin, op. cit.

GLOSSARY

Accurized   A standard production rifle that has been completely rebuilt to the highest possible specifications, often using parts, particularly barrels and triggers, that are specially manufactured.

Action   The part of a rifle containing the bolt and magazine. The barrel screws into the front of the action, the butt to the rear. Also called the receiver.

Ammunition   A generic term covering all small-arms cartridges, each cartridge comprising the bullet, propellant, case, and primer. Also known as a "round." Ammunition can be subdivided into three main types:

AP Armor-piercing. The projectile normally has a tungsten core, capable of penetrating armor plate. AP bullets are usually significantly heavier than normal ball.

Ball Solid lead-cored, copper-jacketed military bullets.

Tracer A bullet containing a phosphorus compound that ignites when fired, providing a visible trace of its flight towards a target.

ART scope   Auto Ranging Telescope. Fitted with a ballistic cam to automatically compensate for the trajectory of a bullet. See also "ranging."

Ball   A spherical lead bullet, aerodynamically inefficient, but easy and cheap to produce.

Ballistic coefficient	(BC) The length of a bullet relative to its diameter and its aerodynamic shape. The more efficient the BC, the better the bullet will overcome air resistance when in flight.
Ballistics	The science dealing with the flight and motion of a bullet.
Barrel	The hollow tube through which the projectile moves when fired.
Barrel wear	The erosion of the rifling by the bullet and the hot propellant gases, causing eventual loss of accuracy. Rifle barrels of the World War I era could erode after 500 rounds; modern stainless barrels can easily exceed 10,000 rounds.
Bases	The mounting pads for a telescopic sight. These are usually screwed or soldered to the top of the action and/or the barrel, depending on scope type. See also " scope mounts."
Bedding	The proper fit of the barrel and receiver into the stock, allowing no movement at all. If loose the rifle will shoot badly.
Bipod	A two-legged support fixed to the fore-end of the stock.
Block	See "breech-block."
Boat-tail	The tapering at the tail of a bullet, first introduced in Germany at the start of World War I. It reduced drag and considerably increased the bullet's stability and range.
Bore	The internal part of the barrel. It may be smooth or rifled.
Breech	The rearmost and strongest part of a barrel into which the cartridge is inserted. See also "chamber."
Breech-block	The hinged or sliding part of the action that seals the chamber once the cartridge is loaded.
Bullet	The projectile fired from the barrel of a weapon. Often incorrectly used to describe an entire round of ammunition.
Bullet drop	As it loses velocity a bullet in flight gradually describes a parabolic curve as it falls to earth. Also known as "trajectory."
Burn rate	The speed at which a propellant ignites.
Butt	The rearmost portion of the stock that rests in the shooter's shoulder.

Cap	A percussion cap, also sometimes applied to the primers of modern centerfire cartridges.
Cartridge	Properly the brass case holding the propellant, but often used to refer to the whole round of ammunition. See also "ammunition."
Centerfire	A brass cartridge with a primer in the center of its base.
Chamber	The machined recess in the receiver into which the cartridge fits. See "breech."
Chamber pressure	The pressure generated in the breech by the ignition process. Excessive pressure can burst a breech, with unpleasant results.
Charge	The amount of propellant used to fire a bullet.
Cheek rest	The raised portion of a rifle stock on which the shooter rests his cheek. A proper cheek rest provides a steadying influence known as "stock weld" and assists the aim.
Clip	A metal strip holding cartridges so that they can be loaded into a magazine.
Cock	The hammer on a flintlock musket, whose jaws contain the flint. Also the expression used to signify preparing a weapon to fire, as in "cocking the action."
Cold-bore shot	The first shot fired by a sniper is normally taken using a rifle with a cold barrel. The bullet should strike the target at exactly the point of aim.
Collimate	Ensuring the telescopic sight and bore of the rifle are perfectly aligned. See also "point of aim," "point of impact," "sighting-in," and "zeroing."
Concealment	A place that is protected from the view of the enemy and from where a shot may be fired in safety.
Cover	Sometimes used in place of concealment, but properly referring to a place of safety protected from enemy fire.
Crosshairs	Intersecting vertical and horizontal lines visible through the telescope. They provide the precise aiming point for the shooter. They can take many other forms, such as a thin pillar or broken lines. Also known as graticules and reticles.

Deflection	The change in the path of a bullet as a result of wind.
Drift	Lateral movement of a bullet in flight away from the line of the bore, caused by its own rotation or by the wind.
Drop	See "bullet drop" or "trajectory."
Elevation	The vertical adjustment on the horizontal crosshair of a scope, enabling the point of aim to be raised or lowered, depending on distance. This is accomplished by the use of an elevation drum on the body of the scope.
Eye relief	The distance from the eye to the ocular lens, important to avoid parallax problems. An average is about 3in.
Feet per second	(fps) The unit of measurement used to determine the speed at which a bullet travels. See also "velocity."
Field of view	The size of image visible through the telescopic sight. Generally the more powerful the magnification, the smaller the field of view. Larger objective lenses provide a better field of view.
Firing pin	An enclosed steel rod, held by a strong spring and retained within the bolt, that strikes the primer of a cartridge when the trigger is pulled.
Fixed sights	The standard metal sights fitted to military rifles, usually adjustable by the shooter only for range. Also known as "open" or "iron" sights.
Flint	A wedge-shaped piece of hard stone, with its angled face designed to strike the frizzen or steel and create a shower of sparks.
Flyer	A bullet that strikes the target well outside of the predicted area of grouping.
Fore-end	The part of the stock forward of the trigger guard in which the barrel rests.
Free-floating	A term applied to the barrels of very accurate target and sniping rifles, where no part of the barrel touches any other part of the rifle.
Frizzen	The flat metal plate on a flintlock mechanism against which the flint strikes to create a spark for ignition. Also known as the steel.

Full metal jacket   The copper-jacketed, solid lead-cored military bullet of the type usually referred to as ball ammunition.

Furniture   A generic word covering all of the fittings on a longarm, such as trigger-guard, butt-plate etc.

Gas-operated   A term referring to certain sniping rifles, such as the M1C & D Garands, M21/24 and Russian SVD, which harness the energy from the propellant gas to automatically unlock the breech-block, recycle the action, and re-cock it.

Glass-bedding   Glass-fiber (or more often now a modern plasticized compound) is applied to the receiver bed inside the stock. The receiver is then fitted, the compound allowed to dry, and the excess removed. This ensures an absolutely perfect fit.

Grain   The measure of weight applied to both bullets and propellants.

Group   The area covered by a number of bullets fired at the same point. The smaller the group, the more accurate the rifle.

Hammer   The cocking piece of a rifle, usually applied to percussion weapons but also to some early centerfire rifles.

Hangfire   The delay that occurs when the trigger is pulled but the cartridge fails to ignite instantly. Seldom dangerous but very unsettling.

Hide   A covert sniper position, usually well camouflaged.

Hit probability   The percentage of chance of a projectile striking its target at a given range. The greater the range, the lower the hit probability.

Hold-off   Compensating for bullet trajectory by aiming above or below the target. Also referred to as hold-over or hold-under as well as Kentucky windage.

Iron sights   See "fixed" or "open" sights.

Keyhole   The result of a bullet striking its target having been deflected, taken from its keyhole-shaped entry hole.

Killing power   The efficiency of a bullet in terms of its ability to kill with a single shot. Larger bullets carrying greater energy generally have more killing power.

Lands and grooves The spiral cuts made inside a barrel in order to rifle it produce a series of high ribs inside it. The raised parts are the lands, the lower ones are the grooves.

Lead The distance in front of a moving target that a shooter must calculate to enable him to hit it. A difficult skill to master.

Line of sight The imaginary line drawn from the shooter's eye along the barrel to the target.

Lot number The serial number allocated by the factory to each batch of ammunition manufactured. In theory, all ammunition with the same lot number will perform identically.

Magnum A cartridge that contains a larger than normal propellant charge, giving it higher velocity and theoretically greater killing power.

Match grade A term applied to both firearms and ammunition, denoting manufacture to specifications well above the accepted norm, which results in improved reliability and performance.

Mil (Mil-dot) A new metric system of angular measurement that equates to 1/6400th of a complete revolution. It is now used to estimate distance and target size based on a formula whereby one mil equals 1m at 1,000m. Mil-dot scopes, used with a calculation chart, can provide the shooter with very accurate range and target size indications.

Minié A conical lead bullet with a hollow base that expands on firing. For military use, it replaced the traditional lead ball within the space of a few years.

Minute of Angle (MoA) A measurement system used to determine the accuracy of a rifle. One MoA equates to 1in at 100 yards, two MoA equals 2in at 200 yards and so on. Elevation and windage drums on scopes are normally set for $^1/_2$ MoA adjustment, so two clicks will alter the mean point of impact of the bullet by 1in at 100 yards.

Misfire A cartridge that fails to fire.

Muzzle The end of the barrel from which the projectile emerges.

Muzzle energy The kinetic force carried by a bullet.

Muzzle velocity The speed at which the bullet leaves a barrel. This decreases rapidly with distance.

Objective lens   The lens at the front of a telescope.

Ocular lens   The lens at the rear of a telescope, closest to the shooter's eye.

Offhand   A shooting position in which the firer stands upright, using no other support than his arms.

Open sight   The rear metal sight on a rifle. See also "fixed" sights.

Parallax   The apparent movement of a target in relationship to the reticle when viewed through a telescopic sight. It is caused by having incorrect eye relief between the eye and ocular lens.

Patch-box   A cavity cut into the side of the butt, closed by a hinged or sliding cover. It usually contained bullet patches but could also accommodate flints or percussion caps.

Point blank   When the distance between a rifle and target is so short the use of any form of sight is rendered unnecessary or impossible.

Point of aim   The part of the target at which the sights are aimed. See also "point of impact."

Point of impact   The part of the target where the bullet actually lands but not necessarily the point of aim. See also "collimate" and "zero."

Powder   Originally gunpowder, but now referring to any propellant charge.

Primer   A percussion cap that ignites the propellant when struck.

Projectile   A bullet or shell.

Propellant   The main charge of a cartridge. See also "powder."

Rangefinder   An optical device that computes distance to a target.

Ranging   The technique used to compensate for bullet trajectory by means of a ballistic cam fitted to an adjustable ranging telescopic sight. See also "ART scope."

Receiver   The part of a rifle housing the bolt and breech mechanism. Also called the action.

Recoil   The rearward thrust generated by firing the rifle.

Reticles   See "crosshairs."

Rifling	The spiral grooves in the bore that cause the bullet to spin.
Round	Another term for cartridge.
Scope	Any telescopic sight.
Scope mounts	Rings or saddle mounts into which the scope fits. These then attach to the rifle by means of mounting bases.
Scout	A soldier who works ahead of the main body of troops to give warning of possible danger.
Sear	The part of a trigger mechanism that holds the cock, hammer, or firing pin in place until the trigger is pulled.
Semi-automatic	A self-loading firearm, but not a machine gun.
Service rifle	An unmodified military issue weapon.
Set trigger	A trigger mechanism having two different pull weights, one normal and one very light. Often visible as two separate triggers.
Sighting-in	The process of collimating or zeroing a rifle.
Stalking	Taken from the hunting of animals, it refers to the tracking of an unseen target.
Steel	See "frizzen."
Stock weld	The proper contact of the cheek with the stock.
Surveillance	The concealed observation of places, persons, or objects.
Terminal velocity	The actual speed of a bullet as it strikes the target.
Trace	The air turbulence behind a projectile, clearly visible as a swirl in good weather conditions.
Tracking	Following a moving target through the sights of a rifle.
Trajectory	The path of a bullet in flight, initially flat, then curving downwards as gravity and loss of velocity take effect.
Trapping	Shooting at a moving target by selecting a fixed point at which to fire, and allowing the target to move onto it. The opposite of tracking.
Trigger pull	The amount of force required to release the sear and fire the cartridge.
Turrets	The caps on the body of a scope which house the elevation and windage drums.

Velocity   The speed of a bullet, normally measured in feet per second or meters per second.

Windage   Originally the loss of propellant gas through loading an undersized ball. In modern use, the adjustment on a telescopic sight to compensate for the lateral motion of a bullet.

Windage drums   The adjusting mechanism to alter the vertical crosshair to allow for lateral drift.

Yaw   A term that applies to a bullet that starts to spin erratically around its own axis, either as a result of loss of velocity or by being deflected.

Zero (zeroing)   Ensuring that at a given range, the point of aim and point of impact coincide precisely. See also "collimate" and "sighting-in."

SELECT BIBLIOGRAPHY &
FURTHER READING

Many of these books are now out of print, but can be fairly easily obtained through the internet.

Brown, M. L., *Firearms in Colonial America, 1492–1792,* Smithsonian, Washington DC, 1980

Chandler, N. and R., *Death From Afar, Marine Corps Sniping, vols 1–5,* Iron Brigade Armory, Maryland and North Carolina, 1992–98

Coughlin, Sgt J., and Kuhlman, Capt. C., *Shooter,* St Martin's Press, New York, 2005

Culbertson, J., *13 Cent Killers,* Random House, New York, 2003

Garavaglia, L. A. and Worman, C. G., *Firearms of the American West, vols 1 and 2,* University Press, Colorado, 1984 and 1994

Gibbore, J., *Soldier,* Brundage Publishing, New York, 2001

Gilbert, A., *Sniper One to One,* Sidgwick & Jackson, London, 1994

Gilbert, A., *Stalk and Kill,* Sidgwick & Jackson, London, 1997

Kugler, E., *Dead Center,* Ivy Books, New York, 1999

Lanning, M. L., *Inside the Crosshairs: Snipers in Vietnam,* Ivy Books, New York, 1998

Marcot, R., *Hiram Berdan, Military Commander and Firearms Inventor,* Marcot Publishing, California, 1989

Pegler, M., *Powder and Ball Small Arms,* Crowood Publishing, Wiltshire, 1998

Pegler, M., *Out of Nowhere: A History of the Military Sniper,* Osprey Publishing, Oxford, 2004

Petersen, H. L., *Arms and Armor in Colonial America, 1526–1783,* Telegraph Press, Pennsylvania, 1956

Ray, F. L., *Shock Troops of the Confederacy*, CFS Publishing, North Carolina, 2006

Sasser, C. W. and Roberts, C., *One Shot, One Kill*, Pocket Books, New York, 1990

Sasser, C. W. and Roberts, C., *Crosshairs on the Kill Zone*, Pocket Books, New York, 2004

Senich, P., *Limited War Sniping*, Paladin Press, Colorado, 1977

Senich, P., *The Pictorial History of US Sniping*, Paladin Press, Colorado, 1980

Senich, P., *The Complete Book of US Sniping*, Paladin Press, Colorado, 1988

Senich, P., *US Marine Corps Scout-Sniper*, Paladin Press, Colorado, 1993

Senich, P., *The Long-Range War*, Paladin Press, Colorado, 1994

Swofford, A., *Jarhead*, Simon & Schuster, London, 2003

Sword, W., *Sharpshooter: Hiram Berdan, his famous Sharpshooters and their Sharps Rifles*, Andrew Mowbray Inc., Rhode Island, 1988

Ward, J. T., *Dear Mom*, Ivy Books, New York, 1991

FURTHER READING

This list covers British, American, and German books on the subject, from World War I onwards. It does not cover the many service manuals and pamphlets issued on the subject or books detailing the general development of infantry rifles. Although the originals of many of these books are long out of print, some have recently been republished. A few are extremely rare and may take some searching! I am greatly indebted to ex-sniper Harry Furness and Iron Brigade Armory for much of this information.

Armstrong, Lieutenant-Colonel N. A. D., *Fieldcraft, Sniping and Intelligence, 1916-1918*, the Outdoorsman's Bookstore, Powys, 1993. Armstrong was commanding officer of the 2nd Army School of Sniping in France, 1915–16.

Avery R., *Combat Loads for Sniping Rifles*, Desert Publications, Eldorado, 1991. Ammunition treatise for sniping.

Crum, Major F. M., *Scouts & Sniping in Trench Warfare*, Cambridge, 1916; *Memoirs of a Rifleman Scout*, Oxford, 1921; *Riflemen, Scouts and Snipers*, Oxford, 1921. Crum was a regular army soldier and Boer War veteran who championed and taught sniping in World War I. They are now very rare books.

George, Lieutenant-Colonel J. B., *Shots Fired in Anger*, NRA, Washington, 1981. A Marine officer who fought as an independent sniper in the Pacific.

Greener, W. W., *Sharpshooting for Sport and War*, London, 1900. Treatise by the famous W. W. Greener on accurate rifles and shooting.

Hatcher, Major-General J. S., *Telescope Sight: Characteristics, Advantages, Disadvantages, Mounts and Reticules*, NRA, Rhode Island, 1962.
A self-explanatory look at the subject of telescopic sights.

Henderson, C., *Marine Sniper, 93 Confirmed Kills: Biography of Gny. Sgt Carlos Hathcock*, Sphere Books, New York, 1990.

Hesketh-Pritchard, Major H., *Sniping in France*, Lancer Militaria, Arkansas, 1993; *A Memoir* (ed. by Eric Parker), Fisher & Unwin, London, 1924. Famous for his first book, but his biography is less well known. He almost single-handedly forced Britain into taking sniping seriously from 1915 onwards.

Hogg, I. V., *The World's Sniping Rifles*, Greenhill Books, London, 1998. A good reference work on the subject of sniper rifles.

Idriess, I. L., *The Australian Guerrilla: Sniping*, Paladin Press, Colorado, 1989; *The Desert Column*, first published 1932. Idriess was a sniper on Gallipoli with the famous Billy Sing. He also served in Flanders and postwar was a prolific writer, although these books are now hard to find.

Laidler, P., *The .303 No.4[T] Sniper Rifle: An Armourer's Perspective*, Skennerton, Margate, 1993; *Telescope Sighting No.32: An Inside View of the Sniper's Rifle Telescope*, Laidler, Oxfordshire, 1989. The most detailed reference books on the British service No.4[T] sniper rifle and its variant scopes.

Law, R. D., *Backbone of the Wehrmacht: Sniper Variations of the German K98k Rifle*, Collector Grade Publications, Ontario, 1996. A detailed history of all of the K98 sniper rifles in use 1939–45.

Long, D., *Modern Sniper Rifles*, Paladin, Colorado, 1988. A good reference for the then current service rifles.

McBride, H., *A Rifleman Went to War*, Lancer Militaria, Arkansas, 1987. Well-known book covering the author's service as a sniper on the Western Front.

Melville, M. L., *The Story of the Lovat Scouts 1900–1980*, St Andrews Press, Edinburgh, 1981. Little known but interesting story of the Lovats, responsible for much of the Allied training in World War I.

Plasterer, Major J., *The Ultimate Sniper*, Paladin Press, Colorado, 1996. Covering US training for snipers, in considerable detail.

Senich, P., *The German Sniper 1914–1945*, Boulder Press, Colorado, 1982.
A large volume covering all aspects of weapons and training for the German armed forces.

Shore, Captain C., *With British Snipers to the Reich*, Lancer Militaria, Arkansas, 1998. Shore was a sniper training officer during World War II, and his book is rich in information and anecdotes.

Skennerton, I., *The British Sniper: British & Commonwealth Sniping & Equipments*, Skennerton, Margate, 1986. The best study of the subject yet written.

Spicer, M., *Sniper*, Salamander Books, London, 2001. Written by a serving British sniping instructor, this is an excellent "how to" manual covering every aspect of the subject.

Tatum, W. H., *Sniper Rifles of Two World Wars*, Museum Restoration Service, Ottawa, 1967. A slim paperback giving basic details on most of the service rifles in use at the time.

Van Orden, Captain, G. A. and Lloyd, C. A., *Equipment for the American Sniper*, US Government Publication, 1942. An exhaustive look at what the US should have done at the outbreak of war.

Wacker, A., *Im Auge des Jagers*, VS Books, Herne, 2005. The harrowing biography of Joseph (Sepp) Allerberger, one of Germany's highest scoring Eastern Front snipers. Now available as an English translation.

Whelen, Colonel T., *Fundamentals of Scope Sights*, NRA, Rhode Island, 1952. An expert treatise on the subject of optical sights.

Zaitsev, V., *Notes of a Sniper* (ed. by Okrent, N.), 2826 Press Inc., Nevada, 2003. Probably the most famous sniper to emerge from World War II, Zaitsev's story was immortalized in the Hollywood film *Enemy at the Gates*. His real-life story was only slightly less dramatic than the film version and makes for interesting reading.

INDEX